Life is a Cabaret

Life is a Cabaret

One man's race against time to meet the stars of yesteryear. Or lose a fortune.

James Innes-Smith

First published in Great Britain in 2007 by Friday Books
An imprint of The Friday Project Limited
83 Victoria Street, London SW1H 0HW

www.thefridayproject.co.uk
www.fridaybooks.co.uk

ISBN – 13 978-1-905548-68-2

British Library Cataloguing in Publication Data

A catalogue record for this book is available from the British Library

Cover design by Nathan Burton
Internal design by Snowbooks Design

Typesetting and colour plate layout by Omnipress Ltd
www.omnipress.co.uk

Printed by MPG Books Ltd
www.mpg-books.com

The Publisher's policy is to use paper manufactured from sustainable sources

www.theweirdandthewonderful.com
www.lifeisacabaret.com
www.jamesinnessmith.com

Dedicated to the memory of Keith Manifold,
Dick Pleasant, Chubby Oates and The
'Almost Famous' Jack Mayes who sadly
never lived to see this book.

Contents

Acknowledgements

A big standing ovation to the wonderful entertainers who agreed to take part in this book – I had such fun meeting you all. Stirring applause also goes out to the Grand Order of Water Rats for all their kind detective work, to the staff at the Victoria Pub in Paddington for letting me use their delightful upstairs room and to everyone at the Friday Project. Love to Henry – thanks for all your support. Special thanks to Nigel Newton, Rosemary Davidson and Showcall without whom this book would never have been written.

Prologue

During my strange odyssey into the world of entertainment-lite, friends kept asking me the same question – why on earth had I become so obsessed with a bunch of entertainers none of them had ever heard of? Why wasn't I chasing after *Little and Large*, Bernard Manning or Ken Dodd? Well I guess it must be the Englishman in me but I've always been more interested in the outer reaches of the entertainment industry – an unforgiving place where hard-grafting comedians and speciality acts ply their trade to rowdy or non-existent audiences in scruffy clubs, end-of-the-pier theatres and pre-gastro pubs.

So you can imagine my joy when an old-school theatrical impresario friend of mine gave me his 1975 *Showcall* entertainers' directory with the words 'hope this comes in useful'. I took one look at it and knew I'd stumbled on something special. The dusty, yellowing book featured hundreds of ancient black and white publicity photographs of bizarre speciality acts from the mid '70s – everything from boxing dogs to comedy monks and yodelling country singers. Each act had a page on which to sell themselves to prospective booking agents, and included a brief description of their act and a couple of enthusiastic local newspaper reviews. From this surreal, half-forgotten world of wacky specs, double entendres, sticky-out teeth and loud check suits, emerged a whole generation of all-round entertainers – cuddly-named showmen like Brucie and Tarbie, who ended up dominating Saturday night TV with their gentle brand of comedy song-and-dance routines. But as I was about to discover, Brucie and his golfing chums were only the tip of a very peculiar, glittery iceberg.

During the 1970s and early '80s when variety still topped the bill, hordes of eager young performers packed out clubs and seaside theatres across the land. These palaces of fun, often perched precariously on the ends of rickety piers, were where the stars of variety TV cut their comedy teeth. However, not everyone who performed there would be lucky enough to go on to become the next Doddy or Manning. But having your own flyer and an ad in *Showcall* was a good place to start, and it told the world you were alive and willing to work.

Their advertising methods may seem quaint compared with the slick marketing of today's *The X Factor* generation, but back then it was a long hard slog to the top. Once you were up and running, however, there were several possible routes you could take. Some artistes enjoyed the rough and tumble of the smoky northern club scene and corporate gig circuit, while others dreamed of Scandinavian cruise liners, holiday camps and hotel lobbies. An infinite world of weird opportunities was theirs for the taking and at the back of it all, the exciting possibility of one day making it big. Although the world of entertainment may have changed beyond recognition in the last twenty-five years, with the celebrity gravy train continuing to dominate popular culture, somewhere out there was a bunch of unsung heroes just waiting to be rediscovered. . .

1. But I'm Not Laughing. . .

'So what's the book *really* about, James?'

My old friend Nick always likes to push for the truth.

'It's a nostalgic celebration of the unsung heroes of variety and light entertainment' I reply.

'Come on James. You know what I mean. What's it really, *really* about?'

'Alright, it's a collection of cheesy light entertainers' publicity material from the 1970s and '80s. You know, comedians, ventriloquists, yodelling bird impressionists, that kind of thing. It's a timely reminder of how media savvy we've all become over the past twenty years. . . '

Nick raises an eyebrow.

'Okay, okay. It's about the loss of innocence – our innocence, the entertainment industry's innocence, everybody's innocence. It's about unbridled change. It's abo. . .'

'Balls. It's about failure and you know it. You're laughing at a bunch of never-beens – yesterday's losers. You're taking your own lack of success out on a bunch of old saddoes who can't answer back. Shame on you, Mr Innes-Smith. Shame on you.' Nick enjoys riding his high horse. He wishes he'd been a big-shot lawyer like his father, instead of the two-bit actor he became.

That evening I pondered Nick's accusations – surely he didn't honestly believe I would go out of my way to be horrible to people I'd never met? All I'd done was gather together a bunch of light entertainers' promotional material, put it in a book, and call it

Reach for the Big Time – it had never even occurred to me that I might be accused of laughing at 'saddoes'.

* * *

Sunday Telegraph Letters Page – November 2004: Large picture of a grinning Kenny Cantor circa 1975

I AM NOT A FAILURE – I MADE THE PALLADIUM

I strongly object to the inference that I am a failure or fallen in your feature from a book about entertainers. To my knowledge three of the fifteen entertainers that you list are still working – and working extremely well. You will have caused great vexation not only to those named, but to those who employ them.

It is amazing, here am I doing no harm to anyone, and am subjected to an attack from a writer who obviously knows nothing about show business. Not every one can get to the London Palladium, although I have worked it on many occasions. Not everyone can have a television series, although I have had my own Play Your Cards Right on Television New Zealand. I have been round the world nine times. I starred on the maiden world cruise of the QE2. I starred at the Sydney Opera House, worked with the very best of entertainers: Sir Harry Secombe, Frankie Vaughan, Val Doonican, Howard Keel, plus many more, not just once but many times.

I am now thought of as an authority on some aspects of variety. We have a very successful business, Cantor's Theatre School & Centre for the Performing Arts, teaching young people about being entertainers. Then you try to destroy it all by saying that I am a failure.

Kenny Cantor
Lowestoft, Suffolk

'Hi James. . . Have you seen the letters page in the Torygraph? Told you your book was about failure.' Nick also enjoys rubbing things in.

'But Nick, this is a disaster – Kenny seems genuinely upset.'

'Listen mate – don't worry – he'll get over it. Now let's go out and get drunk.'

But I didn't feel like getting drunk – I felt like being sick.

All-round light entertainer Kenny Cantor had seen an article about *Reach for the Big Time* in the previous week's *Sunday Telegraph*. Although not mentioned by name, his picture was one of fifteen taken from the book. I admit Kenny's photo may not be exactly flattering but then that was the point: 1975 was a deeply unflattering time for everyone, with fashion still stuck in the late '60s and punk only just within spitting distance. Put it this way, back then you could be thrown in the slammer for *not* having a silly haircut and a bushy moustache. Hey, even Elton John looked silly back in 1975 and just look at him now . . . everything about that year was horrible. Beige was everywhere and home décor consisted of brown sofas (a.k.a. comfy settees), swirly brown carpets and doilies arranged on brown teak-effect cabinets. Larry Grayson wore brown polyester slacks and still managed to be the biggest thing on TV. (Back then brown polyester was *the* 'happening' material, despite the mini electrical fireworks display every time you took it off.) The truth is that a glamorous night out in 1975 meant staying in with *The Generation Game* and a bowl of brown Vesta curry.

So, yes, the photo of Mr Cantor was a little. . . out of date: huge specs and an impressive combover; nothing too ridiculous, just classic '75. And yes, the broadsheet journalist had taken some liberties, as journalists always do.

In the midst of the sleepless night that followed, even the question mark at the end of the article's title – 'That's Entertainment?' – began to seem like a betrayal. Whereas I was convinced that my book wasn't meant to be about laughing at losers, the piece had made out they were all a bunch of bargain basement performers who had never made it big. But what is 'making it big' anyway? Obviously for Kenny, 'big' meant working with Val Doonican. And why not? On the other hand, if you were to read that Tom Cruise was now working regularly with Val Doonican, you might – apart from wondering what strange parallel universe you'd stumbled upon – reasonably assume that Tom's career was on the slide. But who knows, maybe wearing cardies, smoking a pipe and gently crooning in a rocking chair is exactly what Tom has been looking for all his life; the perfect antidote to all that boring standing around on chilly film sets. . . Put Kenny Cantor into a twenty-three-bedroom mansion in Beverly Hills and he'd most likely be bored out of his mind after a couple of days and be pining for his friends and life back in his home town of Lowestoft.

As an actor myself, all those clichéd notions of success and failure were suddenly being brought into question. What is our current obsession with celebrity and success-by-any-means-necessary all about? I admit that I remain somewhat disappointed not to have achieved the whole Beverly Hills mansion thing, and yet it's never really occurred to me to ask whether my cosy if uneventful life padding around the streets of Paddington might actually be more fulfilling in the end.

I deliberately hadn't included any commentary in *Reach for the Big Time*. Didn't need to – the photographs spoke volumes and the text on the performers' publicity flyers – consisting of some blurb about the act and a couple of quotes from local newspapers – was wonderful in itself:

The Shades of Harmony are varied with expression with a facility and correctness which attests their great sensibility. – 1979

Thelma Joyce – Brilliant electronic organist, has own drummer available if required. Will travel anywhere to please. – 1973

Jackie Carlton – the North's answer to Peter Wyngard – good with make-up. 'Since New Faces I haven't stopped working – but would love to get back into show business' – 1979

Comedians we've got, genuine funny men are a rare breed – Jackie is one such rarity. – 1974

Gavin Prime – solo act or Gavamania Comedy Package Show. 'Rapidly building a cult following in the Midlands' – 1981

The Disco Kid (long haired man in his late thirties) – 'Not so much a disco as a happening' – 1978

Chubby Oates – 'Fat and funny' – 1978

Peter Robinson – 'Almost too humorous to mention' – 1980

Chris Chapman – 'Most Pleasant' – 1976

David Noble – 'A smooth Bruce Forsyth that the ladies love to love and the males can't help but admire.' – 1975

The directories from which I'd sourced the material for *Reach for the Big Time* are an annual publication going back to the early '70s, listing all the various variety performers and light entertainers of the day. Each artist or act was given a page on which to sell him or herself to booking agents. The format is pretty much the same throughout and remains so to this day – name at the top, a wacky photo in the middle and as much publicity blurb as you can squeeze onto the page.

The day after the *Sunday Telegraph* article appeared I received a panicky call from my publisher. Kenny Cantor had not only complained to the newspapers, he'd also gone straight to the owners of the source material to demand an explanation as to why his face had been on everyone's breakfast table the day before.

'The directory people are desperate to speak to you, James. Please call them as soon as you can.'

The manager at the directories hadn't yet seen the offending article but had spent most of the morning trying to appease a by now furious Kenny Cantor. I was nervous about ringing; I needed somehow to disassociate myself from the article. I felt sure the MD would understand, after all it wasn't as though I'd written the piece, or indeed written anything derogatory in the book.

'Hello, it's James Innes-Smith, author of *Reach for the. . .*'

'Well, it's all very easy isn't it, to take pot shots at people like Kenny Cantor. But the fact is he's furious. You can't go around laughing at people. . .'

'But he's a comedian. . . '

'That's not the point.'

This was turning into a nightmare. *Reach for the Big Time* was already in the shops – my local Waterstone's had twenty copies proudly on display at the checkout – I'd even signed a few to send them on their way.

I needed to talk to Kenny Cantor; calm him down; tell him I was on his side.

Despite protestations to the contrary I *had* actually been given permission to take the directories away to be professionally photographed for the book. Tracing all the acts, however, had proved extremely difficult and with a publication date looming, the publishers had decided to include a disclaimer to cover our backs should anyone come out of the woodwork:

While the author and publisher have made every effort to contact all the artists featured in this book, the publisher would be glad to hear from anyone they have been unable to reach.

Tracking down the various performers had been particularly hard because the contact details printed at the bottom of the publicity flyers were all hopelessly out of date. Telephone numbers typically read 'Bolton 6473' or 'Wallop-under-Bush 2765' – impossible to say in anything but a 1940s *Brief Encounter* voice – and utterly useless as working telephone numbers. Some did have working numbers but the original occupants had long since moved on – cue a series of embarrassing calls to bemused strangers:

'Oh, hello, I wonder if you could help me, my name's James Innes-Smith, I'm trying to contact Leslie Melville.'

'Who?'
'Mr Melville. . . the bird impressionist?'
'Sorry mate, I'm Geoff. . . '
'Oh.'
'. . . I drive a van. Meat deliveries mainly.'
'Do you know where I might locate Mr Melville?'
'No idea mate. Down the zoo practising?'

'Could I speak to Terry Burgess and his Cavalcade of Fun?'
'Sod off! Never heard of him.'

I needed a large slug of whisky before plucking up enough courage to ring Kenny Cantor. With huge amounts of trepidation I picked up the phone and started dialling.

'Hello, who's that?'

'Hi, it's James Innes-Smith, author of *Reach*. . . '

'Well, young man, I hope you're satisfied. You've caused my wife and me a lot of pain and upset. We haven't slept all week. . . not since it happened. A local paper has picked up on the story and is being very cruel about me. I've become the laughing stock of Lowestoft.'

'Oh dear, I'm so, so sorry. I want to assure you that I had no intention of. . . '

'My son is being bullied at school because of that article. . . '

'Yes but I didn't write – '

'The other kids are laughing at him for having a failure for a father. Can you imagine how that must feel? I can quite honestly say this has been the worst week of my life. And now my business is going to suffer as a result. Why would anyone want to send their child to a Stage School run by a failure? I'm absolutely outraged. . . '

He was in full spate, so I simply listened and made understanding noises.

'I'm not going to let this lie,' he continued 'someone *has* to be answerable for what's happened. I need to clear my name.'

Poor man. . . I sat in silence for a moment, contemplating the mess. What had started out as a nostalgic piece of fun, a light-hearted Christmas gift book, was rapidly turning into a car-crash. . .

Kenny hadn't even seen the book but as far as he was concerned I was still to blame for the fact that someone else had written about it.

Until the issue of permissions was resolved, the publishers decided that the best solution was to remove all copies of *Reach for the Big Time* from the shops and place them in storage.

I had no idea what would happen next. There was talk of

dishing out some sort of financial compensation, but Kenny wasn't interested in cash – he simply wanted his dignity back.

The following day I received a call from my editor.

'We've reached a compromise' she told me firmly. 'If you can obtain permissions from every single performer within one month then the book can go ahead as planned. If not, I'm afraid *Reach for the Big Time* will have to be pulped. As I'm sure you are aware, under the terms of your contract you will then be responsible for all production and pulping costs, which we estimate to be approximately £25,000.'

I didn't even hear the final caveat – I just felt a rush of euphoria. As far as I was concerned *Reach for the Big Time* had been saved. I punched the air like an American sports hero. It was only after I'd poured myself another large whisky to celebrate that the details of the compromise began to sink in. I felt shaky and immediately started flicking through *Reach for the Big Time* – so many expectant faces grinning back at me. This was going to be a mammoth undertaking. But failure wasn't an option. I didn't have £25,000 and there was no way, short of robbing a bank, that I was ever going to get hold of such a large sum of money.

I sat up all night in a dazed stupor, contemplating my fate. The whisky only made things worse. Euphoria had turned to stomach ache. Locating these old timers could take several months, years even. I'd been given a month; four miserable weeks – twenty-eight measly days. . . surely it just wasn't physically possible, not without the help of M15, The Missing Persons Bureau, and a nation-wide billboard campaign. I poured another large whisky, sat at my desk and stared at the cover of *Reach for the Big Time*. Comedian Dick Pleasant, who I'd chosen as my cover-star, seemed to be pleading with me through his waxed pencil moustache.

For the next few days, the spectre of £25,000 loomed over everything I did. I'd walk past shops and beat myself up over all the things I would never be able to afford if the book were to be pulped: twenty plasma TVs, a BMW 3 Series, 25 000 scratch cards, twenty-nine round the world tickets, 83 333 Chunky Kit Kats. . .

But far worse than the fear of bankruptcy was the worry that maybe I really had ruined these poor people's lives; that Kenny Cantor would now be remembered for being 'that loser from the newspaper article'.

I sat around my flat, miserably wondering what all those other light entertainers from the book were up to now. Did northern comic Tony Peers still refer to himself as 'A Very Funny Man'? And was he still wearing that loud checked suit? And what about Keith Manifold, might he still be yodelling and singing country ballads all these years later? Who were the camp-sounding *Gay Duo* and were they still performing 'songs about the gay way of life'? Had I inadvertently ruined their careers as well?

I felt I was entering a 'Lost Key' moment. You know what it's like – you lose your house keys and spend three hours searching in all the obvious places: coat pockets, under the bed, back of the wardrobe, in the washing machine, all to no avail. You've answered 'Dunno' to the well-meaning but fatuous 'where did you lose them?' question. So out of sheer desperation you begin looking in all the really obscure places. The sort of places only a nutter would leave keys: under the floorboards, inside the cereal packet, on the roof, inside the fridge, buried in the garden. You know in your guts it's a waste of time but you can't help yourself, you simply have to look. . .

If I was to do this properly, I needed to be organised. Writing a list seemed like a good idea. I carefully typed out all the names of my entertainers onto a sheet of A4 and then immediately typed them out again in a smaller font size to make the list seem shorter. I then tried to work out what I needed to do logically, using simple mathematics: I had to find a total of thirty-three performers in four weeks – or three weeks and five days as it now was. That was the equivalent of 8.25 performers per week or 1.1785714 per day.

I tried to pull myself together, gee myself up. 1.1785714 per day wasn't that bad – at least it wasn't two. Three weeks and five days suddenly seemed like more than enough time. Detectives are expected to track down muggers, murderers and rapists with only a single hair to go on. Surely finding a bunch of adorably toothy entertainers with names like Dick Pleasant, Ken Joy and Chubby Oates wasn't going to be that difficult. And yet still my heart would sink at the prospect. But then I'd have to quickly remind myself that, in theory at least, it was possible, which meant I had to try. Only this time there would be no disclaimer to fall back on. This yo-yoing effect would remain with me all day. I kept reassuring myself that anything was possible with dedication, hard work and. . . aha!. . . a little help from some friends. Ah, yes, good old reliable friends, surely they'd be delighted to help me out in my hour of need.

'Yeah Justin, all I need you to do is make a few calls; it would be such a help. . . '

'I'd love to help you out mate, I really would, but I'm absolutely frantic right now. I will be free towards the end of the month though if that's any good to you?'

'By the end of the month the book will be lavatory roll.'

I tried my friend Jenny – a fiendishly organised PA who even takes a clipboard to bed with her at night.

'Hi Jenny, any chance you could help me out with a spot of bother? I just need you to Google a few names, just for an afternoon or two. . . '

'What? Hello? Is that Dave? Dave, I'm in New Zealand. Bit of a bad line. . . '

'What, in New Zealand right now?'

'Yes, you've reached me on my mobile numb. . . '

'Sorry Jenny, got to go, can't afford it. Bye.'

No, I'd got myself into this mess – it was up to me to find a way out.

More waves of panic. . .

2. Contact any Leading Agent...

Reach for the Deadline: three weeks and five days to go...
As well as the uncontactable contact details, most of my entertainers had also included agents' details on their publicity flyers. This would be my next line of attack. On closer inspection, however, these tended to be little more than a separate phone line set up in the performer's own house. This was especially true of the more Beverly Hills-sounding agencies:

Terry Butterfoot – Juggler and After Dinner Speaker
Agent: 'International Entertainment Inc.'
Sunny Cliffe Crescent
Morecambe
Lancs.
Contact Terry on Morecambe 2246

Homely addresses were always a dead give-away. Hollywood sounding agent = back room of a bungalow in Bradford. One entertainer had listed his agent's address as:

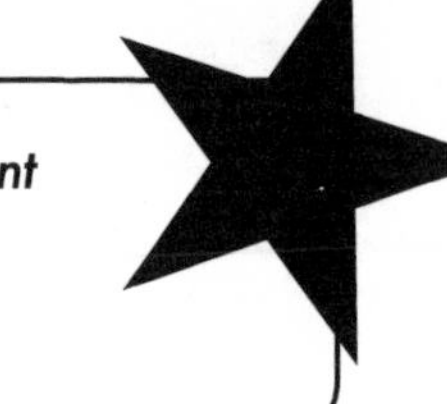

Andy Parfitt International Artists Management
Contact: Room 23
Sea View Hotel,
Scarborough

You can just imagine his wake-up call. . .

I was beginning to learn this lost language of agents and there was something curiously touching about the lengths to which performers were prepared to go to make themselves sound important. There seemed to be several distinct types of agent listed. As well as the small-time talent scouts with bungalow delusions of Hollywood grandeur, there were also the 'no sole agent' listings, which I took to mean 'I know loads of agents but haven't got one. . . yet'. 'Contact any leading agent' meant 'I can't get an agent but lots of them have heard of me.' The most touching entries of all seemed to involve a kindly relative acting as representative to a struggling sibling – someone willing to answer calls from prospective employers using a separate address, thereby giving the whole agent thing a bit more clout:

Ken Mingle (laughter all the way)
Chestnut Way
Cheadle
Contact agent:
'The Mingle International Partnership'
Chestnut Way
Cheadle
Staffs.
Contact: Eric Mingle on Cheadle 3472

Some of the more established agents were still in operation and there followed some pretty surreal phone calls. The boss of an agency in Bolton who had seemed particularly keen to help turned out to be vague in the extreme.

'Ah yes, 'Candy Rock' – I remember them now, they played rock'n roll' on the Northern holiday camp circuit. Must be over thirty years ago. I think the singer – or was it the guitarist – lived somewhere in France, though I couldn't for the life of me tell you where. Alicante possibly? As for the other members of the group. . . actually now I come to think of it, I believe the drummer – oh God, what's his name – moved to Leicester. . . or was it Derby? Oh dear, my poor old brain. . . '

Hopeless. I needed proper leads – street names, current telephone numbers. . . I needed help!

3. Go Forth and Multiply. . .

I still haven't managed to track down a single act from my 'most wanted' list. My entertainer-per-day-ratio has just increased to 3.27. This is going to be even harder than I expected.

The clock above my desk has become my worst enemy. I'm now convinced the second hand has mysteriously speeded itself up just to panic me. Minutes no longer exist; hours zip by like minutes, reminding me that every hour I spend worrying is another hour wasted.

I keep going over my list of names, hoping for inspiration. Nothing. . . but then the following morning something remarkable happens. I receive an unexpected package from an old friend living in Birmingham. It contains a copy of his local newspaper, *The Sunday Mercury*. On the front page he's scribbled 'Turn to pages twenty-eight and twenty-nine – congratulations Jim on a fantastic sounding book!! XXX Andy.'

There on the centre pages is an article about *Reach for the Big Time*, which includes nine pictures and a short appeal from the journalist:

Are YOU one of the acts featured in our article? If so we'd like to hear from you. Call or send us an email.

How could this be? While I've been desperately tearing my hair out trying to think of ways to contact my entertainers, an enterprising young journalist has already put an ingenious plan into action.

But what does he want with my Big-Timers? Had he heard about my quest, or was he simply intrigued to hear from them?

A couple of days later I call him to check if anyone's rung.

'No nothing yet I'm afraid James – but don't forget we're only a local paper with a small circulation. Leave me your number though and I'll call you straight away if I hear from anyone. By the way – love the book. I really hope you can save it in time – if there's anything else I can do to help please don't hesitate to call. And whatever you do, don't give up your search!'

I'm immediately plunged back into misery. If any of my entertainers were going to call they'd have surely done so by now.

That evening, Nick and my girlfriend prize me out from under my desk.

'You need cheering up,' announces Nick 'we're taking you for a Chinese. And for heaven's sake smarten yourself up man. . . you look terrible.'

I haven't been out of the house for days and am beginning to get that haunted, agoraphobic look – the rings under my eyes have turned purple and my hair is a twisted mat from so much tossing and turning.

It feels good to be out of the house at last, although it takes a while for my eyes to acclimatise themselves to the outside world; the harsh strip lighting in the Chinese restaurant is particularly painful. We order half a crispy duck as usual and as usual it arrives tepid and late. We're onto our third bottle of house white when the subject inevitably turns to my impossible plight. Nick is in one of his cocky moods.

'One month – you've got to be kidding right? You'll never do it. It's not possible. Just pay the twenty-five grand and move on.'

'Hey, I thought you were supposed to be cheering me up.'

My girlfriend comes to the rescue. 'Look, we need to think about this logically.'

'But I've already applied logic, it doesn't help!' I cry.

'Alright, calm down – do you have any leads at all?'

'No.'

Nick scoffs and shakes his head.

'What about Actors' Equity, don't they keep records of performers' names and contact details?'

'Already tried them. . . '

'Are there any old time music hall societies you could. . . '

'Dunno. . . '

'Okay, what about Kenny Cantor?'

'What about him?'

'Have you tried talking to him?'

'Yes. He hates me – thinks I've ruined his life.'

Nick snorts loudly as he gulps down another large glass of white.

'Then maybe you need to prove to him that you meant him no harm.'

I'm not sure I like where this is heading.

'But how?'

'Go and see him. . . '

I must admit, the thought had crossed my mind. . . briefly.

'But I'm scared – he thinks I've ruined his life.'

'Hang on a minute; didn't he boast in his letter to the paper that he knew of other entertainers from the book who were also still working?'

'Yes but. . . '

'So?'

'So, he probably hates me even more for ruining their lives as well. . . '

'No, silly. Don't you see? Kenny is now your only hope. You need to go and apologise to him personally, show him the book and make sure he gives you those other contact details.'

'But that still leaves all the others to find. . . '

Nick gets up to leave.

'I say don't waste your time – sod the lot of them. . . ', and on that helpful note, he stumbles off into the night.

'Ignore him. Look, it's a start. Think about it dummy – what's the time-span of your book?'

'Mid '70s to early '80s. But what's that got to do with anything?'

'Don't you get it? You've got thirty or so performers all touring the country at around the same time, right?'

'Right.'

'So isn't it inevitable that their paths will have crossed at some point? They probably all performed at the same clubs and holiday camps. All you need to do is show them your copy of *Reach for the Big Time* and hope it jogs a few memories. And you'll be killing two birds with one stone. You've been obsessed by these people for a whole year – well now is your chance to actually meet them. Kenny Cantor and co. are a dying breed, a forgotten part of the entertainment industry. Go and see them before it's too late and they all end up dead. You'll only regret it if you don't. Who knows, you might even have some fun along the way – and judging by those rings under your eyes you could certainly use some of that right now.'

She was right. Those simple black and white photos had bred

affection in me for Dick Pleasant and his ilk. These were oddball characters without a voice – the flotsam and jetsam of a kinder, more innocent era. It would be great to meet them all. And maybe I could kill three birds with one stone by proving to Nick the Cynic that they weren't all a bunch of failures.

This was the best (and only) plan yet.

4. 'A Hard Act to Follow'

One year earlier...
On hearing the good news that my agent had finally sold *Reach for the Big Time* to a publisher, I decided to go a little crazy. Although the advance had been modest by today's standards, by my standards I was suddenly rich, rich, rich. Considering my current financial predicament, what happened next seems reckless in the extreme. In all the excitement of not being broke anymore, I started throwing my money about in earnest: holiday for two in Cornwall; new suit from an elderly man in Savile Row who called me sir a lot; and a week of non-stop crispy duck from the Chinese. But what I really wanted more than anything was a car – nothing flash, just something to remind me of the book – something retro and fun.

My last car – a four-shades-of-brown 1981 Vauxhall Chevette – seemed to get a real kick out of making me suffer. Oily-fingered blokes from the AA would take one look at my heap of rusting metal and burst into hysterical laughter. All their talk of dented flank-drives, dodgy catterbearings, leaking jenny-whips and rusty minge-pipes used to scare me half to death. That and the fact that 'combustion' and 'engine' were so often used in the same sentence.

Why cars haven't gone digital like everything else is a mystery to me. It seems incredible that we are still merrily driving around in what is the transport equivalent of a horned gramophone player.

To help me choose which car to buy, I turned to my friend Jim, who knows a thing or two about 'motors' as he likes to calls them. I've never been very good at making purchase decisions – I usually end up full of regrets: 'if only I'd bought the bigger one or the more expensive brand or the silver-plated version'.

A hundred years ago, deciding which car to buy was easy – there was only one make; it was called a Ford and it came in one colour: black; one shape: boxy; and one engine size: slow. If you couldn't afford one you shrugged your undernourished shoulders and continued using the tram.

'Hi Jim, I'm after a cheap second-hand car – need your help. What do you think of those old Morris Marinas?'

'Worst car ever made if you ask me – that and the Hillman Avenger. I blame British Leyland for under-investing. . .' and so begins a long tirade about the parlous state of the British car industry in the '70s. Jim just loves talking about cars and will litter his speech with phrases like 'you can't beat a quality camshaft' and 'the standard shemmy-scalp is far superior to the mendip-scat-head'. My pathetic attempts to sound knowledgeable – 'I much prefer yellow cars to blue' – just doesn't really cut it.

I continued down my list of potential car-purchases.

'What about a Morris Ital? My mate's uncle used to swear by his.'

'I'm not surprised, I'd have sworn by mine if I'd been stupid enough to buy one.'

'Austin Princess?'

'Austin "Scurvy Knave" more like.'

'How about a Ford Cortina – they were pretty cool. . . '

'You do realise Cortina means 'tin-can' in Latin? Really, it does.'

I put him on hold while I checked my Latin dictionary. Bloody hell he was right!

'What about a Hillman Imp?'

'Now you're being silly.'

Half an hour later and I was still no wiser about which car to buy. So I asked him again in words of one syllable.

'Jim – which car I buy please?'

'I'm not sure I'm really the right person to ask.'

Not the right person to ask? We gave Jim the nickname 'Motor-mouth' for two very good reasons.

'But Jim,' I whimpered, 'you eat, breathe and smell of car. You've just spent the last half-hour proving how knowledgeable you are about cars. I would have said you were absolutely the right person to give advice on which one to buy.'

'Yes but I'm in a whole different game. You're after something cheap and reliable, whereas I deal in expensive, love-and-labour-intensive motors. My only advice to you is whatever you choose, make sure it's modern, bland and reliable.'

The thought of buying something 'modern, bland and reliable' with my advance made me feel depressed. I wanted something to remind me of the characters in my book, something eccentric and wacky – a '70s classic. Jim promised to keep an eye out and advised me in the meantime to go and buy a copy of *Practical Classics* – a magazine for people who love old cars but hate getting their hands dirty.

At the time everyone kept advising me against buying a car; that in the long run it was much cheaper to travel by train or by coach. But these were people who had obviously never been on a National Express coach surrounded by grumpy, incontinent pensioners. Besides, 'coaches' aren't coaches at all; they're buses. When did you last see a brace of sleek black stallions pulling seventy-nine grumpy pensioners and an undernourished student up the M6? I'm sorry National Express, but coaches are elegant nineteenth century horse-drawn vehicles driven by whip-wielding gentlemen in top hats and billowing cloaks; buses smell of sick and are driven by fat sweaty blokes in yellow-tinted specs and stained polyester shirts. The fact is, all travel in the UK is inefficient and slow, but at least in a car you can sing along to *Deep Purple's* 'Highway Star', bellow-belch and pick your nose to your nose's content – and I wouldn't recommend doing any of that on the 5.45 Virgin Express to Nuneaton.

As I flicked through *Practical Classics*, one article in particular jumped out at me. It told of a middle-aged executive who had traded in his sporty new Jaguar for a late '70s Ford Capri. It was the 'car he'd always promised himself', just like in the advert. This was the sort of car I was after – a car that seemed to sum up everything that was mad about the 1970s – a car that would definitely remind me of my dotty entertainers.

I rang Jim immediately and told him to keep a look-out. A week later he called me back with some exciting news.

'I've found you a couple of cheap Capris in *Classic Car* magazine. Arrange a viewing and I'll come and look at them with you.'

I thanked him and immediately rang the first of the two numbers.

'Hello, I'm ringing up about the Capri – is it still available?'

'Yeah. . . '

'Great – could you tell me a little bit more about it?'

'It's yellow.'

'Yyyyes. . .'

'With a brown roof.'

'Right. Anything else I should know?'

'Dunno.' Cough. . . wheeze. . . splutter.

Here was a man utterly lacking in social skills, but it didn't matter because that croaky voice and phlegmy cough suggested he was old – a good thing according to Jim: 'Old people are much more careful drivers.' I'm not so sure. My father is getting on a bit but that doesn't stop him from driving like a boy-racer in built-up areas and like an old lady delivering cakes on motorways.

'I see – and how many miles has the car done?' I continued.

'Erm. Quite a few.'

'Like how many. . . ?'

'Oh I dunno. . . thousands.'

'I see. And how long have you had it?'

'Had what?'

'The CAPRI.'

Old wheezer was about as communicative as a gerbil. Fortunately, I'd been studying Quentin Wilson's '101 Essential Tips on Buying a Second Hand Car' in *Practical Classics*. Quentin reckoned the attitude of the seller was as important as low mileage, a long MOT and brakes that actually helped you stop in an emergency. 'Sellers should show passion, expertise and charm' advised Quentin. Well, my asthmatic friend had failed pretty spectacularly on all three counts.

'How's the interior and upholstery?' I continued.

'Up-what?'

'Holstery. The cloth. . . how are the seats and the carpet?'

'Fine. . . considerin'. . . '

Considering what – his lack of bowel control?

Despite an unpromising start, I arranged a viewing with Jim for the following day.

The owner, Graham, lived on a grubby housing estate off Kennington Road. Dressed in a baggy grey vest, he was much younger and fatter than I'd imagined. He greeted us at the front door with a plate of toast in one hand and his testicles in the other.

'Thought you was comin' t'morrer.'

'It is tomorrow.'

'Oh. Is it?'

The car was a complete mess – more rust than metal. Great flakes came away in our hands and the interior had a really unpleasant smell that I can only describe as biscuity-feet. He offered to take us for a test drive but we politely declined.

From its description in *Classic Car* mag, Capri number two seemed a much better prospect: only 50 000 miles on the clock and two previous owners.

'I've had every make of Ford ever produced in the UK' said Nick, the owner, as we inspected the interior for rust and unholy smells.

Nick had obviously looked after his old classic – the bodywork was in great nick with only a small amount of rust around the sunroof. But the real clincher for me was the name on the badge. I couldn't believe my eyes when I first saw it – if I'd been looking for a car to remind me of my entertainers this was it – a limited edition Ford Capri Cabaret. I had to have it. The cabaret circuit had kept my entertainers on the road throughout the '70s – and now my Cabaret would keep me on the road throughout the Noughties. For £700, Nick was also willing to throw in his International Capri Club membership card, an invitation to the club's annual knees-up and a couple of cheesy posters from the car's original advertising campaign:

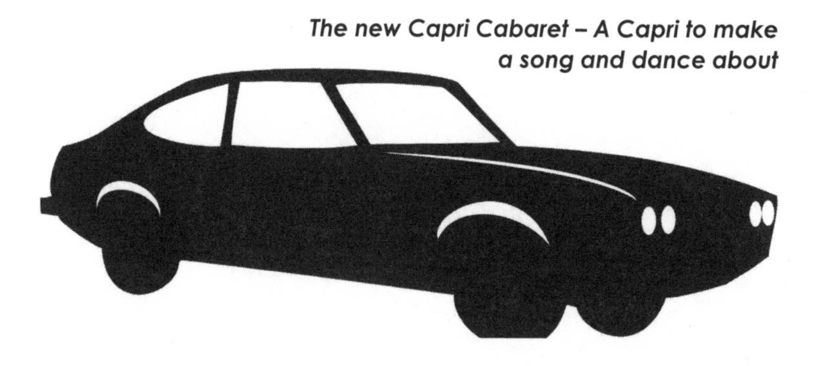

I'd never fallen in love with a car before, but that night I sat at the computer merrily Googling the word Capri. Apart from being a mystical island in the Mediterranean colonised by Caesar Augustus in 29BC, I also learnt that 'Capri' was an acronym for 'Critical Assessment of Prediction of Regional Interaction', described on the website as a 'community-wide experimentation, the comparative of protein – protein for docking for structure prediction' – whatever that means... More importantly, I discovered that nearly every town in Britain had its very own Capri Owners Club. I'd even found a website where people could send in their Capri jokes. I particularly liked:

Q: What's the difference between sheep and Capris?
A: People don't get embarrassed being seen in sheep.

Q: What's the difference between a hedgehog and a Capri?
A: The hedgehog has the pricks on the outside.

and...

Q: How do you get to Wales in a Capri?
A: You won't.

It felt as though I'd joined some weirdly exclusive club. And now, all these months later, I actually had somewhere other than Tesco's to drive to.

Next stop, Lowestoft...

5. 'Up Them All!'

Reach for the Deadline: three weeks and three days to go. For a whole year my only impression of Kenny Cantor had been from that 1975 black and white photo of a zany-looking man in his forties with spectacularly large bottle-lensed spectacles. But now he had a voice, a personality. . . and a vendetta against me.

Like most of the other performers in my book, Kenny had filled his flyer with glowing reviews and vivid descriptions of how brilliant he was:

International Comedy Entertainer Kenny Cantor is funny all over the world – we hope that you will enjoy seeing this musical, singing, dancing, juggling, ad-libbing idiot, who can write, design and direct his own shows.

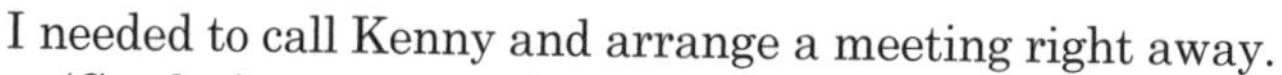

I needed to call Kenny and arrange a meeting right away.

'Good afternoon.'

'Could I speak to Kenny please?'

'Who's speaking?'

'It's James Innes-Smith, author of *Rea. . .* '

'This is his wife. You've got a nerve ringing here. You have no idea how much trouble you've caused.'

'That's why I'm ringing. I wanted to come and apologise, try and explain about the book. Could I have a quick word with Kenny?'

'He's over at the theatre school. You'll have to ring his mobile but I doubt he'll want to talk to you.'

Thankfully Kenny does seem ready to talk. He's calmed down a lot since our last conversation and tells me he's feeling more jaded now than angry. He just can't understand why anyone would want to mock what he does for a living, especially in such a well-respected newspaper ('All my friends read the *Telegraph*').

I ask whether he would mind if I drove over to see him to try and patch things up. He seems reticent at first.

'I'm a very busy man; I can't really spare the time.'

I try and reassure him that my intentions are honourable and that I won't take up much of his precious time.

'All I need is half an hour, just to talk things over.'

'Very well. I'm around first thing tomorrow. But like I say, I'm a very, very busy man.'

Apart from a strange rattling coming from the boot, Cabaret's first big trip up the A12 has gone without major incident. Unfortunately 'Mapquest' hasn't been quite so reliable.

I'm in the small village of Kessingland, five miles south of Lowestoft, and have been driving round in circles for an hour trying to find Kenny's house. By some strange twist of fate I've somehow managed to end up in the car park of a nearby Pontin's Holiday Camp – a place I'm sure Kenny is more than familiar with. An official-looking man at the gates gives me directions back to Kenny's house, but ten minutes later I seem to be heading down an unpromising looking dirt track.

'You're approaching me from the wrong end!' This is the third time Kenny has had to bellow instructions at me down the phone.

'. . .Keep the orchard on your left.'

'What orchard?'

'The one you should be keeping on your left. Oh this is ridiculous. Tell you what, I'll stand in the street and wave, so you know it's me. Toot your horn when you see me.'

'Okay, I'm in a blue "Y" reg Ford Capri.'

He needn't have bothered waving – I recognise him immediately by his massive red-framed Timmy Mallet-style spectacles. He's wearing loud orange and yellow shorts, thin beige ankle socks and brown slip-ons. His mobile phone hangs around his neck like a strange medallion.

'Good grief, what took you so long? I can't wait about all day, I have things to do – I'm a very busy man.' He chivvies me down the garden path towards a bright red front door. But before allowing me inside he decides to test my sense of humour.

'Do you get it?' he asks pointing up at a name etched in wood above the door.

'Get what?' I ask.

'The name of my house, Uppham Hall. Get it?'

'Erm. . . ' I suppose it is quite amusing that this small semi-detached house has been given such a grand sounding name but that isn't the joke. It's actually a play on the words 'up', 'them', and 'all'

'. . . It was named in honour of the incompetent builders who worked on this house.'

'Would you like a glass of water?' Kenny asks, fetching himself a cold beer from a '70s style cocktail cabinet. 'I've been in two minds all day about whether to see you after the all the trouble you've caused. My wife Caron is devastated.'

'I'm so sorry.' I reply weakly.

'But it's not fair. I've done nothing wrong.'

'I know – which is why we need to make sure the book goes ahead. . . '

He looks at me aghast.

'You are joking right? Why in God's name would I want that bloody book to go ahead after what's happened?'

'Because if the book gets pulped, we all lose out. I'll end up having to pay £25,000 in costs and. . . '

'Well that's not my fault, is it, young man? We've all suffered. . . '

'. . . Exactly, but if we can save the book, people will be able to make up their own minds about whether you were a failure or not. Otherwise all those people who mocked might continue thinking of you as "that loser from the article".'

'But I haven't even seen the book – I don't know what it is. Nobody has had the decency to send me a copy. As far as I'm concerned it might be incredibly damaging.'

Crunch time. . .

'. . . Which is why I've brought you my one and only copy to look at.'

It's now up to Kenny to decide whether the book is a piss-take or not. He begins flicking, manically at first, desperate to find his image so he can assess the damage. But it isn't long before he becomes distracted by all those familiar names and faces from the past. I watch as his face turns from concerned scowl to toothy grin.

'You know what?' he says perkily, 'I reckon I've probably met or worked with most of the people in this book. Even this handsome fella. . . '

He holds the open book up beside his face and points to a photograph of a man with similarly large spectacles, a slightly fuller haircut and an identical grin. Thirty years on, Kenny's hardly changed a bit. If anything he looks slightly younger and better looking now.

As he continues flicking and chortling I wander over to the cocktail bar where he keeps all his many trinkets collected over thirty years of touring. A large plastic sign advertising 'The Star's Bar' hangs above a shelf cluttered with Toby jugs, chintzy Planet Hollywood souvenirs and a glass tumbler with 'Sick as a Parrot' written across it.

I stand, quietly looking through an old photograph album, anxious not to impinge on his memories. Perhaps he'll be able to give me even more contact details than just the few working performers mentioned in his letter – maybe he has a little black book with the names and addresses of all the light entertainers he's ever worked with. I savour the fantasy for a moment. Could it be that my quest was about to become a whole lot easier?

Watching Kenny hunched over the book, eyes bulging through three-inch milk-bottle lenses, I feel a sudden pang of affection. It's been over a year since I first uncovered his grainy old black and white photograph and now here he is in front of me in all his bespectacled glory.

It suddenly occurs to me how odd this meeting is. After all, Kenny is largely responsible for the pickle I now find myself in. And yet here I am sitting in Uppham Hall, desperately wanting to give that very same man a hug for possibly being the only person alive able to save my book.

He places *Reach for the Big Time* on a small leatherette pouffe and announces that he has to go and pick up his daughter, Shani.

I ask if I can come along for the ride.

He remains tight-lipped as we drive over to Beccles where Shani is practising some dance routines for a forthcoming talent contest.

Shani is still on stage when we arrive, so Kenny suggests a pint in the pub opposite.

'So what exactly do you want from me?' he asks, tucking into a bag of crisps.

I brace myself. 'In that letter you wrote to the newspaper you said you knew several of the other acts from the book. I'd like to be able to apologise to them too – ask them personally if they'd like to be in the book.'

'And you want me to give you contact details right? Well I'm not so sure. What if they're dead against being included?'

'It's completely up to them. If they choose not to be part of it then the book will be pulped at the end of the month as planned.'

'Look, as long as none of this reflects badly on me.'

'I promise.'

'Okay, I'm in. . . '

Brilliant – now all I had to do was convince him to sign a publisher's release. A worry, as many of the sub-clauses can seem baffling and intimidating to the uninitiated:

I hereby irrevocably give permission for my image to be used in all media whether now or hereafter known or devised for the full period of copyright and all extensions and renewals thereof (insofar as is possible) in perpetuity throughout the known universe and beyond. . .

Kenny scratches his head as he reads through the convoluted paragraphs.

'I don't really like signing forms' he says nervously.

A couple of pints later Kenny has become quite excited about my journey into his wacky world of entertainment and is happy to sign on the dotted line.

He even suggests turning my quest into a TV reality show. 'We're all mad in this business you know.'

I feel I've found a new ally in Kenny as he starts rifling through a pile of paperwork looking for the first of his three contacts. . .

'How could that *Telegraph* journalist call Kenny Baker a failure? The man's a major movie star for heaven's sake.'

This is certainly news to me. I only know Kenny Baker as one half of dwarf double act, *The Mini Tones* – featured on page ninety of *Reach for the Big Time.*

'Haven't you heard of *Star Wars*?' he rolls his eyes.

I have of course heard of *Star Wars* but am probably the only person left on earth not to have actually seen any of the films. I still have no idea who Luke Skywalker is or how Darth Vader became a Lord. Kenny shakes his head in disbelief.

'You've heard of R2-D2 right?'

'Was he the skinny camp robot or the squat wheely one?'

Kenny throws his hands over his face in utter despair.

'Kenny Baker has played the 'squat wheely one', as you call it, in all six *Star Wars* movies. He's a legend!'

But hang on. Isn't that a bit like calling Stanley Bates a legend for being the bloke inside the Bungle suit on *Rainbow*?

Kenny suddenly starts scrabbling through a pile of old papers and pulls out a Sunday supplement magazine from the week before. On the back is a full-page advertisement for *Star Wars Episode VI – Revenge of the Sith*, including details of a 'spectacular' premiere taking place in Leicester Square, a mere two days from now.

'If you look carefully you can see his name, just there, under the title. You should get yourself an invitation to the premiere.'

I like where Kenny's coming from but I'm not so sure it's possible to wangle your way into a film premiere on the pretext that you're simply dying to meet the contents of a small robot.

'By the way, have you seen this?' He hands me a cutting from a recent copy of *The Sun*. On page five is a large picture of Kenny Baker being pursued by photographers outside a courthouse. It appears Kenny's recent conviction for drink driving has resulted in a ban and some unwelcome tabloid intrusion.

'You see? I told you he was famous.'

Unfortunately Kenny C can't find Kenny B's contact details so he suggests I try contacting him through his website.

While he's firing up his PC I nip next door for a drink. I notice the walls of his sitting room are covered in clown paintings – some in mid flower-squirt, others dragging lonely suitcases. Turns out Kenny is from a long line of circus folk (his grandfather was head clown with a large travelling circus). There's definitely something of the clown about Kenny as he makes a space for me at the computer.

Kenny B's extensive website has only been up and running for a couple of months and is dedicated to all his many fans around the world:

Hi. It's Kenny Baker here and welcome to my official website. I have had this website developed for you my fans, so we can keep in contact every hour of every day throughout the year and not just at conventions.

Knowing how notoriously obsessive *Star Wars* fans can be I'd say this was quite a brave move on Kenny's part. Should he really be asking all those sci-fi-spods to keep in contact EVERY hour of EVERY day? I hope he doesn't mind total strangers turning up on his doorstep claiming to be R2-D2's illegitimate son.

Kenny even has his own online shop – twenty-five quid gets you a signed photo of Kenny's head poking out of R2-D2's neck. Also included is a list of last year's *Star Wars* convention appearances and a link to a not very good picture gallery with blurred shots of Kenny signing autographs at a convention. My favourite part of the site is the FAQ page:

Frequently Asked Question: 'How hot is it inside the costume?'

Frequently Answered Answer: 'Once on location in Tunisia someone fried an egg on R2-D2's shell. The hottest it ever got while I was inside was 127 degrees Fahrenheit.'

George Lucas – if you're reading this – please provide Kenny with an electric fan for Episodes 7, 8 and 9.

FAQ: 'How do you get into and out of R2-D2?'
FAA: 'The head is lifted off, and I am lowered in by two people, there is a seat inside which I can sit on.'

Sounds like some kind of weird medieval torture. . .

FAQ: 'What do you do inside R2-D2?
FAA: 'I sit inside and listen to instructions, it can be very noisy in there at times, so I have to be alert. I have two levers to enable movement from side to side, but I can only move three inches at a time.'

And you thought veal calves had it bad. . .

Finally I click on the 'Send Kenny a message!' link and start typing furiously.

Dear Kenny

I hope you don't mind but I recently included your 1974 Mini Tones *publicity photograph in my book about light entertainers. The book is called* Reach for the Big Time *and is a collection of publicity material from the '70s and '80s. You may have seen some of the recent press coverage. Anyway, the book has had to be withdrawn until I've secured permissions from everyone involved. I know this may sound strange seeing as you are already in the book but would it be possible to meet up so that I can show it to you and get your personal approval? I was thinking maybe before or after the* Sith *premiere later this week? I'm fascinated to find out more about you and your band,* The Mini Tones*. We could also have a chat about the robot if that's not too boring for you.*

Best wishes

James Innes-Smith

Meanwhile Kenny C has found me leads for yodelling country singer Keith Manifold and night club performer Bunny Lewis. To celebrate I suggest a stroll down to Pontin's.

On the way, Kenny talks openly about his hopes and dreams. Beneath that wacky exterior lies a rather serious, thoughtful man.

'So why the extreme facial furniture?' I ask.

'Because big glasses are funny of course. Don't you think they're funny?'

'They're certainly unusual' I reply.

'But do you think they're funny?'

'I'd say they were more startling than funny.' Kenny seems slightly irritated by this revelation.

'You probably don't understand – in show business, you need to have something unique in order to get noticed – something nobody else has got. These glasses became my unique something – my signature if you like. And I have plenty more pairs where they came from.' (Later he shows me a drawer packed with every conceivable shape and colour of spectacle.)

But did he, I wonder, own a normal pair of glasses for wearing around the house? His mood suddenly changes as he hurries off down the driveway towards the crazy golf course. I have to run to keep up. He doesn't seem to like the term 'normal'. It seems some of the more conventional residents of Kessingland don't appreciate his eccentric dress sense. But, why, he argues, shouldn't he be different and wear wacky specs if he likes? What's so great about being 'normal'? Continuing to wear the specs reminds him that despite what anyone else thinks, he's still an entertainer at heart. But what sort of entertainer is he? He seems reluctant to be pigeon-holed.

'The trouble with me is I'm talented at too many things. Being an all-rounder has done me no favours, especially in this damn country. Agents never know where to place me – "Is he a juggler or a comedian, a singer or a dancer, a designer or a director?" All of the above, I tell them, but they've never really understood. Part of me wishes I'd stayed in Australia or South Africa. At least I was appreciated there.'

For all his bragging ('I was more popular than Bruce Forsyth when I hosted *Play Your Cards Right* in South Africa'), Kenny seems uncertain about his place in the annals of entertainment. He's not bitter exactly, more confused – why had Britain never woken up to his talents? After all, his father Terry 'Toby Jug' Cantor, had been lauded for being an 'all-rounder', so why not Kenny?

Although he has never performed at this particular Pontin's, he seems to know his way around. I keep expecting to hear the laughter of small children emanating from the tatty adventure playground, but out-of-season holiday camps can be pretty desolate places. We head over to a large concrete theme bar but the place is deserted. Faded posters advertising last season's entertainment still cling to the walls. How odd that of all the Pontin's in all the world, Timmy Mallet should choose to perform his 'Mad Hatter Show' here: 'Timmy will entertain you with his opinions, loud looks and good humour. Just keep out of the way of his mallet!' Last season you could also have seen twice-daily performances by The Supremes (sans Diana Ross), The American Four Tops (as opposed to, say, The Lowestoft Four Tops) and Milli Munroe – a Tina Turner tribute act who looks suspiciously like a man in an ill-fitting Afro wig.

A security guard has spotted us loitering outside the 'Captain Croc Play Area' and tells us to leave immediately. As we make our way back up the hill towards Uppham Hall, I ask Kenny which entertainers he admires most and without hesitation he tells me Cannon and Ball are still the best double act around. He's also a big fan of Richard Digence and used to enjoy Jim Davidson before he turned 'blue'. Of the more modern crop of entertainers he quite likes Lee Evans and Joe Pasquale, but on the whole he feels his clean, family-orientated style of entertaining has been cruelly overlooked by the mainstream.

'I realise now I will never be a star but it must be so hard for performers like Stan Boardman and Freddie Starr – all that rubbish about biting hamsters – Freddie was the biggest thing on TV, and then suddenly he just wasn't there anymore. Okay, so he can be a bit unpredictable at times, but that can easily be dealt with.'

I suggest that maybe Freddie's style of knockabout humour just isn't considered funny anymore. But Kenny doesn't agree – he feels there's been a conspiracy against a whole generation of performers and that it's now up to entertainers like his daughter Shani to keep the colourful flag of light entertainment flying.

Shani is calling from the other room. She wants dad to come and see some of her latest moves. Meanwhile I check my inbox but disappointingly there's still no word yet from the whistling wheely-bin.

I head back into the sitting room where Shani is performing a particularly complex show-tune. . . Kenny is so proud of is daughter and hands me a promotional flyer:

A Young STAR in the making
Shani –
The latest singing sensation

Young Shani seems to typify the sparkly, never-say-die face of modern light entertainment – a world of clean-cut karaoke kids and *Pop Idol* wannabes who believe anything is possible if only you BELIEVE. It's all a long way from the grim, penny-pinching, flock-wallpapered world of the 1970s entertainment scene from which Kenny emerged. Whether Shani is actually a star in the making remains to be seen, but I wonder if her father had such high expectations when he was starting out?

'All I cared about was staying in work. Becoming a star was never an issue.'

These days Kenny is busy running his very own light entertainment empire. He hands me a brochure to prove it: there's Kenny the toastmaster: '*Have gavel will travel – I am also one of the cheaper toastmasters around*'; Kenny the children's entertainer, '*Ken Can! – He's dynamite with kids! Songs, games, madness*'; Kenny the compere: '. . . *he can fill in the gaps with amiable chat or perhaps a song*'; Kenny the after-dinner speaker: '. . . *the subject of his talk is "The business that there is no business like"*', and Kenny the panto dame '. . . *has appeared at the Empire Grantham – birthplace of Margaret Thatcher*'.

But it's '*Cantor's School for the Perfoming Arts*' that takes up most of his time these days. He hands me a copy of the latest brochure made out of a single sheet of A4 folded in three. Inside are some pretty lofty claims: '*"Cantor's Theatre School" goes on to be probably the finest seat of learning in the area. Don't miss out for your children – bring them to Cantor's.*'

The main aim of the three-year course is to teach children '*how to become stars*'.

So how does Kenny turn the good people of Beccles, Lowestoft and Halesworth into stars and what exactly does he mean by the word '*star*'?

'Well, we allow kids to push their identities so that they can be. . . you know. . . extreme in what they want to do.'

I'm confused.

'What I mean is, children are generally ebullient but there are some kids who are very, very quiet. We teach the quiet ones to be up for it. We've had kids go up for all sorts of things, like that programme *The X Factor*. Personally I think it's over-rated but all the kids seem to want to appear on it and so we teach them how.'

So Kenny's idea of becoming a star involves auditioning for a TV talent show, but had any of his students gone on to become 'stars' in the old fashioned sense of the word?

'Well, one of our girls played Annie in the musical.'

'Where was that?'

'Oh, you know – at our theatre in Beccles.'

Apparently a couple of his students have also appeared as roller skaters in *Starlight Express*.

Kenny's wife Caron has just returned from picking their son up from school.

I feel awkward; maybe now would be a good time to leave. Kenny agrees. There's evidently been some heated discussion about my visit and I know that Caron has been incredibly protective over her husband throughout this whole furore. As he walks me back to my car he looks up and smiles broadly.

'Caron really is brilliant you know. She's so good at pulling talent from kids.'

I'd been dreading this meeting with Kenny for obvious reasons but I'm glad he's found it in his heart to forgive me.

'Let me know how you get on and give my regards to everyone,' he says cheerily as I pull out of his drive '. . . tell everyone Kenny says "hi". They all know me – everyone in the business knows Kenny Cantor.'

I wind down the window and ask if there's any chance of seeing him perform sometime soon.

'Of course. I say you should only retire when the phone stops ringing.'

6. Long Ago in a Working Men's Club Far, Far Away. . .

Unfortunately I haven't been able to scam my way into the *Sith* premiere ('I don't care if you've lost your ticket – the fact is you're not on the list') but there is some excellent news waiting for me on my computer. Kenny Baker is intrigued to hear about my book, but would like to meet me and find out more before committing. Although he's gong to be in London for the *Star Wars* premiere he has to leave for a convention in Huddersfield early the following morning, and then he's off to San Francisco, Japan and Scandinavia for more conventions.

Having failed to reach Kenny on his mobile, I've driven over to Leicester Square to see if I can somehow collar him on the red carpet. As I pull into Charing Cross Road Nick rings to check on my progress.

'Still looking for losers?' he asks.

'Actually I'm just on my way to a film premiere in Leicester Square to meet one of them now.'

'Ha, ha, very funny.'

'No really – one of your so-called 'losers' just happens to be starring in the biggest movie of the year. Have you heard of *Star Wars*. . . ?'

Stunned silence on the other end of the line.

'. . . Anyway gotta go – tell you all about it later.'

Despite heavy rain, the fans are out in force to celebrate The Force and Mr Lucas has put on quite a show for them. Several bored-looking Stormtroopers stand around the edges of the square wondering how on earth they're supposed to pee in all that moulded white plastic. The Royal Philharmonic Orchestra meanwhile is belting out an endless loop of the famous theme tune.

My view of proceedings is almost completely obscured by herds of nerds sheltering under drippy umbrellas. The whole square is heaving with creepy middle-aged men clutching plastic light-sabres and Morrisons shopping bags. All strain for a glimpse of *Star*-dom. A middle-aged dad hoists his son onto his shoulders for a better view.

Dad: 'What can you see, Darren. . . what can you see?'
Son: 'Nothing Dad. . . just people walking along a carpet.'

Ah yes, the glamour of the movie premiere. . . last time I attended one of these, I'd been the one walking the carpet. After months of stagnation, my career had been on a bit of a roll – I'd had three good theatre jobs in a row, done a nice TV cameo and to top it off, scored a peachy little part in a spoof '007' movie starring Rowan Atkinson as a bungling secret service agent. I'd been cast as a swarthy James Bond-type character, who ends up being killed by John Malkovich's evil cartoon baddie in a spectacular pre-titles sequence worthy of a real James Bond film. My action-packed scenes were shot in and around St Michael's Mount in Cornwall, and involved me jumping over walls and tearing along darkened corridors (every boy's dream) looking for the evil Malkovich.

Apart from falling off a rope and bruising my backside, everything seemed to go fairly well. But several weeks after completion, the director called me back on set. It seemed there had been a problem with my hair. Every time I moved, clouds of dried product could be seen emanating from the top of my head. I would have to shoot the scene again, without the use of hairspray.

But my dodgy barnet wasn't the only worry. Rowan Atkinson had seen the rushes and wasn't happy with the way I delivered my final line of dialogue. Apparently he didn't think it 'worked' – in other words it wasn't funny. The 'line' in question was in fact a single word – 'Bollocks!' – which was spoken just after Malkovich had shot a set of deadly arrows into my chest. Rowan felt the scene needed more of an ironic Oh-dear-what-a-bummer-I'm-about-to-die kind of 'Bollocks!' (the way Blackadder would have said it), whereas I had blurted a more realistic Shit-I'm-about-to-die! kind of 'Bollocks!'

Now, Rowan Atkinson knows a thing or two about comedy, so when he tells you something isn't funny, you'd better believe it.

Indeed, he'd already vetoed a 'comic' scene involving a horse falling over at a polo match, after announcing that horses, by their very nature, just aren't funny.

I reckon you could say the same about cats, rats and pigeons. Whereas dogs, ducks, and monkeys – by their very nature – *are* funny.

Anyway, where was I? Oh yes, I was talking 'bollocks'. I must have repeated that word over a hundred times using every single type of inflection. By the end of the day, the word had lost all its meaning, and yet I still had no idea whether any of my interpretations had even registered on Rowan's comedy barometer. But because I didn't hear from Rowan again after the shoot, I assumed he must have liked at least one of my 'bollocks.'

A year on, an invitation to the premiere of the now-named *Johnny English* landed on my doormat, and a couple of weeks later Nick the Cynic (a big fan of Mr Bean) and I were trotting along the red carpet in our finest Top Man suits.

As the Empire Leicester Square lights went down, my heart rate shot up. Over a thousand people, including Rowan Atkinson and my idol John Malkovich, were in the audience, and about to witness me in the opening scene. But which one of my 'bollocks' had Rowan decided to use? The 'ironic' bollocks, the 'comedy' bollocks or the 'serious' bollocks? Nick turned and whispered in my ear. 'Your time has come mate - I'm proud of you.'

Cue brooding music. Night. . . an owl hoots. We see the dramatic silhouette of a large spooky castle. As we zoom in closer, a shrouded figure is seen leaping over some ivy covered battlements, loaded pistol at the ready. He shoots a look to the left and then to the right – have the brutal-looking guards with machine guns seen him?

I try to suppress a smile – I'm the man.

Cue dramatic music:
. . . dum dum. . . dum dum. . . dededede dum-dum, dededede DUM-DUM.

The man's face is suddenly lit by a bright spotligh. . .

Hang on a minute, that's supposed to be my face suddenly being lit by a bright spotlight! Why do I look like Rowan Atkinson? Hang on – that is Rowan Atkinson! What the hell's he doing climbing all over my battlements, or more importantly, what the hell's he doing climbing all over my part? And then it hits me like a pair of scissors hitting the cutting room floor. I had been cut, and replaced by the biggest cop-out of them all – a dream sequence, in which the bungling Johnny English acts out his fantasy of being the glamorous secret service agent. Rowan had obviously decided that there wasn't enough Rowan at the beginning of the film. And so I'd been replaced by a Blackadder-cum-Mr Bean hybrid in a dinner jacket.

I know, I know – actors get cut from films all the time. Indeed, this wasn't my first experience of being scissored. I'd already lost my arguing-in-a-jeep-with-Tom-Hanks scene from *Saving Private Ryan* and my kissing-Julianne-Moore-at-a-party scene from *The End of the Affair*. So yes, I was well aware of how cruel the movie business can be, but couldn't someone have at least told me I'd been cut BEFORE inviting me to the premiere? This was serious salt-in-the-wound stuff. I could hardly bear to look at Nick's face – he was laughing all over it.

Although I've been standing next to the blood-red Axminster of Evil now for nearly an hour, I still haven't recognised any of the so-called celebrities shimmying along its twisted pile. I guess the real stars don't arrive until the very last minute.

I ask a greasy-haired anorak standing next to me if he knows what a Sith is – he reckons it's an anagram of shit. Apparently the reviews have been less than ecstatic.

Suddenly through a gap in the brollies I catch a glimpse of Ewan McGregor's ankle sliding out of a silver Merc. At least I assume it's McGregor's ankle, judging by the sudden surge of hysteria. The expensively socked leg is gently brollied across the red carpet and into the warmth of a waiting Odeon. The crowd quietens down for a moment before bursting back into hysterics again as a small official-looking man hovers nervously with a clipboard. He doesn't look remotely famous but the crowds don't seem to care – he's the right side of the barrier and his feet have touched the sacred carpet – therefore he must be worshipped.

Three squat Essex girls are standing directly behind me screaming in discordant union – all they can see is a wall of wet umbrellas and the back of my waterproofs, but they don't seem to mind as long as they can have a good old shout. I ask one of them if she's ever heard of Kenny Baker. 'Aggggghhhhhhhhhhhh' she replies, but I'm not sure whether that means 'Yes, he's great' or 'I really, really fancy Ewan McGregor.'

It seems the red carpet possesses magical, sexual powers, turning even portly, middle-aged actors like Ian McDiarmid into objects of lust. Some would call it witchcraft. . . talking of which, I've just spotted Christopher Lee emerging from another silver Merc. No sign of Kenny yet, although I'll need to pay attention – apparently he's only 3'8" tall. . .

It's getting late – the Stormtroopers have stopped storming and the orchestra have packed away their instruments. But there's still no sign of Kenny. I ask a tall, skinny man in *Star Wars* face-paint whether he has by any chance seen a 3'8" dwarf pass by.

'Yeah, there were four of them – came past a couple of minutes ago.'

'How many dwarves are there in this film?' I ask.

'Well, there are all the Ewoks for a start. . . '

'Did any of them look like R2-D2?'

'No they just looked like dwarves in suits.'

Kenny must already be inside the cinema. I have no idea what time he leaves in the morning for Huddersfield, but without his permission I may as well give up my quest right now. I leave yet another panicky message on his mobile.

I'm about to give up and go home when the skinny man with the face-paint suddenly taps me on the shoulder.

'Over there, look. Dwarves!'

In a far corner of the square an official is guiding a low umbrella along a line of screaming fans. Could this really be him? I push my way to the front of the crowd where a group of pale, balding men are straining their necks for a better view.

'Excuse me, is that Kenny Baker' I ask, trying to sound like a *Star Wars* fan.

'Yes, that's him' says the tallest of the three men. 'I wish he'd come over here – Gareth's desperate for an autograph, aren't you Gaz?'

'Too right. . .'

Hmm, that gives me an idea.

'Hey guys, I'm a big fan of Kenny too. Let's see if we can attract his attention. How about we all chant his name on the count of three?'

'Yeah, good idea.'

'Okay. . . and, one, two, three. . . Ken-NY! Ken-NY! Ken-NY. . . !'

It seems to be working. The tiny umbrella is moving this way.

'Come on, louder!' I yell.

'Ken-NY! Ken-NY! KENNN-NY. . . '

Gareth suddenly surges towards the metal barrier with biro and paper at the ready.

'Kenny, hi Kenny. Excuse me, could I, sorry – Kenny could I have your autograph please? The name's Gareth.' His voice is quivering with excitement.

The umbrella is lowered to reveal a grinning Kenny in a tuxedo. He smiles and obligingly takes the small scrap of paper and attempts to make his mark – but the paper has been seriously rained on.

'Sorry mate – paper's too wet.'

Gareth is beside himself. He's been waiting all day for this moment. Luckily I have some dry paper on me and hand a couple of sheets to Kenny, taking the opportunity to introduce myself.

'Hi Kenny, I'm James Innes-Smith, the author of the book about light entertainment. You said we could meet sometime today.'

'Oh yeah. God, I completely forgot. Sorry mate. I'll give you a call later tonight. I'm not allowed to tell you where I'm staying for security reasons – but we'll talk later – I've got your number haven't I?'

He hands Gareth the signed piece of paper and is gently ushered on towards the next lot of outstretched biros. Gareth is overcome with joy as he carefully slips the precious piece of paper into an inside pocket. 'All I need now is Christopher Lee' he sighs.

Gareth reminds me of some of the autograph hunters who used to hang around back stage when I was on tour. I could never understand why so many strangers wanted my autograph – it wasn't as though I was famous, but that never seemed to bother them – some would even send me creepy notes such as:

Dear James

Please could you send me a signed full-length photo of yourself as I very much enjoy the way your legs look on stage.

Thanks

Yours sincerely

Howard

PS. Please find enclosed a stamped addressed envelope.

And. . .

Dear James

My mates and me all go drinking at The Three Stars pub in King Street on Saturday nights. We'd love it if you joined us. We'll be over in the far corner by the cigarette machine from 8pm onwards.

We all think you're gorgeous by the way. . .

Tracy and mates xxxxxxxxx

Hey, what can I tell you? I was on tour, I was lonely and I fancied a drink – so I went along to The Three Stars. Well I learnt a valuable lesson that night – there's always someone out there lonelier than you. The Three Stars turned out to be a hardcore gay bar and the sexy sounding Tracy was actually a fifty year old man named. . . Howard.

Some of the creepiest backstage hangers-on were the ones I met during my time as Darcy in a terrible touring production of *Pride and Prejudice*. Even though we had hit the road several years after the Colin Firth TV adaptation, there were still armies of unrealistically romantic Chardonnay drinkers unwilling to accept anyone else in the role – they were the female equivalent of *Star Wars* fans but with more facial hair. His Royal Colin-ness had unwittingly created the definitive portrayal. As a result, ladies of a certain age would often wait for me backstage – not because they wanted to rip my shirt off and ravish my nipples – that was left to lonely men like Howard – but to give me a damn good talking to. Who the hell was I to mess with their ultimate male fantasy? 'Darcy has curly hair – everyone knows that. You can't possibly play him with straight hair like yours. . . ' was one typical response. An anguished lady named Janet wanted to know why I had decided to cut the coming-out-of-a-lake scene. I tried to explain that apart from the technical problems of building a lake on stage, the famous Darcy-dunking had only been added to the TV adaptation to titillate ladies like Janet. But she wasn't having any of it and demanded a refund. On another occasion a middle-aged woman in unsuitably tight leather trousers attempted to convince me that Darcy was in fact some kind of early rock 'n' roll super-stud. She was furious that I hadn't grown my hair long or learnt to ride a Harley on stage. She was obviously confusing Mr Darcy with Lemmy from *Motorhead*.

Later that night I receive a call from Kenny – he's still at the *Sith* party and sounds a little worse for wear.

'If you still want to come and see me I'll be at The Whitehouse. . .'

'*The White House*?' I ask incredulously.

'No, no, no. Not *The* White House! The Whitehouse – a hotel just off Regent's Park. Meet me there tomorrow morning at ten.'

That night I dream of strange robots.

Kenny is loading two large suitcases into the back of a cab when I arrive at the hotel. He seems a lot smaller in the daylight but remarkably young for a man in his seventies. He has smooth skin and a wicked glint in his eye. I introduce myself but he doesn't recognise me.

'You remember we met yesterday? You told me to meet you here at ten.'

'Did I? Sorry, there was a bit of a party last night. Listen mate, I'm really sorry but I've got a train to catch. We're going to have to do this another time.'

'But you don't understand, I really need to talk to you before you go away.'

'What about?'

'My book, *Reach for the Big Time*. I need your permission remember?'

Kenny's girlfriend overhears our conversation and comes to my rescue.

'If it's that important why don't you hop in the cab with us – we're only going as far as Marylebone but maybe we can have a chat on the way.'

Marylebone Station is only a mile or so down the road so I'll need to work fast. It's not often you find yourself praying for gridlock.

Kenny is struggling to get into the cab – the step up is too high. The world it seems doesn't cater well for homunculi. Many aspects of his life have had to be specially adapted, from the height of the bed to the positioning of doorknobs. Even his car has special stacked pedals and an extra low steering wheel.

Being an asthmatic, Kenny tries to avoid using his legs wherever possible. Losing his driving licence has been a real headache – public transport just isn't a practical option – 'far too many steps.' Kenny's none too keen on hotels either: 'I used to tour theatres and clubs with a luxury caravan strapped to the back of my Rolls – it was a damned sight more comfortable than any hotel.'

Kenny's career has inevitably been dominated by his size. He spent his early days performing comedy song and dance routines designed specifically for those of a smaller disposition. Back then it was still just about okay to snigger at the vertically challenged.

It was during his time with *The Midget Review* at the Metropolitan Variety Theatre in Edgware Road that he met his *Mini Tone* partner Jack Purvis. With Kenny on mouth organ and vibraphone and Jack on trumpet, the diminutive duo spent twenty years touring northern working men's clubs and end-of-the-pier theatres.

'We were the only musical dwarf act in the business so we always attracted a lot of attention. I miss being able to play my instruments – I'm too much of a physical wreck these days. Playing the vibraphone gives me backache, leg ache and everything else-ache and the asthma means I no longer have enough puff to play the harmonica.' The mere mention of the word asthma sends him into a fit of wheezing.

The Mini Tones came to an abrupt end after Jack's car collapsed on top of him while he was tinkering with the exhaust. The freak accident left him paralysed from the neck down and he sadly died a couple of years later.

'Everything went wrong for me in the late eighties. My wife died of epilepsy soon after Jack's accident and for a while I felt totally alone. Terrible, terrible times.' He grips his girlfriend's hand and squeezes. '*Star Wars* has been a real lifesaver although I'm not a great fan of sci-fi. The special effects are good on *Sith* but it's not my type of film at all. I prefer something real, with real actors. *Star Wars* is mainly about the scenery. . . mind you Yoda's computer-generated hair is amazing. . . it moves just like the real thing.'

As with Yoda's hair, the character of R2-D2 has become increasingly CG'd over the last three films, meaning a lot less work for Kenny.

'There are still certain close-up movements only I can do convincingly. It's all about giving R2 a personality and CGI can never really do that. Besides, George Lucas likes to keep his friends onboard.'

Kenny's relationship with fellow robot actor C3-PO's Anthony Daniels remains somewhat strained.

'We've never really hit it off. It's such a shame because C3-PO and R2 are the two characters fans most want to talk to. They assume we must be best buddies and are always disappointed when they find out we're not.'

Kenny isn't particularly looking forward to the next round of conventions.

'I find them exhausting these days but the fans still seem to enjoy coming. I guess it's a great way for them to make new friends, swap stories and compare merchandise – someone even brought in a *Star Wars* condom the other day, I couldn't believe it. Some of the fans can be a bit weird but they've provided me with a decent pension so I can't really complain. They think I'm a star but I'm not so sure. R2's the real star, I just happen to be inside bringing him to life. I'd like to do more film work but I'm a bit sick of being typecast. I've played more mini people than you can shake a very small stick at: I was 'Fidgit the Midget' in *Time Bandits*, a 'village goblin' in *Labyrinth* and a 'plumed dwarf' in *The Elephant Man*. I suppose it would be quite a stretch to cast me as a regular-sized guy but you never know. . . '

The traffic on Marylebone Road is solid in both directions – unfortunately we're able to avoid the crush by zooming up the bus lane, meaning even less time with Kenny. We're already nearing the station, and with only five minutes to go before the train leaves, Kenny is beginning to panic. Suddenly his phone rings.

'It's Terry Seabrooke. . . ' he mouths to his girlfriend.

I recognise the name immediately. Could this really be the same Terry Seabrooke featured in my book? This is so exciting – I open *Reach for the Big Time* at Terry's page and gesture to Kenny not to hang up.

'. . . By the way Terry, you're not going to believe this but I'm looking at an old photograph of you from the 1970s. There's someone here I think you should talk to. . . ' – he hands me the phone.

Poor Terry only rang to give Kenny some advice on how to break into the after-dinner speaking game. And now all of a sudden, he's having to listen to some nutcase gabbling on about a ludicrous quest.

Terry remembers reading about the book but is somewhat taken aback to find out he's actually in it. The worrying news is, he's flying to Los Angeles in the morning and won't be back for six weeks. He's agreed to sign the release but only after seeing the book. I need to get to Terry before he gets to La-la land.

'What time do you fly in the morning?' I ask.

'I need to be at Heathrow for eight.'

'What about tonight? Can I come and see you tonight?'

At this point of course I have no idea where Terry lives – he might be in the Orkney Islands for all I know.

'Can't see you tonight I'm afraid – I'm doing a private gig for the Waltham Forest Jewish Friendship Club and won't be back until very late.'

This is so frustrating – fate has just delivered Terry to me on a silver salver – I can't afford to lose him now. I offer to make him breakfast and drive him to the airport in the morning. Astonishingly he agrees to my plan and we arrange to meet at his place at 5am. Meanwhile Kenny is pulling at my arm, trying to grab his phone back. I hand him the release and the book and tell him I'll run on ahead to make sure the train doesn't leave without him.

The guard is standing beside the train with his whistle poised as I skid across the platform with Kenny's bags outstretched.

'Please don't blow that whistle!' I yell, 'R2-D2 can't miss this train – he has an important convention to attend.'

The guard obviously thinks I'm deranged as I run at him, cheeks blazing.

'Can I see your ticket please sir?'

'No you don't understand – these aren't my bags, they belong to Kenny Baker, you know – R2-D2 from *Star Wars*. He's a dwarf and can't run very fast but he and his girlfriend will be here any second and then you can blow your whistle, I promise.'

'If you're not travelling with us today sir could you leave the platform please, the train is about to depart.'

Why do officials always insist on calling you sir when they so obviously mean 'wanker'? I just need to somehow keep him talking – stop him from blowing that damn whistle.

'Erm, are you a *Star Wars* fan?' I ask, desperately trying to make conversation.

'Yes, but I prefer *Star Trek'* he replies flatly.

'Ah yes *Star Trek*, very good – errrm, who's your favourite character, Captain Spock? Doctor Shatner?' (As you can tell, I'm no Trekkie).

'Could you leave the platform please sir, you're causing an obstruction.'

Where the hell's Kenny – how can it be taking him so long? I'm not going to be able to keep this charade up for much longer.

'. . . I bet you like the Scottish one best' I continue, 'you know, what's-his-name – Scotty. "I cannay hold the ship any longer captain. . ."'

It's not a great Scotty impersonation but at least it's distracting him from his whistle. At last Kenny and his girlfriend come tearing across the concourse, tiny legs whirring.

'Look, there – you see – I told you! R2-D2!'

A wheezy Kenny races onto the platform.

'Are you really R2-D2?' asks the stunned guard.

'Used to be – not any more.'

'Where's C3-PO then?' he giggles, prodding a fellow guard who's come over to see what all the fuss is about.

'Dunno' replies Kenny as he attempts to launch himself onto the train. Once safely onboard he hands me back the book and the release with an extravagant signature scrawled along the bottom.

'This is for Jack too. I reckon he'd be dead chuffed to know he was being immortalised in print – good luck with the search and don't forget to send me a copy when the book's back in the shops.'

I suddenly remember that Nick the Cynic is a huge *Star Wars* fan.

'Could I have your autograph' I yell above the noise of the diesel engine – 'it's for my friend Nick. I have paper but no pen.'

The train starts to slowly pull out of the station. Kenny hunts around in his pockets. I'm having to run now but the end of the platform is looming. No longer able to keep up, I stop to catch my breath. A small white business card flutters from the train window. On the front is a photo of Kenny with his arm round R2 – on the back he's written in wobbly handwriting 'To Nick – from us both – all the best!!'

I hadn't been expecting any fresh leads from Kenny (the Seabrooke connection had been thrilling enough) but that evening I find an email from him with two more contact details attached: ventriloquist Jack Mayes (a fellow Water Rat) and impressionist Victor Seaforth (an old chum from variety days).

With new leads coming in thick and fast it's time to set to work on a *Reach for the Big Time* family tree, which should help me keep track of where I've been and where I'm going next with this crazy old journey.

7. Terry and Johnny

Reach for the Deadline: three weeks to go...
Fortunately I haven't had to jet over to the Orkney Islands to meet magician Terry Seabrooke – he lives in the glitzy, showbiz town of Bushey in Hertfordshire (apparently George Michael lives just up the road).

Terry is busy packing when I arrive. I haven't properly woken up yet and nor has Terry – he's still wandering around bleary eyed as I hand him a Danish pastry.

Terry Seabrooke
Comedy Magical Entertainer
The comedy act that gets your audience going...
to where, it is not known!!!!
Booking through 1975
All enquiries: Melton Management

'I never know what clothes to take with me on these long trips – six weeks is a lot of underwear' he says, chucking several pairs of pants into a bulging suitcase. Terry's a big fan of Los Angeles and wishes he could go for longer.

'I come alive when I'm out there.'

Considering how horribly early it is, Terry is remarkably on the ball. He's much tubbier of cheek than in his 1975 publicity photo, although he seems a little frail. He has a slight limp and suffers from acute back pain brought on by, would you believe, his love of Ford Capris.

'I haven't driven one for years on the advice of my doctor. He calls my condition 'Capri-back' – apparently the car has a very bad driving position. It seems lots of men of my age have the same complaint because so many of us drove Capris back in the '70s. Always use a cushion for long journeys is my advice.'

Terry is trying to decide which of his many illusions to take to LA with him – he specialises in close-up card and coin tricks and is keen to try out some new material at the Magic Castle – the magicians' Mecca in Hollywood.

He takes me up to what he calls his 'Magic Den', a large attic room where he keeps all his magician's paraphernalia. The floor is littered with elaborate contraptions for 'removing' fingers and hiding cards. Retractable knives covered in fake blood, some tatty wands and several brightly coloured silk handkerchiefs lie scattered about the place; a dusty black cloak hangs like a shroud in the corner.

'I should throw most of this stuff away but it's just so difficult – my whole life's up here.'

He surveys the mess fanning out in all directions.

'Maybe next year I'll go through it all and have a chuck-out. . . '

I tell him he must keep it all for posterity and start sifting through a pile of dog-eared posters advertising some of the many shows he's appeared in. Terry has supported everyone from Harry Secombe to Norman Wisdom but his all-time favourite entertainer has to be Bob Monkhouse. 'He used to stand in the wings and give me notes on my performance.' He hands me a piece of crumpled cardboard with hand-written gag suggestions from the great Monkhouse himself.

'So Kenny Baker tells me you're off to see Jack Mayes – you know he lives up the road in Stevenage?'

I've already left several messages on Jack's voicemail but so far he hasn't got back to me.

'So, do you reckon you're going to get all your permissions in time?' asks Terry with a mouthful of Danish pastry.

'So far so good' I tell him, offering up my copy of *Reach for the Big Time* and a release.

'You know you really should have asked my permission first, but . . .'

He begins flicking.

'Good heavens, just look at all these wonderful old acts. Well, well, well.'

I apologise for not tracking him down earlier but he's already fallen in love with the book and is more than happy to sign the release. He also has a couple of leads for me, the first of which comes with a health warning.

'Comedian Johnny Clamp lives over in Dunstable but I have to tell you, they don't come any more eccentric than dear old Clampy.'

Sounds a bit worrying but I'm willing to take that risk if it means securing another permission.

'I've also got a number here for my mate Chubby Oates – he lives down in Kent but he does occasionally come up to London to visit his club. I'm sure he'll be pleased to hear from you.'

Despite the health problems, Terry's a real trooper, and it's comforting to know he's still out there plying his magical trade after all these years. Tomorrow will be his 127th visit to the Magic Castle and he's as excited as ever.

Before leaving for the airport he gives me a quick demonstration of his latest disappearing coin trick – a remarkable sleight of hand that ends with him removing a specially marked coin from one of my inside pockets. On the way out he gives me a copy of his autobiography entitled *Seabrooke's Book – Around the World with a Baking Tin*. As well as his fascinating life-story, the book contains some of Terry's favourite magic tricks, including 'visible sawing through a woman', 'the magic chattering teeth' and 'how to turn a tennis ball into a face'. Also included are some useful tips on how to keep your props in tip-top condition – 'make sure all head-choppers, wrist-guillotines and cremation-illusions are free from grime and dust at all times.'

At the last minute Terry has decided to pass on my offer of a lift – 'Capri-back – Doctor's orders!' – and has settled for a more comfortable cab ride to the airport.

I'm quite relieved not to have to give Terry a lift as it now means I can head straight over to Johnny Clamp and maybe squeeze in Jack Mayes as well if there's time. Three permissions in one day would be quite an achievement, but as I enter the second week of my quest I'm going to have to start upping the ante.

Johnny Clamp
Comedian
'A gag on any subject'
Vocalist - Compere - Guitarist – Actor
Enquiries: Johnny Clamp

A very FAST and FUNNY COMEDIAN who is constantly employed at night clubs, theatres and on luxury liners in all parts of the world.

He has worked with numerous stars including Diana Dors. He has acted in Doctor Who *and appeared on other TV shows.*

He has a fine singing voice and like all top comics can get laughs by pulling faces. He specialises in asking the audience to choose a subject, he then tells a gag on the chosen subject.

He is dedicated to comedy and his ambition is to have his own TV series.

Once again fate is on my side. Although I'm still having problems getting through to Jack (could he be deliberately ignoring my calls?), I do manage to get straight through to Johnny Clamp.

Terry's right, he does sound rather odd on the phone and seems incapable of giving me simple directions to his house without turning everything into a joke. The good news is that he's happy for me to come over to talk about the book, as long as I allow him to try out some of his latest material on me.

Johnny lives on a small low-rise '60s housing estate on the outskirts of Dunstable – it's one of those respectable-looking estates often seen in old *Carry On* films. As I pull into the car park, I can just imagine saucy Joan Sims in a pink fluffy negligee, flirting with the milkman from an upstairs window.

Johnny greets me in the chilly stairwell of his apartment block and immediately tells me to follow him outside. He's clutching a trumpet to his naked, barrel-like chest. His eyebrows have been plucked to extinction, and there's an oily slick of jet-black hair boyishly combed forward into a high fringe. The reason he's brought me outside is because he wants to give me a short recital – 'Don't worry, the neighbours know when to keep their windows shut!' he tells me with a grin. I feel self-conscious standing out here in the middle of a housing estate with a semi-naked, trumpeting comic. What on earth will people think?

On the way back to his apartment he can't resist bombarding me with trumpet gags. So this is what he means by a gag on any subject. . .

'I learned to play at twenty-two you know, which was a

bit annoying for the people living at number twenty-four. My neighbours tell me the trumpet is an ill wind that nobody plays any good – but I beg to differ.' Johnny bills himself as a professional ad-libber but his gags seem pretty well rehearsed to me.

Although he's in his sixties, Johnny behaves like an excitable boy who's just been let out of school early.

'Come up to the hovel – I want to sing you my latest love song.'

He doesn't seem remotely interested in hearing about my book and is just so pleased to have a captive audience. He certainly takes his gag-on-any-subject boast seriously. Even as he's making tea I can see him mentally flicking through his joke-encyclopaedia searching for the file marked 'hot beverages'. Several tea-inspired jokes come spilling out in quick succession – 'This is Jewish tea you know – He-brew! I went into this café the other day, I said "Do you have tea bags?", they said "We call them waitresses here"'. I resist the urge to bang on my imaginary cymbal, but I seem to have made the mistake of laughing a bit too heartily – he's now on a roll and can't stop. He asks if I enjoy sport – which I take to mean 'I'm about to gag you to death with football jokes'. When I tell him I'm a cricket fan, he barely pauses: 'My father was a big cricketer you know – I was his first slip. . . ' I actually don't really like or understand cricket and have to force a giggle. But Johnny's been around long enough to know a genuine laugh when he hears one.

'No need to pretend. Some of my gags work, others are just fertiliser. You'll like this one though – I made it up this morning. Bloke goes into a shop and sees this girl playing with herself – bloke says to the shop assistant, "What sort of establishment is this?" and the assistant says "It's a do-it-yourself shop."

By now I've actually forgotten how to laugh, so he offers me a custard tart instead. I'm finding all the quips exhausting so I hand him the book and a copy of the release; I really need to leave. But he's not going to let me escape that easily. After all, I promised to listen to one of his love songs. As he pours me another cup of tea I ask him what the secret of a good comic is.

'You've got to be erratic; geniuses are always erratic. Inside every comic is an innocent baby trying to get out – I am that baby. I've never lost my vulnerability and I'm a romantic at heart, which I think is important. We all need a bit of romance right? And with that he brings out his tatty guitar.

I feel bad about wanting to leave – Johnny is like an old circus horse, he just can't stop performing and is only doing what comes naturally. He starts strumming as I flick through some of his old publicity material. Johnny has a pure, rather mournful falsetto voice and sings with passion about a lost love. He has a sad, faraway look in his eyes – nothing like the face-pulling goon in *Reach for the Big Time.*

After such a heartfelt song I ask him if there's anyone special in his life at the moment. . .

'Of course – he's right there looking back at me in the mirror every morning! Only joking.' It's hard to know when Johnny is being serious as he tends to punctuate most sentences with little phrases like 'Only joking', 'God's honest truth', 'This is no fertiliser' and 'I wouldn't tell you any bull.'

As far as I can make out Johnny has lived with several women over the years, although judging by the single-maleness of his poky flat, I rather wonder. Despite his veneer of self-assurance, he's philosophical about his life and doesn't expect to ever get married. 'When I go, the world won't miss a beat'.

I worry about Johnny. He needs an audience for all those thousands of gags rolling around in his head, but I fear work has been pretty thin on the ground of late. He does the odd gig here and there but his dreams of one day having his own TV series have long since evaporated.

He eventually signs the release without even glancing at it. All Johnny really wants to do is show me how funny he is.

'Give me a subject – go on, any subject. . . '

'Okay, how about Ford Capris. . . ' I reply, starting up the engine.

After a long pause he shakes his head and scowls. I seem to have flummoxed him.

'I'm so sorry but I just can't think of any jokes about Ford Capris. I promise you this doesn't normally happen.' He seems genuinely peeved.

'Not to worry – there are plenty online. . . '

8. The Rats

Reach for the Deadline: two weeks and five days to go. . . I leave Johnny Clamp's flat with a heavy heart. I hope he manages to find a more permanent and appreciative audience than me.

For all I know Jack Mayes, who lives up the road from Clampy in Stevenage, might be baying for my blood. The fact is he still hasn't returned any of my calls and I'm starting to worry. I've been lucky so far but who knows how many potential Kenny Cantors are still out there?

Seeing as Jack is so close, I've decided to stick around Dunstable for a while until I make contact. I head to a nearby Little Chef and order myself an 'American style' breakfast of oily eggs and deep-fat hash browns. After leaving several more messages for Jack, I try phoning Kenny Baker's other lead, impressionist Victor Seaforth. Kenny warned me to be especially gentle with Victor as he's in his late eighties now and somewhat fragile. Cold calling total strangers to apologise for something they may not even know about feels risky – any one of them could stymie my quest by simply telling me to bugger off. Frankly I'm amazed anyone has agreed to see me at all. I'm not sure I'd be willing to welcome a total stranger into my house on the back of some bizarre quest.

Victor Seaforth

Comedian, impressionist, vocalist and compere

Victor Seaforth has completed over three hundred broadcasts and twenty-one television transmissions to date, including the Black and White Minstrels *television show. He has played all the leading theatres throughout the country, also all the top night clubs. Other credits include ten summer seasons, four pantomimes, hundreds of one night concerts and cabarets and commercial television.*

Taking bookings through 1977

Poor Victor is confused; he thinks I'm calling from his local library about an overdue book, and is being terribly apologetic. I explain that it's I who am trying to apologise to him about something quite other. But the late return of the book has obviously been playing on his mind, and he seems genuinely concerned that I might be about to ask him to pay a fine of thirty-seven pence. When he does eventually latch on to the reason for my call, he immediately becomes defensive. Why hadn't he been told he was in a book, and why hadn't he received a copy – and what the blazes was it all about anyway?

I suggest that maybe the best thing would be for us to meet.

'I'm moving to a retirement flat in Bexhill-on-Sea at the weekend so I can only see you the day after tomorrow. I still don't understand how I ended up in a book without knowing it.'

'All will be revealed', I assure him.

Jack Mayes is driving up the M1 when I eventually get through, some four cups of coffee and a slice of strawberry cheesecake later. He sounds flustered.

Jack Mayes

The laugh along – sing along Comedy Act
With a few balloons to blow up the audience with laughs!

Bookings: QE2; Caesar's Palace Luton 1973

'What is it you want? You'll have to be quick, I don't want to be stopped by the police.'

'Shall I call you back?' I ask.

'No just tell me what you want, but hurry.'

Fluster has turned to irritability. Trying to explain about my strange quest is hard enough at the best of times – under pressure and at speed it all sounds slightly dodgy. But thankfully Jack is quick on the uptake.

'Sounds interesting but I'd like to see the book first obviously. I'm afraid I'm busy most of this week and then I'm off on holiday for two weeks. I'll be up in London tomorrow for the Water Rats' annual boat-trip if that's any good to you. Actually if you're doing a book about light entertainers you should try and come along – it's our biggest knees-up of the year. Maybe some of the performers from your book will be there. Tell you what, give the organiser John Adrian a ring. Tell him I sent you. I'm sure he'll be able to squeeze you in somewhere.'

Jack Mayes – ventriloquist, ex-balloon artist, captain of the Vaudeville Golf Society – you're a genius. But will John Adrian be able to give me an invitation to such an illustrious-sounding event at such short notice? There's only one way to find out.

John doesn't sound hopeful when I ring.

'I'm afraid invitations were sent out months ago – there's a seating plan and everything. But leave it with me and I'll call you back this afternoon if I'm able to slot you in. The book sounds fascinating by the way.'

An hour later he rings back with some excellent news.

'We meet at Embankment Pier at 5:15pm – the boat leaves promptly at 5:45. You may be interested to know that Paul Daniels and Debbie McGee will be attending as will Melvyn Hayes, who is our new King Rat. As we sail up to Greenwich, supper will be served on board. On the way back there'll be a cabaret show. Let's hope some of the people in your book turn up. Did I mention Bob Holness was also coming? Should be a great night.'

Not *The* Bob Holness? Not the 'Can I have a "P" please Bob?' Bob Holness of *Blockbusters* fame? I used to worship at the altar of his Hol(i)ness. Part friendly geography teacher, part teddy bear, Bob was by far the nicest of all the '80s game show hosts. As a teenager I used to dream of one day being a contestant on *Blockbusters*: all those silly furry mascots; the appalling prizes (an adventure weekend in Plymouth) and of course the naughty way students would ask for the next letter ('I want "U" Bob'; 'Can I have an "E" Bob?'). Apparently the show was so popular in Dubai, shops and offices would close early so people could rush home to watch it. I would rush home to watch it too.

John Adrian and I have agreed to meet on the gangplank of the 'Natacia' but I'm having trouble spotting him as most of the men boarding the vessel seem to fit his description of himself as 'over sixty with balding hair and a beige jacket'. A rotund, northern-comic type (over sixty, balding hair, beige jacket) sees me loitering on the gangplank and comes over for a chat.

'You look as if you're waiting for someone too', he says in a broad Yorkshire accent.

'Yep – John Adrian – do you know him?'

'Course I do. Everyone knows John. He's already onboard I believe.'

'Who are you waiting for?' I ask.

'Brian Johnson. Have you seen him?'

'Not sure. Who is he and what does he look like?' A sixty-year old man with grey, balding hair and a beige jacket no doubt.

'Have you heard of a group called *AC/DC*?'

'Of course.'

'Well, Brian's the lead singer.'

And there was I thinking this was going to be a celebration of 'light' entertainment. Mind you those *AC/DC* boys must be pushing sixty. I bet even wild axe-man Angus Young has swapped his funny school uniform for a beige jacket and tasselled slip-ons – he probably winters in Bournemouth these days. Even hard rockers go soft in the end.

'He's bloody useless is Brian. I told him what time he had to be here. His wife must be away – she organises his whole life for him these days.'

Brian has no connection with the Grand Order of Water Rats other than being the northern comic's guest for this evening's festivities.

'By the way I'm Tony Barton – comic. That's not my real name you understand. My real name's Tony Norfolk – used to be in a double act with a comedian called Johnny Goode. We became *Norfolk 'n' Goode*. Couple of years later we joined forces with Charlie Still and were *Still, Norfolk 'n' Goode*. You may have heard of us?'

Tony's sudden, unexpected launch into stand-up routine takes me off guard. I don't get the joke at first and respond with a polite nod and an 'Oh really, how interesting'. If he'd introduced his gag with 'I say, I say, I say. . . ' or 'You'll like this one, –' at least I'd have known he was telling a joke and could have pretended to laugh. You just don't expect total strangers to be quite so pally, but that's light entertainers for you all over – always up for a lark and a crack. Generally I find professional comedians uncomfortable to be around – especially the ones who feel they always have to be 'on'. The desperate need to be 'funny' all the time feels more like a desperate need to be loved; or it could just be that comics are terrified of shutting up for more than two minutes.

Becoming a member of the ancient Order of Water Rats requires over ninety percent approval from existing members. And for that you need to be well respected in the entertainment business (Mr Barton it appears is highly regarded on the northern club circuit and is proud to be a semi-regular on that popular comedy series *Coronation Street*).

The Grand Order of Water Rats came into being in 1889 after a small group of entertainers bought a race horse as a way of making a bit of extra cash. The horse, Magpie, was a great success and kept on winning races. Everyone was happy except for one member of the group – comedy writer and joint owner, Wal Pink. Wal was a religious man and didn't approve of gambling, so after much moral-high-grounding he managed to persuade the other owners to donate their winnings to charity. Knowing they were helping the needy seemed to give the group more of a kick than pocketing the cash and so the following year they turned themselves into a benign brotherhood. It was Wal who came up with the Water Rats name. Magpie and he were trotting down the street one day in a violent rainstorm. A bus pulled up beside them and the driver leant out and yelled 'Call that a horse? Looks more like a bleedin' water rat!'

Wal was then heard to declare 'That's it. . . that's what we've been looking for – Water Rat, the most unloved little creature of all . . . let's give it some respect. If you turn the word Rats backwards the word Star is revealed. . . we'll elevate the lowest to the highest in the firmament of good fellowship and charity. A Rat is a Vole and Vole is an anagram of Love and that's what we'll be ... a Brotherhood of Love.'

I guess you could say Wal was the first hippie.

At the start of each year a 'King Rat' is elected to oversee events, such as the annual boat trip. Melvyn Hayes took over the mantle this year from skiffle-supremo Chas McDevitt, who apparently had a hit in the '50s with 'Ridin' the Freight Train'. I've never heard of Chas and have no idea what he looks like but I do recognise Melvyn chatting away to Paul Daniels at the entrance to the boat. As King Rat, it's Melvyn's job to welcome us all aboard with a royal handshake and a 'Have a great evening.' 'Who the hell was that?' I hear him whisper as I filter through.

A three-piece jazz band portside is playing 'Put on a Happy Face' as we all mill around the long central buffet table, nibbling on various nibbles.

Apart from a few more wrinkles and a far less camp demeanour, Melvyn Hayes hasn't changed a bit since he was 'raising the rafters with a hey, hey, hey' on *It Ain't 'Alf Hot Mum*. He's still small and compact with a broad, ready smile. Apart from John Inman and Larry Grayson, Melvyn was about the only obviously gay character on TV in the 1970s. I reckon any aliens watching television at the time must have assumed all gay men skipped about in floppy wide-brimmed hats and chiffon scarves, pinching shop mannequins' bottoms. Although in real life Melvyn Hayes is far from gay (he's on his second marriage), it seems he will be forever remembered as camp cross-dressing 'Gloria', the frustrated musical theatre queen who spent every episode running around in a skirt shouting 'I'm a star! I'm a star!' It may be deemed unacceptable to like it now but at the time I remember absolutely loving *It Aint 'Alf Hot Mum*. The series ended up being plagued by accusations of homo-racial stereotyping and was eventually consigned to the BBC incinerator along with *The Goodies* and *Mind Your Language*. By the early '80s the TV cultural-revolutionists had banned from our screens all traces of limp-wristery, facial boot-polish, mammy-waving minstrels and exaggerated ethnic impersonations ('Yeah mon, dat swingin' from de trees is reeely great mon'). I couldn't believe it when I found out that the actor playing the lead Indian character in *Ain't Half Hot* was actually a posh white actor. Mind you the only other Indian man I'd ever seen on TV was Peter Sellers, so I didn't have much of a racial yardstick.

Melvyn hasn't always played the camp clown. He started out in the '50s performing the Indian Rope Trick for 'The Great Masoni' – a top magician who had a long-running show at the Comedy Theatre in London. But it was as Bombardier 'Gloria' Beaumont that he made his name; well, that and *Summer Holiday* with Cliff Richard, but I'm not sure he likes to be reminded of that.

Once on board I head straight for the seating plan pinned up next to the ladies' loos. Five names immediately jump out at me and I can hardly contain my excitement – a whole clutch of Big-Timers all under one roof. Terry Burgess, Charlie Smithers, Ken Joy, Keith Simmons and Jack Mayes have all spookily been seated at the same table along with my childhood hero Bob Holness and his wife.

I'm sitting at the table opposite next to a glamorous looking lady named Caron Gardner. She has one of those pretty, pouty faces synonymous with the swinging end of the '60s – all high-cheekbones, masses of mascara and thick strawberry blonde hair. Her skin is tanned and clear and she has one of those velvety Rank-starlet, Chelsea-girl voices straight out of 1966. I tell her why I'm here and how excited I am about the table opposite and she suggests I go forthwith and introduce myself before they all get stuck into the buffet. She's probably right – nothing should come between a light entertainer and his tummy.

Too late. The captain of the ship is making a speech. He'd like us to put our hands together and raise a glass (not easy) for King Rat. The elderly crowd goes wild as Melvyn suddenly bursts in through a set of glass doors, followed closely by a little man blowing into a set of bagpipes. We all grab our handy-sized Union Jack flags (left on every place setting) and start waving furiously. After a comedy Groucho Marks-style stomp round the tables, Melvyn heads upstairs to where many of light entertainment's royalty have been seated (Paul Daniels, Tom O'Connor and guitarist Bert Weedon amongst them). Bagpipe-man is having trouble keeping up with Melvyn's rodent-like pace. They eventually come to a breathless standstill on a raised platform where Melvyn is about to make a speech.

'Ladies and gentlemen, please raise your glasses for the man with the best set of pipes in the business: Mr Ken Joy!'

So that's what Ken looks like now. Not quite the cheeky young whippersnapper featured on page seventeen of *Reach for the Big Time*. The goggle-eyed gurner riding a comedy bike and spinning one of those old-fashioned football rattles is now a grey little man in his sixties. He has retained a certain goofiness I suppose – instead of the obligatory beige jacket, Ken is wearing one of those brightly coloured, harlequin patterned waistcoats favoured by 'zany' uncles at weddings.

After several boozy toasts to various notables on board, we all stand to attention to sing the Ratlings' signature tune, a rousing little number about loyalty and commitment to the cause. I seem to be the only one who doesn't know either the tune or any of the words so to show willing I mouth along like a badly dubbed actor, making sure no sound passes my lips.

The captain of the ship (Captain Birds Eye without the beard) runs through the onboard safety procedures and reminds us not to panic should the worst happen. We all cheer again as a loud belch of black diesel smoke tells us we're on our way (an awkward gust of wind blows the noxious fumes straight back in through an open window resulting in a mass outbreak of spluttering). With throats cleared it's time for Melvyn to make the announcement everyone's been waiting for.

'Would tables Y, W and D please make their way to the buffet?'

That's me. This could be a good opportunity to introduce myself to the Big Time table opposite before they too are summoned to the buffet cart. I approach with caution. Mr Joy is looking anything but joyful, hunched up in the corner, puffing on a stubby cigar; he's probably exhausted after all that chasing about after Melvyn.

I'm only able to recognise who's who by surreptitiously checking each performer's photo against the real thing and then adding thirty years. Jack Mayes is the easiest to spot – his teeth are still large and protruding and the carefully positioned thatch of ginger hair (could be a wig) is just as carefully scraped across his walnut head. He also seems the liveliest of the bunch, merrily waving his Union Jack just for the sheer pleasure of it. Terry Burgess is still handsome, a bit like an old fashioned GP, but much greyer now of course, and smaller than I imagined. He's busy demonstrating one of his card tricks to Keith Simmons of the *Simmons Brothers* (catch phrase 'Have a Fish!'). From his dapper 1977 photo – all black tie and side parting – I imagined Mr Burgess to be rather grand; posh even. But in reality he couldn't be more cab-driver-cockney if he tried. Charlie Smithers also seemed rather dapper in his 1973 photo – a bit like Terry Thomas but without the gap – but he too is a broad Londoner just like Terry. Charlie is the least recognisable from his photo and I'm shocked by how frail he looks. According to my table partner Caron, he's one of the longest-serving comics in the business, and it shows. Next to Charlie is dear Bob Holness. I'm sad to say, Bob is looking frail these days. Both ears are hooked up to hearing aids and he seems rather lost – nothing like the confident game-show host I remember with such fondness from my youth. I never imagined Bob might one day become old – he always seemed so timeless. It's upsetting to see him like this.

Keith Simmons on the other hand looks remarkably fit for his age, despite the shock of dyed curls framing his long, narrow face. He's clutching a pristine hardback copy of James Herbert's horror novel *The Rats* to his chest. I decide to use this as my way in.

'Excuse me – are you Keith Simmons?' I ask nervously.

'Yes I am; who wants to know?'

'Sorry to disturb you but I couldn't help noticing your copy of *The Rats*. I just thought you might be interested to know I nearly got expelled from school for reading that book – my headmaster was so appalled by all the sex and violence he took the book outside and burned it in front of the whole school. He told me I was a bad influence.'

'Well I think it's a fantastic book and so appropriate for this evening. Look at this. . . ' (he points to the inside cover) '. . . signed by the author himself. I'm asking all the ex-King Rats to sign it for me so I can auction it off for charity. Who are you by the way?'

I ask if I can have everyone at the table's attention.

'Sorry to bother you all. You don't know me but I recently featured you all in a book about light entertainers called *Reach for the Big*

Time – you may have heard of it, there was quite a lot of press coverage a couple of weeks ago. . . '

Blank faces stare back at me.

'. . . Anyway, I'd like to apologise to you all. It was wrong of me not to get your permission first. Anyway the upshot is, I'm now in a bit of a pickle. . .' and so begins my tale of woe. I'm growing in confidence with each telling but in front of such an illustrious audience I'm feeling particularly nervous.

I hand *Reach for the Big Time* to Keith who has a good old belly laugh when he sees his picture on page twenty-three. He passes the book to Charlie Smithers who can't believe he ever looked so young; Ken Joy is amused by his gurning 1977 alter ego. Even Bob Holness seems to be enjoying seeing so many familiar faces from the past. Terry Burgess, however, has remained worryingly tight-lipped.

Melvyn Hayes has just got up to make another announcement.

'Would tables A, L and C please make their way to the buffet table now. No pushing please and that includes you, Mr Holness.'

I've never seen a bunch of seventy-year-olds move so fast. They're like eager little boys racing to be first in line at the tuck shop. Despite headmaster Melvyn's plea for calm, there's plenty of pushing and shoving going on and a lot of competing to see who can come up with the funniest quip. These old timers just can't resist the opportunity to show off; you can see it in their bright eyes, always on the look out for a crafty gag or a well-placed put-down. But the thing I find most refreshing about being in their company is the total lack of cruelty and cynicism. There's a generosity of spirit and a big-heartedness that my generation of sneering miserablists seems to have lost. Knee-jerk cynicism may have made us more sophisticated but we seem to have lost much of our humanity along the way.

There's still a backlog of hungry entertainers queuing from the first round of tables; the trays of meaty stews are looking dangerously depleted. I take my place in line behind Jack Mayes. A stout little man with a loud pink suit tells me to 'get a move on before it all runs out.' I fear he may be too late – those at the front of the queue have resorted to scraping the crispy bits from around the edges of the meat trays. Order eventually descends as a matronly waitress fights her way through the crush, armed with a steaming tray of fresh stew.

Seventy-three year old Jack wants to know whether he can buy a copy of *Reach for the Big Time* from me. I feel terrible not being able to give anyone a copy, especially when I think of all those thousands of copies gathering dust in a dank warehouse in Middlesex.

I've been slightly wary of Jack so far. He has quite a stern manner and hasn't been particularly friendly towards me. In an effort to try and bond, I ask him what he's been up to since his 1973 publicity photo was taken. Although officially semi-retired he's pleased to tell me that he still works as an occasional children's entertainer in and around Stevenage. For the past thirty years he's been known amongst his fellow entertainers as 'The Almost Famous Jack Mayes' and it's a badge he seems to wear with pride.

'I still have it printed on all my publicity material' he tells me with a grin, 'I was never afraid of failure – not that I consider myself a failure you understand. It's just that I was never really interested in the whole fame game. Mind you, everyone around Stevenage seems to know me. They come up to me in the street and say 'How's that Hairy Harry of yours?'

Jack has been performing with his strange ventriloquist puppet with the enormous thatch of hair (made from real mountain goat) for over forty years.

'Kids today still love my old Hairy Harry even though he's a bit tatty now and can be very naughty at times.'

Jack's photo in *Reach for the Big Time* has him proudly displaying an enormous balloon sculpture of. . . well I'm not quite sure what. It certainly isn't your typical sausage-dog-cum-rabbit balloon animal – more a bunch of differently shaped balloons randomly stuck together. I show Jack the photo but he only has the vaguest recollection of it being taken. Although he does remember the wig. . .

'I stopped wearing toupees when the Falklands War broke out – I felt guilty about being so vain when our boys were out there dying in battle. The thing is I was never really that bald, just very thin on top – the wig gave me more volume.'

Jack's not in the least bit surprised by the crap-ness of the so-called balloon animal in his photo.

'You could get away with a lot more in those days – kids weren't as clued up and sophisticated as they are now. I used to tell them they could have any animal they liked as long as it was a dachshund or a giraffe. All my animals were the same really, you just had to view them from different angles and call them different names – the kids would believe whatever you told them.'

He may not remember much about the photo being taken but is he angry with me for using it without his permission?

'I'm not angry exactly, but why didn't you ask first?'

'I couldn't find any up-to-date contact details for you. I did try. Are you sure you're okay about me including you in the book?'

'Yeah, I don't mind. Just a bit of nostalgia isn't it? Us old-timers won't be around for much longer – I don't mean to be morbid or anything but we're none of us getting any younger. I suppose it's nice to know we'll be forever remembered in your book.'

Jack has a melancholic streak – you can see it in his sad, thoughtful eyes. My next question of course is whether he remembers any of the other acts from the book.

I watch for signs of recognition as he slowly turns the pages. Jack has a wonderfully expressive face – part clown, part old-fashioned country parson. With his long, lugubrious features and crooked chin, he can seem quite fierce but once he starts smiling his whole face beams. I recognise that twinkle in the eye – it means he's recognised someone.

'Chris Smith – another vent act – works with a giant duck. Known him for years. Blimey that's not a very flattering photo of him is it? I've got his number right here in my mobile. Would you like it?'

'Thank you so much – you have no idea how much this means to me.'

'£25,000 wasn't it?'

I'm really warming to Jack – he isn't fierce at all – he's a sweetie.

'I haven't spoken to Chris for a while. . . I think he lives on his own out near Reading.'

Shepherd's Bush boy Jack has also been living on his own since his wife Mavis died earlier in the year. He's been finding it hard to come to terms with the sudden loss.

'When you live on your own you lose your life. I'm just not used to it. Mavis was a wonderful woman and did everything for me – looked like Doris Day – one of the reasons I married her I suppose. She'd always accompany me on stage during my dove act to brighten up proceedings. The audience loved her.'

Jack is proud to have been the first magician in the UK to incorporate doves into his act (Jack started out in magic before moving across to ventriloquism). Despite being a one-time member of the Magic Circle's inner circle, he's happy to share some of his secrets with me.

'Working with doves was very cruel really. Four or five bewildered birds would be carefully secreted about your person in various strategically placed pouches sewn into a specially adapted suit. You'd come on stage looking like a fat bloke with all these birds stuffed inside your suit and by the end of the act, when all the birds had flown, you'd be this little skinny geezer in a baggy suit all covered in bird crap. The poor old doves had to be folded really tightly in order to fit into the pockets. You'd never get away with it these days. You should talk to Terry Burgess – he used to specialise in doves, did Terry.'

The venerable looking Mr Burgess is just ahead of us in the queue. He's busy shovelling ladlefuls of buffet onto his plate. Jack looks on anxiously, worried that he might be missing out – food, it seems, was hard to come by when Jack was a lad.

'We was so hard up I had to eat the rubbish out of dustbins, literally. I never had no shoes neither – used to walk up and down the Scrubs Lane in bare feet, all weathers. So did a lot of other kids on my estate.'

I resist the urge to shout 'LUXURY – when I was a lad we used to dream of eating rubbish out of dustbins' in a broad Python-shire accent.

'I never resorted to begging though. . . ' he continues proudly, '. . . not like so-called "poor" people these days. They don't know the meaning of the word poor.'

Hitler must have had it in for young Jack. During the War he and his mum were bombed out of three consecutive houses, all within a couple of miles of each other. The two of them eventually ended up eking a meagre existence on a run-down war-torn estate behind the BBC in White City, the sort of salt-of-the-earth place where everyone looked out for one another and nobody ever locked their front doors, 'not that there was anything worth nicking'.

Terry Burgess is eyeing me suspiciously from across the mixed vegetable tray. I don't think he likes me and I'm beginning to wonder whether it has something to do with the book.

Terry's entry in *Reach for the Big Time* is irresistible:

Terry Burgess
And his
CAVALCADE OF FUN

Ideal entertainment for the after-dinner show, club, cabaret, theatre show. An act to suit all occasions. With audience participation. Fast moving with laughs all the way. Comedy magic with an emphasis on the comedy. Terry Burgess has an act you can sit back and enjoy. A very visual and colourful entertainment that can be performed anywhere, surrounded. An up-to-the-minute act that makes the audience roar with laughter. A brand of humour that is adapted to the audience. Musical accompaniment is not essential. Terry Burgess has appeared in London's leading hotels. If you are wondering what kind of entertainment to provide at your next function, liven things up with Terry Burgess and solve your problem.

All enquiries to: Terry Burgess.

And there was I assuming 'musical accompaniment' was a compulsory part of every self-respecting light entertainer's canon. Not quite sure what a 'surrounded' performance is but I suppose it's reassuring to know that whatever it is can happen anywhere. I'd like to 'sit back and enjoy' Terry Burgess if he'll let me. I throw him an extra large grin from across the trays of carrots and potatoes but he ignores me and carries on shovelling. I approach with caution.

'Hi Terry, can I just ask – are you annoyed with me about something?'

'You could say that – yes.'

'Is it about the book?'

'Yeah. I think it was wrong what you wrote. I heard all about it.'

'But I didn't write anything. Who told you I'd written something?'

'I can't reveal my source. But I sympathise with him. I reckon you was having a laugh at our expense.'

Oh dear, it sounds to me like Chinese whispers.

'I'm very sorry that you feel that way but I assure you I didn't actually write anything derogatory and I certainly wasn't out to have a go at anybody. As you can see, apart from the short introduction there isn't any text in the book. Are you sure your friend wasn't upset about the newspaper publicity?'

'I dunno. But it's not right to mock us.'

'I agree. But I think you're referring to an article written by a journalist. I assure you I had nothing to do with that. Please look through the book again, I'm sure you'll agree it wasn't meant to be cruel.'

He has another cursory flick and manages a small smile. I'd hardly describe Terry as a 'cavalcade of fun' right now although seeing the book for a second time seems to have calmed his fears somewhat. On the way back to his table he slips me a calling card made of that freaky 3D material that makes your eyes go weird. It reads: 'Terry Burgess: To Amuse and Confuse'.

'I'll agree to be in your book on one condition' he tells me. 'You send me a copy when it's back in the shops.'

You've got it Terry.

Excellent – so that's four new Big-Timers signed up within the space of an hour.

Jack has at last reached the front of the buffet queue and has piled his plate with enough beef to feed a whole army of 'Hairy Harries'. Sadly 'Hairy' won't be joining us for supper as he has a prior engagement in Jack's loft.

'You'll have to come up to South Hertfordshire if you want to meet my Hairy' he says temptingly.

What is it about Hertfordshire I wonder that attracts so many of my Big-Timers? With the two Terrys – Burgess and Seabrooke – up there in Pinner and Bushey, respectively, Jack Mayes across the M1 in Stevenage, and Mr Clamp over Dunstable way, I'm wondering whether it might have something to do with the quality of the cheesecake at that Little Chef I visited.

With a dangerously full plate of buffet I return to my table and sit back down next to Caron.

'So you've managed to introduce yourself I see'. She says with a cheeky smile.

I'm sure I recognise Caron from somewhere. . .

'Why do I know your face?' I ask.

'Well, I was a Hill's Angel for a time in the '70s – maybe you remember me from that?'

Doubt it – I was never much of a fan of Benny Hill and his panty-wielding pom-pom girls.

'You may have seen me in *Monty Python* – the saucy vicar sketch?'

Nope, don't remember any saucy vicar sketch. . .

'If you were watching the shopping channel QVC last week you may have seen me modelling underwear for the over fifties.'

Now that's something I would have remembered. Trouble is I'm not really a huge fan of QVC although I did once sit through several hours of a collagen-clad woman trying to sell me a 'cleavage-enhancement-system' consisting of a pair of uncooked chicken breasts sewn into a bra. The lady claimed I'd never have to feel lonely or flat-chested ever again. After three hours I nearly believed her.

'No I haven't watched QVC for quite a while', I tell her.

'In that case you must have seen me in *The Evil of Frankenstein* with Peter Cushing – I was the scantily dressed girl running around screaming a lot.'

Ahh, now you're talking. I used to love all those old Hammer films. Although I tried sitting through some of the *Hammer House of Horror* TV series again the other day and was sorely disappointed by the lack of horror – nostalgia it seems has a nasty habit of lying about the past. The only episode that was even remotely scary the second time round was 'The House That Dripped Blood' in which a posh couple are menaced by some dodgy plumbing.

Caron looks at me wistfully. 'You know it's funny, I keep thinking I've retired from showbiz and then the phone rings with a job offer and I just can't stop myself.'

A tipsy Tony Barton suddenly appears at our table – he wants to tell me how jealous everyone is that I'm sitting next to 'the most beautiful woman in show-business.' John Adrian has obviously seated me at the captain's table.

The sun is disappearing behind a vast steel tower block as the Natacia is slowly manoeuvred back round for her return journey. I'm just about ready for some live cabaret.

The only Big-Timer I haven't managed to speak to properly yet is Charlie Smithers:

Charlie Smithers
Comedian
Stage Award Winner 1972
Mecca Agency International Ltd, Bromley

When I do eventually pin him down outside the gents' loo (he's been a frequent visitor all night) I'm delighted by how friendly he is. Everyone I've spoken to about Charlie holds him in great high esteem. He's one of the very last of the old postwar comics – his repertoire still consists of jokes about doodlebugs and rationing. It's taken a lot of persuading on the part of the organisers to convince Charlie to get back on stage tonight.

'I've been in two minds all week about whether to perform. I haven't been too well recently and wouldn't want to disappoint my old comedy muckers with a sub-standard show. I don't do much comedy these days so it's quite nerve-racking being here.'

Melvyn is asking for everyone's attention again downstairs. Charlie looks anxious.

'Oh dear that's me – they've put me on first would you believe. I suppose I'd better get back. By the way I'm very happy about you using my image in the book. I hope it's a great success for you. Come and visit me anytime. I've got lots of stories to tell. Mind you I have been in the business longer than forever, you know. . . '

Charlie struggles onto the small makeshift stage and introduces himself – not that he needs any introduction. The whole place erupts with hoots and cheers as he grasps the microphone with his small bony hand.

Although a little shaky to begin with, he soon loosens up but I'm finding it hard to hear many of the jokes – his delivery is a barely audible whisper. The few jokes that I do manage to catch, I don't really get, although everyone else seems to be laughing. As well as the wartime references there are lots of in-jokes about fellow performers I've never heard of. But it doesn't matter, everyone is thrilled to see him up on stage again – after all there can't be many

Charlie Smithers left out there.

So far, tonight's cabaret has been aimed squarely at the over-sixty-fives – a good ninety-five percent of the audience. But that's all about to change. The organisers are keen to remind us that light entertainment isn't only for the ancients, even though the vast majority of Water Rats are well over retirement age.

Poor old Charlie hasn't even returned to his seat before the sombre lighting is transformed into flashing red and blue disco. From innocent postwar comedy to knowing post-modern disco in less than a minute – the relentless beat of Kylie Minogue pumps from a mighty speaker. The mood couldn't be more different as a tight-bodied young woman with heavy make-up, low-slung, botty-crack revealing jeans and a skimpy top skips across the floor, gyrating and pouting her way through a backing track of 'Can't Get You Out of My Head'. Bob Holness looks on in pained bewilderment – he's not the only one. Charlie's fingers are firmly embedded in his ears and Ken Joy looks more sepulchral than ever. Everywhere I look, mouths loll open in astonishment as young Victoria Clusky shamelessly shakes her shapely bootie at us. Those that can, make a hasty retreat to the relative peace and quiet of the upper deck. It's all a world away from the gentle routines of Messrs Smithers and Mayes. The current light entertainment scene is dominated by the caterwauling of a million karaoke-kids dreaming of becoming fully-fledged tribute acts. Miss Clusky does a perfectly serviceable approximation of Miss Minogue, but frankly who here really cares? She's performing to a room full of elderly men who wouldn't know a Kylie if it jumped up and bit them on the hip-replacement. It's a well-known fact that all old people hate pop music. They only refer to it as 'pop' because they think the word sounds imbecilic and derogatory – listen to the way they spit it out. Oldies can't differentiate between 'rock', 'techno' and 'house' – to them it's all just 'an appalling racket' or 'that dreadful noise'. Most old people, by whom I mean the over-seventies, are likely to have passed through a cultural cut-off point from which they cannot escape. My father has certainly heard of the Beatles and the Stones but he couldn't hum or name you a single track by either band. He sort of remembers punk but more as a silly haircut than a musical revolution. Anything after that – forget it. Dad's true musical cut-off point came in about 1939. Music hall and Mozart are what he likes; everything else is referred to as 'that terrible pop.'

'Sorry everybody, I suppose I should have eaten something before the show – maybe my trousers would have stayed up!' Miss Clusky is obviously aware of the erotic side effects she's having on her flabbergasted audience. All those energetic thrusts and leaps have exposed more buttock than she bargained for. Just as the annual Water Rats boat trip is in danger of descending into a full-on porno show, Melvyn brings on the next act, a comic called Andy Brown. Andy can't be more than thirty but his amusing repertoire of gags all focuses on the indignities of old age: 'I see The Incontinence Society of Great Britain has set up a website. . . ', he jokes, '. . . it's called www.slashslashslashslashincontinence.co.uk.' The world of the internet has obviously passed many of these old timers by, judging by the deathly hush that greets Andy's rather brilliant joke. He struggles on gamely. '. . . All I can say is thank God for the recent mild winter – one cold snap and I might have been performing to an empty boat this evening.'

You'd think the last thing elderlies would want to be reminded of is their ever-increasing fragility, but Andy has touched a comedy nerve and everyone is falling about laughing – I suppose it's reassuring to know they're all in the same boat, so to speak. After a couple of so-so gags about the revitalising effects of Viagra, Andy welcomes to the floor the soul sensation that is Jamie Heath (think of a Midlands version of Lenny Henry's soul-loving, bed-hopping ladies-man Theophilus P. Wildebeeste). Freddie, with his exotic knee-length dinner jacket and immaculately sculptured hair, has toured with 'amongst others, Kool and the Gang and The New Four Tops'. I doubt many in the audience will have heard of either of these bands and I suspect The New Four Tops may be one of those end-of-the-pier outfits living on the back of the one remaining member of a group who had a hit once, back in the mid-seventies. Young Freddie gives us a run down of his favourite soul artists before launching into a slightly off-key version of 'Papa Was a Rolling Stone' performed with the aid of a backing tape (inevitably).

I make my escape and head upstairs for a chat with Victoria Clusky. She's managed to change into something slightly less revealing and is enjoying a large glass of Chardonnay. . . Turns out Victoria is the daughter of Dec Clusky – one time member of '60s beat band The Bachelors. She's exceedingly proud of her dad and tells me to 'check out his website', which I do later that evening. I discover that Dec now runs an online service for aspiring musicians who want to make it big in the music industry. According to his website 'makehits.com' the process is pretty straightforward – although worryingly he still refers to the charts as the 'hit-parade'. According to Dec all you need to do to ensure a guaranteed number one hit is spend £227 on a series of books entitled *How to Make a Million From Your Music* by Dec Clusky. Dec works in association with a group known as 'The Serious Writer's Guild' who sound like an independently respectable set-up until a Google search brings me straight back to. . . makehits.com. The 'guild' is run by, you guessed it, our friend Dec and consists of 'a bunch of highly successful music makers and song writers under the personal direction of. . . Paul McCartney.' Only joking – I mean Dec of course.

The makehits.com site is full of grandiose claims and even grandioser promises, all of which come straight from the Bachelor boy himself:

Dear Music Friend

So you fancy yourself as a Song Writer, a Mega Star, or possessed with Incredible Music Writing Talent? Maybe you want to produce or compose? If so, this might be the most important letter on the music business you have ever read.

How many times have you been told by friends, family, loved ones that you should be in the Hit Parade? Every time you or anyone else sings your stuff everyone says: "You should be in the charts instead of that rubbish I hear on the radio".

Well, why aren't you? I'll tell you why...Because you don't have the first idea how to, that's why! Oh, you might convince yourself that you know all about it (or at least your pal Charlie knows). BUT DO YOU REALLY KNOW?

Trust me, you haven't a clue. But here's the GOOD NEWS:

I DO! And I will help you ... that's a promise.

And I know it all. (Now – there's a title for a song) That's not just bullsh*t confidence ... it's the truth.

Dec goes on to tell us all about his remarkable, amazing, incredible and outstandingly awesome career in showbiz ('we were bigger than The Beatles for a while') and a personal thesis on why people want to become pop-stars. He knows that what every hard working musician really wants (amongst other things) is:

. . .loads and loads of money – plus a lifetime stream of income. You can always give it away, if the idea offends you!

as well as, of course,

. . .a music "money making machine" which is FUN as well as being HIGHLY LUCRATIVE with little or no investment.

Sounds pretty good eh? What's that? You wouldn't mind a slice of this action yourself? You see ... I was right all along... OK, so all these people call me and ask if I know how they can be successful. And I answer with a letter saying: "Yes, I DO know as it happens!"*

If you are still in any doubt about Dec's ability to turn you into a one-man hit-making factory, take a look at some of his past success stories posted on the website. Steve Zaborski from America claims to owe Dec 'a debt of gratitude' for giving him the opportunity to purchase 'my very first BMW'. Good on you Steve and I look forward to hearing your song in the hit-parade very soon. John, from Peterborough, would also like to thank Dec for steering him towards a 'six-figure income'.

I'm tempted to put Dec's claims to the test myself, but right now I'm not sure I could afford the £227 subscription fee. Besides, I own a 1982 Ford Capri Cabaret, what could I possibly want with a shiny new BMW?

The Natacia has arrived back safely on the shores of the Embankment. Everyone seems in high spirits – the laughter and general air of tomfoolery can probably be heard all the way up the Strand. As I trip back down the gangplank I have to keep reminding myself that I've just spent several hours partying with pensioners. I wonder how they've managed to retain such youthful optimism and wide-eyed innocence. It's as though they've somehow managed to avoid the vagaries of the modern world. Never feeling you have to grow up probably helps – after all, 'being sensible' is an anathema to most Big Timers – their job is to entertain through silliness and there's certainly been a lot of that this evening.

Who'd have thought that. . .

Ken Joy
*Visualist * Instrumentalist * Funniest*
K.A.J Productions

. . . would now be entertaining diners at a Beefeater restaurant in Bromley? Or that Keith Simmons of. . .

* For all advice on success in the Music/Songwriting industry contact Dec direct at dec@makehits.com and visit the website: http://www.makehits.co.uk

The Simmons Brothers
Comedy Entertainers
'Have A Fish!'

. . . would still be sporting such a massive hairdo? I was particularly taken by Keith, not simply for his love of trashy horror novels, but for his keen interest in my book. He rings me the following day to tell me how much he enjoyed seeing so many familiar faces and to ask if I'd like to attend a special tribute lunch that he's organising in honour of drag-artist supremo Danny La Rue – 'He's celebrating his fiftieth year in showbiz – everyone will be there. . . even John Inman.'

How could I possibly resist. . . ?

With five more signatures and a new lead in the shape of Chris Smith and his enormous duck, I head back home to add to my ever-expanding Big-Time Family Tree.

But I was about to receive some extremely distressing news. . .

9. Rollin', Rollin', Rollin'

Reach for the Deadline: two weeks and three days to go...
After such a successful trip up the Thames, the email waiting for me back home seems doubly devastating. Ventriloquist Chris Bylett, one of the fifteen acts featured in the article, feels his career has been so undermined by the recent press coverage that as far as he's concerned the book deserves to be pulped and the sooner the better – what's more, he doesn't seem prepared to negotiate.

I'd been expecting some hiccups but this seems so sudden and so final. Carrying on with my quest now seems pointless. The deal is all or nothing and without Chris on board I may as well have nothing.

I feel angry and let down. What's so special about Chris that he won't even speak to me? I call my girlfriend, confident she'll know what to do next. But even she seems at a loss.

So it would seem the fun and games are over. I need to start preparing for the worst. I call my lawyer friend Phil for some advice on how to file for bankruptcy – that evening he brings over a thick file of notes for me to look at. I barely make it to Page three, Clause II, subsection vii: 'Possessions – the removal thereof'.

The thought of gathering together my meagre belongings – CD collection, a few books, ancient laptop, a couple of old table lamps – and handing them over to some faceless 'retrieval' company in Northampton seems so pathetic. And after the contents of my flat have been removed and sold at auction, I will presumably be marched from the premises by a gang of burly skinheads with crowbars. And then what? Mumping on friends for the rest of my life – or worse – a soiled, polyester sleeping bag in the doorway of Dixons? Maybe living on the street would do me good – toughen me up a bit. I pour myself a whisky – and then another. But the more I drink, the more the idea of destitution terrifies me. What if I die on the streets – will anyone care or even notice? And then there's the whole question of soup – I can't stand soup – I'd rather die than live on soup handouts.

'Jim. . . Jim! Wake up.' I open a crusty eye to find my girlfriend desperately trying to scrape me off the floor.

'Leave me alone. Let me die. . . ' I moan, rearranging the soggy newspaper pillow under my head. She brings me a glass of water and attempts to haul me into an armchair.

An empty bottle of Famous Grouse has been flung across the room and there's a Chunky Kit Kat wrapper stuck to my left cheek. The last twenty-four hours begins flooding back – the boat trip, incontinence websites, James Herbert's *The Rats*, making a million from music, skipping down the gangplank, Hairy Harry – I'm trying to piece it all together. I know that somewhere down the line something has gone terribly wrong and then it all starts to trickle back: Chris Bylett; bankruptcy; bailiffs; Dixons' doorway; soup; vomit; ruin; death. I start sobbing into my whisky-stained shirt. I really do need to toughen up. . .

A long bath and several aspirin later my girlfriend plonks me down in front of the computer and forces me to send an email to Chris Bylett, asking him to reconsider. Two hours later there are six new emails waiting in my inbox. Precisely none are from Chris, one is from a debt clearance company (could be useful), four are offering to extend my penis by up to three inches (could be even more useful) and the sixth has 'Re: your book!!' written in the subject bar. I click, assuming the worst – no doubt it's from another distraught entertainer. I couldn't have been more wrong. . .

Yodelling country singer Keith Manifold has emailed to say he's heard all about my plight and is desperate to help save the book. Unlike Kenny Cantor, Keith feels honoured to have been included in *Reach for the Big Time* and has just bought three copies from Waterstone's (which is more than I've been able to do). What's more, he's thrilled about his recent appearance in the national press: 'Friends and colleagues have been ringing to congratulate me – they want to know who my publicist is! And now a local newspaper is keen to do a follow-up where-are-they-now piece!'

Best of all, Keith has some contacts for me and has invited me up to Macclesfield to see him perform.

I want to give Mr Manifold a big hug right this minute. How

can I even think about giving up my quest now? This is no longer about me losing a fortune – it's about Keith having something to be remembered by.

So that settles it – the journey continues. I'll deal with Chris Bylett and his comedy duck 'Desmond' once everyone else is on board. I ring Keith to tell him I'm on my way.

But before hitting the M1 heading north, I have a prior engagement with Victor Seaforth in South London. Victor can only see me for an hour because he has a doctor's appointment plus he's busy packing up his belongings in preparation for an imminent move to Bexhill-on-Sea.

Victor Seaforth

Impressionist – the man of a thousand voices!

Victor has completed over three hundred broadcasts to date, including the Black and White Minstrels television show. He has played all the leading theatres in the country also all the top night clubs. Other credits include ten summer seasons, four pantos, hundreds of one night concerts and cabarets.

Enquiries direct to Victor Seaforth

The traffic on Streatham High Road is the usual slow, agonising shuffle. At this rate I'm only going to have about ten minutes with Victor.

While Streatham still feels like gritty inner city London, Norbury, less than a mile down the road, is pure suburbia. Victor lives on a pleasant 1920s crescent with a neat garden where several rosy-cheeked gnomes are doing a spot of fishing. Victor, dressed in a smart black suit, looks much younger than his eighty-eight years. Despite arthritic, slightly bowed legs he's fit and lively and has a soft London accent with a hint of elocution – straight out of a 1940s war movie.

Hanging in pride of place in the hall is a large photo of his glamorous wife, Zuma – an accomplished acrobat.

'She died two years ago today. I miss her like mad and think of her every day' he tells me quietly.

One of the reasons for Victor's move to Bexhill is to extricate himself from all the memories.

'This was our house – now that she's gone I don't feel I belong here any more.'

Victor is excited and a little nervous about the imminent move. He shows me a glossy brochure of a swish new apartment complex.

'It's specially designed for older folk like myself. All very luxurious – twenty-four-hour carers on site and a very nice lounge. Everything is catered for.'

He hands me a cup of tea and a plate of Bourbons – I hand him *Reach for the Big Time* and a release. His face immediately lights up.

'Gosh, I've represented several of these acts over the years.'

'Represented?'

'Yes indeed – I'm still officially an agent you know – although I've cut back a lot recently. These kinds of acts were my bread and butter – I'd book them for working men's clubs and such like.'

This is exciting news – I had no idea Victor had also been an agent. Presumably that means he must have files, contact details, telephone numbers. . .

'If you'd come to see me two weeks ago I'd have been able to give you plenty of numbers. But I had a clear out last week and threw most of my old paperwork away.'

Agggh! Why is he telling me this? Surely he must know the whereabouts of some of his ex clients? I ask him to have another look through the book – just in case he's missed anyone. Every now and then he looks up from the pages, gazes into the middle-distance, opens his mouth as if he's about to reveal something vital – and then nothing – just a shake of the head. Two pages from the end however, his eyes suddenly light up.

'Aha, now then – The Shades of Harmony – great little vocal duo. The guitar player is my nephew and I was the group's agent for many years. Ian and his wife Felicity moved to Malaga several years ago. Unfortunately I don't have their telephone number but I can give you their address.'

The Shades of Harmony are one of my favourite acts from the book. The blurb on their flyer has kept me amused for months and I've been desperate to find out more about them:

The Shades of Harmony

The Shades of Harmony *are gifted – varied with expression with a facility and correctness that attests their great sensibility. When listening to these two young artists, one recalls the magic of Nina and Frederick, others that come to mind are Miki and Griff, but they have their own originality in the presentation of their act.*

To make your cabaret complete why not book The Shades of Harmony? *Cabaret, clubs, variety, radio and television.*

'Varied with expression with a facility and correctness that attests their great sensibility' sounds like something you'd find in a Nazi handbook on etiquette. Victor has no idea who wrote these priceless lines but he does agree they sound bonkers. Now that I have an address, maybe I'm about to find out at last.

Although 'Seaforth Entertainments' is still officially in business, Victor's once extensive client list has shrunk to just one, but it's a biggie.

'I organise British Airways' monthly in-house bash. But I find it exhausting these days. I've decided to phase myself out of the business (I think he means he's retiring) – I just can't be bothered with it any more. I'm eighty-eight years old; I've done it all, seen it all. The thrill of work no longer exists for me.'

But he's not retiring just yet and is busy booking an act for next month's BA bash.

'They want me to book this tribute band which imitates a pop group from the '70s called Elow – never heard of them myself.'

Neither have I but they sound intriguing.

'Apparently they were quite popular and used to play classical instruments.'

He shows me the name scribbled down on a piece of paper – aha, he means *ELO* (as in *Electric Light Orchestra*).

Victor hasn't performed in public for over two years but this morning he's keen to give me a demonstration of his skills. He's even brought down an old dressing-up box full of costumes.

'The press christened me 'the man of a thousand voices' but I didn't like that. Audiences would take it literally and want to hear every single one of them. Well I just didn't have the repertoire. So then I became known as 'the man of a hundred voices' but that was still an exaggeration. I preferred the 'Man of Many Voices.'

In fact Victor is a man of very few voices but each one is like an entire act in itself. First up is his twenty-minute rendition of Winston Churchill's victory speech. Rising to his feet he starts giving it the full Donald Wolfit – plum red cheeks, spittle flying, voice a tremulous boom. Just as he reaches a dramatic climax the phone rings, making us both jump. He picks up the receiver, still in Churchillian mode. . .

'Good afternoon'. . . *(long pause)*. . . 'No, I'm sorry I'm not interested!'

He slams down the receiver.

For the past couple of weeks, Victor has been plagued by unsolicited tele-marketers and is clearly at the end of his tether.

'They get on my nerves these people. Always trying to sell me things I don't need, or to tell me I've won a prize I don't want. . . and some of them talk in this strange sort of language. . . you know. . . bad English I call it. I tell them to speak more distinctly but they don't understand what I'm saying. It's all such a waste of time, such a terrible waste of time.'

He takes a deep breath, finishes the rousing Churchill speech and collapses on the sofa, exhausted and emotional. I don't know whether to cheer, make a nice cup of tea or call a doctor.

'I must have listened to Mr Churchill's speech over a hundred times' he says breathlessly, 'and I'm still word-perfect you know.'

Seconds later he's on his feet again, face contorted, one eye closed, body hunched. His energetic Quasimodo impression lasts even longer than Churchill and has plenty of references to 'the bells, the bells'. He's really going for it – tears rolling down his cheeks, drool dribbling from both corners of his mouth. But he's not finished yet. After a short breather, he opens up the scruffy dressing-up box and starts rifling through piles of old hats and scarves.

'I'd like to show you my Toulouse Lautrec' he says, carefully removing an enormous black cloak and a pair of two-foot long, specially adapted shoes. 'I call them my Toulouse-shoes. Could you give me a hand putting them on please?'

It's not so much a case of putting them on as carefully lowering him down into them. By kneeling on the long padded shoe extensions Victor is able to magically transform himself into the diminutive five-foot Frenchman. A hurriedly stuck-on beard, tatty top-hat and gold tipped walking cane complete the look. With a 'hor-he-hor' froggy French accent his bizarre impersonation takes flight. Again I'm worried – what if he can't get back up? I know his right knee has been giving him gyp and I don't want to be held responsible for causing him serious injury. He struggles on gamely but I wish he'd do some less physical impersonations – I'd be happy with a bit of Frank Spencer or Larry Grayson. He wrinkles his nose at the mention of Larry.

'I supported Grayson back in '73 – I'll never forget it – he came into my dressing room one night, marched straight up to me and kissed me full on the mouth! Can you believe it? I was spitting for weeks after that.'

I help him off the floor and start packing away the cloak and beard. He then takes out an old straw boater and tells me to follow him through to his kitchen-cum-dance studio.

'I'd like you to see my James Cagney Yankie-Doodle-Dandy dance routine before you go. I practise tap dancing every morning here in the kitchen – the lino floor sounds marvellous underfoot.'

Unfortunately his tap shoes are with the menders, so this morning he'll be tapping in a pair of slippers. Halfway through his splendid routine the phone rings again – this time it's the hospital wanting to know whether he's still on for this nine-thirty appointment. It's now nearly ten o'clock and Victor is in a panic.

I offer to drive him to the hospital. On the way he seems distracted.

'You haven't seen my Shirley Temple impression yet.'

I try and picture Victor, hair in bunches, singing 'On the Good Ship Lollipop'.

I wave goodbye to him at the hospital gates and feel a pang of sadness. In all the rush and confusion he's forgotten to change out of his slippers. . .

I hope he finds an appreciative audience at the 'Rosemont Apartment Complex – Catering for the Needs of Seniors' in Bexhill-on-Sea. I think he may have rediscovered a taste for performing. . .

10. Commercial Breakdown

Reach for the Deadline: two weeks and two days to go. . .
I hardly recognise my theatrical agent's voice when he calls to tell me I have an interview for a commercial – it's been so long since we spoke. Because of the stress of recent events I've completely forgotten that I actually need to continue making a living as an actor. Right now an advert would be perfect and because of the quick turnaround, it wouldn't take too much time out of my hectic schedule.

'I've got a casting for you this afternoon. If you get it, you'll be flying out tomorrow morning.'

'Great – what's it for?'

'Dog in the Fog' – a new beer for Polish TV. Says here they want you to wear something typically English to the casting – so I'd recommend tweeds and brogues, that sort of thing. Are you available and are you okay about working with dogs and wind machines?'

'Yep, that's all fine. And I'll dig out some old Harris tweeds.' I tell him.

'Good, because we need you to get this one. I appreciate you haven't been going up for much recently and I'm sorry about that, but the fact is we're scaling down the agency and will shortly be deciding who to keep and who to let go. . . '

Great – so no pressure then. . .

All across mainland Europe, respectable classically trained British actors are donning vegetable outfits and silly wigs in an attempt to sell cooking sauces and hair conditioners to gullible Europeans. Hundreds of commercials are filmed every week for the continental market – a large proportion of them will star British actors. I've wasted a large chunk of my life attending hopelessly unsuitable commercial castings, but I have a good feeling about this one.

Sadly, you only make the really big money if you appear in a UK ad, where fees are based on repeats – the more the ad is shown the more you make. But most 'serious' actors treat these big commercial jobs with contempt, and for good reason – long-running campaigns can kill a promising career stone dead as you go from 'the greatest Hamlet of his generation' to 'that poncy bloke from the Cheesy Wotsit ad.' It happened to a contemporary of mine. His career had been going extremely well with lead roles at the National Theatre, a couple of good TV sitcoms and a small part in a Hollywood movie. But then he was offered an irresistibly lucrative advert, to play the new anti-dandruff shampoo man. Little did he know that he'd just accepted one of the longest-running campaigns on TV. A year later he'd given up opening the repeat fee cheques piling up on his doormat – he had more money than he knew what to do with. He'd also given up hope of ever regaining his once glittering career – no serious director would go near him. Then one day while he was out throwing his money at girls and martinis, he discovered the joys of a different kind of powder, not dissimilar in appearance to dandruff. To top it all, he started hanging out with an idiotic crowd of powder-sniffing city boys, and by the late '80s he was supplying half the square mile with the white stuff. Then the crash of '89 happened and the whizz-kids traded in their wraps for cappuccinos. My friend still had a great brick of the stuff in his wardrobe, but with all his customers now drying out in clinics, there was nowhere left for the powder to go but up his severely damaged single nostril. Last thing I heard he was working in 'Spud U Like' on Tooting Broadway. Most druggies can blame their addiction on poverty, depression or weakness – few can put it down to an anti-dandruff shampoo.

There is a way of making a fast buck from ads without being laughed out of the business or ending up in casualty. Foreign commercials may not pay as well – a one-off fee usually – but at least snobby UK directors don't get to see you prancing across the screen dressed as a comedy carrot. Plus you get the added bonus of a three-day break in Madrid or Amsterdam thrown in, all expenses paid. And what could be more enjoyable than working on a storyline that makes no sense, with a director who speaks no English, and a crew who insist on boozy three-hour lunches? Bring it on Polish beer ad.

Although my hit rate for commercials is low – I average about one a year if I'm lucky – the job itself is always a hoot. So much fun are these foreign forays that even Hollywood superstars like George Clooney and Harrison Ford are getting in on the act.

Over the years I've appeared in several surreal European classics. You probably never saw my starring role as 'lazy man' in a French lifestyle magazine commercial featuring a hard-working dog who sees to my every need, or as the mad scientist with a hippo-fixation in a beer commercial for Spain. I was particularly good, I thought, as the one-legged pirate bellowing 'Chip Ahoy' in a Dutch cookie commercial – but slightly less convincing as the 'annoyed man' in a pasta sauce ad.

So why are so many classically trained British actors being hired to sell foreign goods to foreigners? The answer is simple – we're cheap (European actors working in their own country demand the same high repeat fees as Brits). I always liked to think it was because we were so good, which is partly true. We're good at not demanding to know what our 'motivation' is and we're also pretty good at not complaining about having to wear ridiculous costumes (unlike the Italians, who wouldn't be seen dead in a giant squirrel outfit).

Before being offered one of these little gems, actors have to go through the bizarre ritual of the casting session. First up is the call from your agent to confirm that you are indeed being considered for the part of a talking chorizo sausage – 'Fingers crossed darling and don't forget to wear something sausagey!'

The real fun, however, starts when the casting director hands you the 'breakdown', faxed over from the host country. These unintentionally hilarious story and character descriptions (written in Pidgin English by a non-English speaking secretary working in the foreign production office) are meant to make the actor's life easier but merely add to the confusion.

For the last few years I've been collecting some of these priceless foreign breakdowns, and I now have several of them hanging in my loo to remind me that life is simply a series of absurd occurrences.

Here are a couple of examples courtesy of my lavatory wall. First up is the breakdown for the one in which I played the lazy bloke with the charming dog:

French Magazine TV Advert; 'Garden':
A garden. Inside a man nearly lied down and exagerately relaxed watches a portable television. His dog is making him company. Suddenly he makes a light whistle and his dog understand as an order. Obedient, he brings him a cold

beer, sniffing and also wagging. The passive protagonist continues watching TV. He makes another whistle with a different tone from his lip and the serviceable dog bring him a plate with panchitos and sausage. Another different whistle and the dog brings him now a TV remote control. When he have the remote control he changes the channel, and in the new channel we see the fantastic mag with the prize of a Porsche Boxter.

Curious he looks over the table where he has his mag. Looks at the dog. The dog looks at him and he look again at the mag. They repeat the looks and surprisingly he makes an unimaginable effort to stand up of the hammock to take his mag himself.

The only person (apart from me) who could speak any English on this particular job was the director, but he only knew about three words. Halfway through the shoot he decided to add a scene in which the dog refuses to fetch me a beer from the fridge. As the laziest man in the world this naturally makes me rather upset, and I start berating the poor hound.

Unclear how much reaction to give to the scene, I threw my arms in the air and shook my head to indicate I needed help. The elderly director gently took me to one side, put his arm round my shoulder, thought for a moment or two, then fixed me with a look and said in all earnestness,

'I want you to make for me a face of shit.'

Here's one I didn't get for a Finnish bed superstore. . .

Beds TV:

A man and a woman are preparing breakfast. They behave as a couple during their honeymoon. Everything shows us that they just had a wonderful night. They flirt, they fidget each other, the woman smacks the man on his bottom.

They only have eyes for each other and lie on the bed. We see him looking at her bosom. Two hands gently embrace each other. They're eating a croissant whilst kissing. He puts a flower in her. She smiles naughty. Throws her head in her neck. She lets her leg slide along his leg. His hand through her hair. They are relaxed, pink. Her hair is loose and lewd. She doesn't have make-up and glooms. She has a beautiful and cheery face. He's wearing a loose shirt, hardly buttoned. He's looking rough and sexy. A very sunny room. She stands up and kisses him in the back of his neck. A

**dancing tune is coming up on the radio. She swings her hips in the music. He can barely resist to join.
They smile.**

I have a feeling I may have missed out on this one for two reasons. Firstly I couldn't for the life of me work out how to kiss *and* eat croissant at the same time, and secondly, I was nervous about 'putting a flower inside' the shy young actress who was up for the female role.

This next one is for a Spanish mortgage company:

Restaurant:
There is a couple in a luxury restaurant, reading the menu. A sort and friendly waiter asks them what they are to eat?
Waiter: 'Good night, have you already decide?'
Man: (Still reading) 'Eeeee, yes. . .'
Woman: (more decide) 'Yes, some barnacles for me.'
Man: . . . 'yes, as well for me. . . barnacles.'
When the waiter hears it he morphs to a bank man.
Banker: 'Yes of course barnacles, it's great. And then what? Lobster? And after this some dessert, then a little coffee, a cup, a cigarette, and after that all who is going to pay this?'
He takes from his jacket a paper and moves it very fast opposite the man and woman faces.
Banker: 'Hellooooo, eooooo, have we forgotten it once again? Let's see. . . what is more important, a little handful of molluscs or pay yours mortgage?'
Title: Doesn't your mortgage let you live?

Well the good news is my agent has rung to tell me I've been offered the 'Dog in the Fog' beer ad. All I had to do at the casting was grimace at the camera and say 'Not the best walking weather is it?', and for that Oscar-winning performance I've been rewarded with two days at the Grand Hotel in Lodz (pronounced Vwooosh), a couple of hours south of Warsaw. The not-so-good news is that for much of the filming I will be dangling from a set of aerial wires whilst being blown about by two giant wind machines. This is all good according to my agent as I can expect plenty of overtime. He emails me the breakdown and storyboard but as usual it makes little sense.

We are in England. Two men are walking down the street. They are unnaturally bent . . . About 45 degrees caused by extremely strong wind. The gale is fierce.

(Cue mighty wind-machines).

Man shouts to other trying to hold hat on. We see a strange looking hairy dog shifted backwards by the wind, despite of his efforts to cling the ground with his claws. . .

(Excellent, that'll be more overtime then – animals invariably act up during filming. The dog in the French magazine ad refused to let go of the beer bottle to the tune of £400 in overtime). The breakdown continues. . .

Men reach a pub. They struggle to open the door. Once they manage to do it, one men politely lets the other enter first. They fly in fast.

Our men are inside with beer. Outside they see a passer by clinging both hands to the street lamp – like a flag. A sudden gust of wind makes him change the position.

I arrive in Warsaw the following evening slightly concerned about what I've let myself in for.

Lodz is a dreary industrial town with a recently tarted-up main street full of shoe shops and Mexican restaurants. The Grand Hotel seems pretty grand from the outside but inside it's full of Eastern Bloc promise. My room looks and smells like an old people's home – lots of stained wood, a filthy pink carpet and a small rickety table with a torn doily stuck to it. A clear-glass, 40-watt bulb hangs miserably from the ceiling.

I head for the swish-sounding 'Cocktail Lounge' on the third floor where three elderly prostitutes – mouths caked in badly applied lipstick – perch on stools, ready to swoop on unsuspecting tourists. They throw me a cursory glance but soon realise I'm not worth the effort. I move into the snooker room next door, a dark windowless place with nowhere to sit and a vague smell of urine. Two enormous Germans with bushy moustaches are contemplating a game, if only they could be bothered to haul their lardy arses off the floor.

Several ludicrously cheap beers later I stumble off to bed – as I leave the bar, one of the bleary-eyed tarts winks at me over a scrawny shoulder.

The next morning I struggle down to a breakfast-buffet of variously iced buns in the 'Sun-Lounge'. I grab a couple of buns 'to go' and head for the waiting driver who whisks me off to the studio.

The first assistant director gives me a tour of the impressive set which he describes as a 'typical' London street full of oil lamps, red pillar boxes, a tatty Tardis-style police box (when did you last see one of those on the streets of the capital?) and a perfect recreation of a Victorian London pub, featuring faded black and white photos on the panelled walls and lanterns swinging from the ceiling. I wonder if the set designer has ever visited a typical London pub?

The assistant director leads me through a maze of corridors to the costume department where Gavin, another British actor and my side-kick in the ad, is being squeezed into a pair of brown brogues, two sizes too small. He's having a bit of a hissy-fit about having to wear thick tweeds. Gavin, it seems, is a bit of a fashion queen – more used to chest-hugging leather than fusty old tweeds.

'God, I look like a fucking farmer!' he screeches. 'Don't they realise English people stopped wearing this stuff like, forever ago?'

There's nothing actors enjoy more than complaining about their costumes. Gavin has flown in from the West Indies where he's been shooting *Pirates of the Caribbean 2* with Johnny Depp. He's seriously jet lagged and suffering from a bad case of anticlimax. Gavin is no stranger to commercials – I recognise him instantly as 'Mr Bacterium', the human embodiment of 'friendly bacteria' in the long-running Yakult yoghurt drink campaign. I can't resist congratulating him on his brilliant portrayal of human-being-as-bacteria. He responds by showing me some of the fruits of his yoghurty labour – a gold Rolex watch, Dolce and Gabbana leathers and a set of bespoke shirts courtesy of Jermyn Street.

'Please to come through onto set. We must be tying you to the ropes now.'

Back on set, the 'ropes' are actually thin wires attached to pulleys hanging from the ceiling. Gary, one of the British stuntmen hired to guide us through the process, carves a hole in the back of my Burberry coat and attaches the wire to a hook sewn into the lining. Gavin looks horrified as another burly stuntman, Rich, strings him up by his loose-fitting tweed jacket.

The story, as far as I can make out, is meant to be about English reserve and resilience in the face of adversity – in this case a particularly vicious gale. But being plucky Brits, our characters are determined to make it to the pub despite the inclement weather.

On 'action' the two jet-engine-size wind machines are turned up to force ten. Gavin and I fall forward into the hurricane while the two stuntmen prevent us from landing flat on our faces by pulling hard on the wires from off-set. At the same time another crew member is hurling buckets of dead leaves into our faces. It's at this point that we begin to encounter problems. Gavin and I are big blokes, whereas Gary and Rich are both on the weedy side. So each time Gavin and I lean forward into our forty-five-degree starting positions, we end up on the pavement with Gavin cursing the day he ever accepted the job and the poor stuntmen dangling in mid-air. Twenty-three takes later and we're nearing overtime – it's taken virtually the entire day to walk fifteen feet down a fake cobbled street.

At last we manage to make it to the 'pub'. Gavin and I have one more scene before Gary and Rich take over for the 'being-blown-through-the-pub-doors' stunt shot.

But before any of that can happen, we have to shoot the 'strangely hairy dog playing with an umbrella' scene (seeing as this is a foreign commercial I decide not to ask too many questions). Roger, the dog-handler, has flown in from Kent specially and is an unpleasantly sweaty little man with a foul temper. He has his own stunt company specialising in fully trained studio-friendly animals, including dancing llamas and performing lizards. He even has access to more fierce creatures such as leopards, tigers and apes – all hand-trained by Roger.

Our very sweet rough-haired terrier is having problems with the wind machines. He's terrified of the deafening noise and tries to run away every time they're switched on. He's also refusing to play ball with the umbrella despite words of encouragement from the exasperated director. Roger meanwhile is becoming seriously frustrated. If his animals get a reputation for being 'difficult' it reflects badly on him. Of course it's not the poor dog's fault – why should he want to play with a stupid umbrella – it's not as if he's getting paid or anything. It doesn't take much for Roger to lose his temper, as he starts swinging the poor mutt round by the scruff of the neck and dragging him head-first across the cobbles.

While the director tries to figure out what to do with the stubborn terrier, the rest of us gather round Roger to find out more about his winning way with animals.

'And what is it to be a good person with the dogs?' asks one of the Polish lighting crew.

'Patience, first and foremost' replies Roger, yanking violently at the terrier's lead.

Suddenly the stressed-out director comes up with the ingenious idea of attaching a morsel of food to the umbrella handle. The unappealing glob of gelatinous meat seems to be doing the trick and the dog soon forgets about his fear of wind machines.

Two hours and thirty takes later the shot's in the bag and we're on to the final scene of the day – an interior shot of the pub with me ordering and then drinking a pint of foaming 'Dog in the Fog' beer. All sixty extras involved in this scene have been hand-picked and clothed by the director; as a consequence, most are groin-achingly beautiful models dressed in obscenely short mini-skirts and dangerously high stilettos. Although none of them speak a word of English, they've all been assigned a single line of English dialogue to repeat during the scene, to give the impression of a lively London bar.

What follows is one of the most surreal moments I have ever spent on set. Sixty baffled Poles repeating, parrot-fashion, various lines of English gobbledygook. A leggy blonde next to me has no idea what 'Hello mister, I'm in Leicester Square with the fish and chips' means but she's happily repeating it to a chap whose response is 'You are drinking with me yes? You are drinking with me yes? You are drinking with me yes?' Sitting at a nearby table is a young couple, also deep in Ponglish:

'I am liking the Queen, I am liking the Queen, I am liking the Queen.'

'. . .Yes this beer is fine, and yours is fine too? Yes this beer is fine, and yours is fine too'.

An older extra sitting at the bar is merrily gabbling into a mobile 'Goodbye – I'm on my way to Piccadilly Circus, Goodbye – I'm on my way to Piccadilly Circus, Goodbye – I'm on my way to Piccadilly Circus. . . '

At some point during this insane cacophony I'm supposed to nonchalantly stroll up to the bar and order a pint of beer.

Back at hair and make-up Gavin is yelling down the phone to his agent. 'From Orlando Bloom to this!' he cries.

After shooting a couple of close-ups of me sipping warm, flat 'Dog in the Fog' beer I spend the rest of the day at Lodz airport waiting for my delayed flight. The good news is I've managed to clock up six hours of overtime, thanks to a disobedient dog, a stunted stuntman and some gratuitous time-wasting from Gavin.

I can now return to my quest secure in the knowledge that nothing in my life is normal at the moment. . .

11. 'For Those About to Yodel – We Salute You'

Reach for the Deadline: thirteen days to go...

On Nick's advice I've kept Cabaret at a steady sixty mph and made three rest stops along the way. I'm on my way to Derbyshire – ELO's 'Mr Blue Sky' is buzzing from the old push-button radio-cassette. Rediscovering my dusty old tape collection after all these years has been a mixture of embarrassment and delight. I'd forgotten how appallingly cheesy my taste in music was back in the mid-eighties – endless home-made compilation tapes (recording directly from the radio saved money) featuring tinny over-produced bands like Johnny Hates Jazz, China Crisis, The Cutting Crew and Mr Mister. My primitive recording technique involved placing the 'compact' cassette player next to the portable radio in the kitchen and pressing play and record simultaneously (on some of the tracks you can hear my mother doing the washing up in the background). I must have spent hours listing all the track details on the back of the cassette boxes – I've even given star ratings and short reviews for certain tracks – '"Broken Wings" by Mr Mister: Dave Lee Travis show March 1986. * * * * * Wow!!! Great lyrics and nice guitar solo!!!'

I've also unearthed a whole bag full of unedited recordings I made of the *Friday Rock Show* with Tommy Vance (in the early '80s I was quite the metalhead). Although the sound quality is appalling – Radio One was still going out on medium wave back then – I inadvertently recorded some pretty decent driving music

– Rush, Deep Purple, Yes, Zeppelin. It's kind of spooky though, hearing all the old Radio One jingles again ('Rock! With Tommy Vance, Rock! With Tommy Vance!!!') and the mellifluous Mr Vance himself, introducing his favourite tracks: 'You are gonna love this... the sensational new single from SAXON – "Wheels of Steel".'

Sadly, Cabaret's wheels of steel aren't quite what they used to be. These days she's much more comfortable on 'B' roads so I've decided to come off the M1 early. The final leg of my journey to Keith's place in Matlock (he's invited me over for a late lunch) will take me via my old stomping ground. Avoiding grey old Derby I head north, skirting the stuffy suburbs of Duffield and Darley Abbey, and on through the lush undulations of the Ecclesbourne Valley. The B5023 north of Derby is a fantastically pretty route through a patchwork of thorny hedgerows and tree-topped knolls. The landscape changes dramatically as you near the village of Idridgehay, where it all becomes decidedly northern. The lilting fields and lush hedgerows suddenly give way to ancient quarries and crumbling dry stone walls. Continuing north through my hometown of Wirksworth, I pass signs to long-forgotten villages – 'Weston Underwood' (or 'Vest and Underpants' as Dad used to call it); 'Whatstandwell' ('Weebles!' I'd cry 'Because they wobble but they don't fall down!'); 'Hognaston', 'Shottle', 'Cowers Lane', 'Knockerdown' (where our local vicar used to go to get tanked up before evensong), and on through Matlock Bath, a spectacular village situated at the bottom of a deep Alpine gorge. Geographically, Matlock Bath is about as far from the sea as it's possible to get but for us midlanders it was the closest thing we had to a seaside resort – there was even an aquarium, a couple of amusement arcades and a man selling candy floss in the street.

Every Saturday afternoon, this genteel spa resort would undergo a bizarre transformation as hundreds of hairy bikers from all over the Midlands descended on the town to admire and covet each other's Suzukis, Kawasakis, Hondas and Harleys. My best friend Bun (short for Bunither – real name Jeremy) and I would stroll up and down the Parade clutching polystyrene trays filled with chips and curry sauce, pausing every so often to drool over a gleaming piece of hardware.

Bikers - also known as 'greeboes' – all adhered to the same strict dress code. Hair was worn long and straggly while denim jackets became mobile billboards for all their favourite rock bands. It took my mother several weeks to sew Rush, Judas Priest, Status Quo and Led Zeppelin badges to the back of my faded denim jacket – sadly there wasn't enough room for Van Der Graaf Generator.

AA Peach, the motorcycle specialist on North Parade, was the place to buy all the latest gear – mirror shades, Honda Gold Wing badges and testicle-hugging leather biking trousers. To me these scrofulous forty-year-olds seemed like the coolest dudes on earth – I later discovered that the biking fraternity consisted mainly of dull middle-managers and overweight blokes from accounts.

Not much has changed as I pull up outside Harry Hall's Amusement Arcade where I wasted so much of my youth and pocket money. Some of the original arcade games are still here, exactly where I left them twenty years ago – an old Asteroids machine sits forlornly in the corner unplugged and unplayed. Memories pile in – the bobbly pockets of my grey polyester school trousers weighed down by so many 2p coins; the sharp smell of copper on my fingers.

The cramped booth where we used to exchange our grubby one pound notes for '10s' and '2s' is still there. The only obvious difference now is the clientele – noisy groups of excitable teens (presumably at home beating the crap out of each other on Playstation 2) have been replaced by a handful of lonely fifty-year-old men with boozy faces. A little bald man – the owner, by the looks of things – is sitting cross-legged on the floor, fiddling with the wiry intestines of an old Space Invaders machine.

'I virtually lived here as a boy' I tell him proudly.

'If I had 2p for every thirty-something male who came in here to tell me that. . . '

After a disastrous attempt to relive my arcade glory days (hand/eye co-ordination has sadly diminished over the past twenty years), I head across the street to another of my boyhood haunts, The Petrifying Well – housed in an old stone hut next to the river Derwent. For 46p you could gaze for as long as you liked at a collection of everyday household objects encrusted with limestone deposits from the mineral-rich waters bubbling up from the well below. Locals would leave their unwanted household objects in the water and watch in wonder as bowler hats, coins, gloves and shoes slowly, magically turned to stone. There was even a limestone-encrusted cat – the poor thing had obviously been petrified in more ways than one, judging by the astonished look on its face.

The old building surrounding the well is still there but I'm distressed to find it is now a fish and chip shop called 'Garry's'. There's no sign of the well as I approach a surly-looking fish and chip seller in a batter-spattered apron.

'Where's the well?' I ask.

'What well?'

'You know the well, well. I'd like to see the petrified cat please.'

'This is a chippy mi duck. Don't know what ye talkin' about.'

Hang on a minute. Petrifying wells don't just up and disappear.

It has to be here somewhere – maybe Garry is secretly siphoning off the limestone deposits as a cheap batter-substitute.

I bet the owner of Harry Hall's will know. . .

'Oh God – that old thing closed down years ago' he tells me with a chortle.

'But why?'

'Too old fashioned I suppose.'

'Too old fashioned? But it was great – and only 46p to get in. What happened to all those bowler hats?'

'A local builder bought them and sold them off as gatepost adornments.'

'And the cat?'

'What cat?'

'The petrified cat of course.'

'Hmm, don't remember any cat. . . oh well,' he sighs, 'nothing lasts for ever.'

I'm happy to report that Matlock's other main attractions – the Heights of Abraham (a Victorian lookout tower with excellent views), Gulliver's Kingdom (tatty miniature village made of plastic cottages) and a cable car going from one side of the valley to the other, have all made it safely into the twenty-first century.

I continue north along the A6. The market town of Matlock, a couple of miles north of Matlock Bath, is about as far from Hicksville USA as you can get. And yet in an unassuming Victorian terraced house on Bank Road, right in the centre of town, lives my next Big Timer – yodelling country singer Keith Manifold.

I've lived with Keith's photo now for over a year and I almost feel I know him – the gentle smile, the generous thatch of hair, the jet-fighter shirt collars and the granny specs. All I really know about him of course is what he does for a living but his photo has implied so much more, which is why I feel so anxious pulling up outside his house. Will he be anything like the Keith I've come to know and love? I hope the years have been kind. . .

Keith Manifold
Country-Western Vocal Guitarist
Yodelling, Monologues,
Compère Op Knocks 1974.
Appeared Wembley Festival 1977.
Available Sole or with full backing band for tours and cabaret at home and abroad.
No sole representation.
Contact Les Manifold

Alice, Keith's wife, greets me at the door. She's a shy librarian-type with a soft voice and kind eyes.

'Keith's upstairs in his office, go straight up. Hope you like roast beef?'

'My favourite' I reply hungrily.

The portly man who greets me at the top of the stairs bears only a passing resemblance to the man in my book. Gone are the curly locks, the granny specs and the patterned shirt – the current Keith is more your friendly lorry driver type with sensible M&S jumper and pleated slacks. The only residue of his former extravagant '70s self is a small blow-dried quiff of sandy hair atop a high forehead. His accent is broad Derbyshire, though I'd half expected a slow Texan drawl.

He welcomes me into his study – the nerve-centre of the Manifold household. The walls are testimony to a man in love with country music. Several of his own album covers hang in frames above his desk. All feature photos of Keith in various stages of perm – 'Having curly hair was all the rage back then, especially amongst the Country music fraternity. I spent a small fortune on curls' he tells me.

I love some of the album titles – 'Yodelling Just For You', 'I'm Casting My Lasso', 'Old Folks Home' and 'Let's Sit Down'.

'They weren't major releases you understand – we used to sell the odd copy here and there at country music events around the midlands. They look impressive framed though don't they?'

I notice a copy of the *Reach for the Big Time* article blu-tacked to a cork-board. The book itself lies open on his desk.

'I think it's disgraceful what's happened, I really do. I keep getting all these phone calls from friends wanting to buy a copy of your book and I have to tell them it's no longer available. I don't understand, you'd think everyone involved would be grateful for the publicity. When you get to our stage in the game, any kind of recognition is welcome. My phone hasn't stopped ringing – I've never known anything like it – not since I appeared on *Opportunity Knocks* back in 1974.'

During lunch we chat about his *Op Knocks* experience.

'Highlight of my career. . . ', he says, tucking into a large slice of roast beef.

'. . . although I didn't win in the end of course. Ended up coming second to Lena bloody Zavaroni.'

Opportunity Knocks and *New Faces* were gentler 1970s versions of *Pop Idol* and *The X Factor*. Appearing on these shows was seen as a real achievement and the ultimate ambition for many a light entertainer. Although most of the acts in my book would have put their names forward to appear on the shows, only a few would ever have made it past the first round. So coming second was actually quite an achievement. For several weeks, Keith was the Will Young of his day. According to Alice it was quite obvious to everyone who should have won that night. . .

'The week following *Op Knocks* saw the largest amount of mail ever to go through Matlock sub post office and as far as we know that record still stands. Nearly every letter was addressed to Keith. And they all said the same thing – 'He should have won.'

Alice is still emotional about that night. Proud certainly, but also irritated that Keith should have lost out to such a young whippersnapper (Miss Zavaroni would later go on to rub salt into an already salty wound by hosting her own long-running TV show).

During pudding Alice puts on a rare vinyl pressing of Keith's *Op Knocks* entry song 'The Yodelling Granny', a song about – you guessed it – a granny who yodels. It's a cheerful little ditty with some impressive yodelling towards the end. The 'B' side, 'Cascading Dreams', is a much bleaker song about a man sitting in a waterfall watching his broken dreams cascade over the horizon.

I'd always associated yodelling with tinkling cowbells, Heidi in frills and Bavarian men doing that poncy thigh-slapping dance. I had no idea this strange vocal gymnastic was so popular with big butch country singers. Although you'd hardly describe Keith as butch, he's one hell of a yodeller.

'It's all about relaxing your throat and just going for it', and with that the whole kitchen reverberates as he shimmies up and down the harmonic scale. He tries to give me a lesson but I end up sounding like a demented Jimmy Savile.

Lately Keith has been branching out from the whole country music scene. His Roy Orbison tribute act has been attracting good audiences down at the local social club – he even wears the outfit, complete with frilly black shirt, RayBan sunglasses and a black lid-like wig.

'Contrary to popular belief, Orbison wasn't actually blind, he was just a bit short-sighted. He only wore the shades to make himself stand out from the crowd – but in the end they became his signature.'

Seems Kenny Cantor was right – to survive as an entertainer you really do need a pair of silly specs.

Keith performs mainly in pubs and old people's homes these days but he still believes it's important to maintain certain standards.

'If I'm doing 'an Orbison' I always put the costume on before leaving home because I absolutely refuse to get changed in pub toilets. So many venues these days expect you to change in the toilet but they'll not get me in there. A toilet might be all fine and dandy at the beginning of the evening, but come the other end of the night – well you don't know what's been happening in there do you?'

Before heading upstairs to prepare for tonight's show, Keith is keen to give me contact details for northern comic Tony Peers, who coincidentally just happens to be Keith's opposite number in the book. For the last couple of years Tony and Keith have been organising country music events for Haven Holidays and the Grand Hotel chain as well as special Elvis Presley short breaks designed for holidaymakers who enjoy a bit of 'Love Me Tender' with their half-board. Keith also works in close association with 'The King Elvis International Fan Club' based in the unlikely town of Rhyl in North Wales.

'Tony was telling me this morning that he's also been getting loads of positive feedback from your book. I know he'd be delighted to meet you and sign the release.'

I thank Keith and add Tony's number to my rapidly expanding *Reach for the Big Time* contact book.

Although Keith is keen to share with me his many triumphs over the years, he appears to be refreshingly free of ambition.

'For me it's always been about the music.' (Very rock 'n' roll.) 'I was never interested in becoming a superstar or making millions of pounds although I am proud to have played Wembley back in '77.'

Wembley? Wow! How?

Seems a Nashville impresario had heard Keith play and chose him to appear as a supporting act at the Wembley country music festival. Keith played to over fifteen thousand people that night. The previous day he'd been yodelling to a handful of old men at a pub in Bakewell.

'I've never been so scared in all my life – people from round here aren't supposed to play Wembley. If you come from my sort of background you're meant to stay put. That's what I've always been told.'

'Knowing your place' and 'not getting above your station' are obviously still strongly held beliefs in this part of the world. Who knows what might have happened if Keith had made the break and moved to London or Nashville? But he's a Midlands boy through and through and fiercely proud of it.

'Don't you worry' he tells me 'I've had my fair share of fans. . . '

While Keith is upstairs warming up for tonight's gig, Alice shows me round his old study – a narrow broom cupboard of a room with a small cell-like window at one end. The walls are covered in faded posters of some of the many gigs Keith has played over the years: 'Peterborough Festival'; 'Chilworth Community Halls' and the annual Matlock Bath country music festival.

'This is where we keep all our memories' she says, unhooking a spangly sequinned cowboy jacket hanging next to a pile of dusty Stetsons.

'This was Keith's pride and joy. He spent weeks sewing on all the sequins. I'm not sure he could fit into it now.'

She brings down a tatty cardboard box with 'KM fan club – bits and pieces' written on the side. The Keith Manifold fan club was set up in 1975 by a couple of local admirers, Pauline Mycock and Margaret Elias. These tireless ladies would type and staple the quarterly magazine and answer any queries from fans. At its height the club had around a hundred members – mainly locals – from nearby nursing homes, pubs and clubs where Keith did much of his performing. Alice has now taken over the running of the club and has recently renamed it 'The Friends of Keith Manifold' which she thinks sounds less formal.

'Keith's certainly had his ups and downs over the years' she says, handing me one of his old Stetson hats to try on, 'appearing as the cabaret act in between strip shows was probably his lowest ebb. After supporting twenty-eight different strippers in one week poor Keith was ready to throw in the towel. But he battled on. We've never had very much money but we've always been there for each other during the hard times and we've had some laughs along the way.'

The Manifold box of memories is stuffed with fan mail along with several telegrams wishing Keith luck for his forthcoming *Op Knocks* appearance. 'We're rooting for you Keith! All the best mate – Les and Janet.'

Alice hands me a pile of the old Keith Manifold quarterly. The spring 1982 edition is full of on-the-road gossip and features a small pencil drawing of Keith on the front. The usual manual typewriter errors are in evidence – unpredictable spacing, rogue capitals and problems with the letters 'a' and 'o':

In January i had the pleasure once again of playing at the Smokey Mountain Country Music Club just south of Birmingham   in the Wythall Park Hall   along with a fine Staffordshire based band called the "Saddletramps". Then came a short tour of Kent with dates in Faversham, Hollingbourne and Pegwell Bay Nr Ramsgate.

***

I have been engaged to appear at a small village near Fleetwood called Knott End and although the weather was bitterley cold the atmosphere inside the Over Wyre Leisure Centre was electric and with artistes like the 'Naden Brothers', 'Snuffy Garret' and 'White Line Fever' we couldN't help but have a good dAY. . .

I wonder what 'Snuffy', Keith and 'White Line Fever' got up to backstage at those wild Knott End gigs? Keith was to appear with 'Snuffy' and 'White Line Fever' several weeks later at the 'Southport Football Club Festival of Country Music':

we had what I can only describe as a great night. . .

***

September 20th sees the last of my shows at the Trusville Holiday Centre in Mablethorpe. . .

***

I'm on my way to the White Horse Country Music Club in Wiltshire it's the 21st October and John Denver has been on the Gloria Hunniford programme. There was a surprise waiting for me at the venue. When I finished my spot Mick Chandler stepped on the stage and presented me with an award for being voted the best solo artiste at the club in 1981-82, it makes me feel very proud and also very humble to know that country music followers think enough of me to put me in the number one place.

***

mid november sees the recording of a new album and this time I move to a new label as well, it's a Doncaster based company called Future Earth and the results of our labours sound very pleasing indeed and hopefully this will be the start of a new recording career.

From Fanzine dated spring 1983:

One pleasantry I had was on the 19th April in the Paddock Suite at Uttoxeter Racecourse, where duringt he evenings entertainment I had the job of crowning Miss Uttoxeter.

***

At the Royal show in Chesterfield I was working alongside Benny from Crossroads and Grotbags from Rod Hulls Pink Windmill show. It is a great experience and was in a nice relaxed atmosphere

The KM fanclub was far more than just a quarterly newsletter though. Holding regular 'Keith Manifold Fun days' was a good way for Keith and his wife to keep in touch with loyal fans.

'We'd set up the caravan at country music festivals and sell all kinds of Manifold merchandise – key-rings, badges, T shirts, that kind of thing. Long-time fans would be invited to join us in the "hospitality" suite – a fenced off area round the back of the caravan where we kept a stash of lethal home made wine. People used to get so drunk we had to put up a warning sign: "We are responsible for the strength of this wine but we are not responsible for how much you drink."'

One of the highlights of Keith's working year was when the Central TV Roadshow came to town. These were a bit like the old Radio One Roadshows but without the embarrassment of Gary Davis in a pair of pink Hawaiian shorts. Sold as a platform for local talent, the Roadshow was little more than a cheap PR stunt for Central TV. Few Midland towns escaped the sad spectacle of regional 'personalities' such as Judith Chalmers, Benny from Crossroads and Zippy handing out free biros to bored shoppers. For Keith though, it was an opportunity to be seen.

'Us local acts rarely made it to broadcast but at least we had the chance to perform to whoever happened to be walking by.'

After some tea and digestives I help Keith load up his bright orange Transit van. But before heading off to Macclesfield, he has to pick up some equipment from a friend's house so we agree to meet at the venue.

Macclesfield is an hour's drive from Matlock across the notoriously treacherous 'Cat and Fiddle' pass – always the first road to be cut off by snow in the winter. With only one of Cabaret's headlights working, I have to drive like an old codger through the sheeting rain – nose pressed against the windscreen. Breaking down on these lonely moors would be a disaster.

At last the orange glow of Macclesfield appears over the horizon. As I hit the outskirts of town, I pass a playing field with a large sign next to the gate declaring:

Macclesfield Samaritan Fun Day!!
Saturday 23rd at 1pm

I wonder if there'll be a 'pin the tail on the depressed man' competition?

'The Journey's End' is a typical pre-gastro inner-city run down pub on the corner of a long Victorian terraced street. A large blackboard hanging outside lists the various entertainers for the week. Little shooting stars have been chalked next to each name. Last night saw The Heartbeat Duo take to the makeshift stage, tomorrow it's the turn of Mickee D. But tonight belongs to Keith, who is over at the bar chatting to a group of elderly ladies. Keith blames the recent cold snap for the low turnout. I feel sad that more people haven't made the effort to come and see him.

'Not quite Wembley is it?' he giggles 'but these gigs are my bread and butter money these days. I don't mind how many people show up as long as they have a good time. Wembley was a one off – this is the reality of what I do now.'

The tiny stage is only just big enough for Keith and a microphone stand. He's his own roadie these days and has spent the last hour setting up a couple of lights, a backing tape, mixing board and two large speakers. At the front of the stage some of his merchandise has been carefully laid out – home-made CDs mainly, including '15 Country Greats', 'Keith Sings Orbison' and 'Keith Manifold sings Wild Montana Skies'.

The Journey's End feels like a relic of the 1960s – all strip-lighting, brown ceilings, clouds of Embassy smoke and a motley group of locals ale-ing it up at the bar. It's early evening but the elderly female bar-flies are already pretty sozzled. But it's a good-natured sort of merriness – lots of giggling and 'Oooh, haven't seen you here before young man.' Sitting next to me at the bar is Dolly, a tiny old lady with a fixed perm and a creamy polyester blouse.

She's desperate for Keith to start so she can have a dance. Keith, meanwhile, is busy tuning up his guitar so while we're waiting I ask Dolly about life in Macclesfield – had the place changed much over the years?

'Oh aye. Used to be such a nice town, didn't it Freda?'

'Eh? Ye what?' Dolly's friend Freda is at the other end of the bar cackling into her pint.

'I said Macclesfied – used to be a nice town.'

'Oh aye. Smashin' little place. Not any more.' Freda slides down the bar with her two mates – both in their mid-sixties with wobbly upper arms, overpowering perfume and a lovely willingness to chat to strangers.

'None of us dare go near the town centre any more. It's become like a battle zone at night ant'it Bet?'

'Ye what? Oh aye. This pub's okay though int'it? One of the few places left round 'ere where old farts like us can go for a quiet drink without feeling scared. All the other pubs have been taken over – I'm right aren't I Barbara?'

'Ay, overrun by them bloody binge drinkers and druggies. So much fightin' in the streets. I don't know what's happening to this country I really don't. And the girls – unbelievable – bosoms out and bare legs all weathers.'

'You occasionally see them in 'ere – the druggies – don't you Dolly – slumped in a corner with sick all over them. Terrible – really terrible. Landlady soon gets rid of 'em though. . . don't you Tracy?'

'You what?'

'You'll not put up with druggies in 'ere, will ye Trace.'

'No way. Not in 'ere.'

'Thing is ye never hear about any of the violence and drugs on the news do you Betty?'

I ask them why they think that is.

'Well it's everywhere now int'it. All towns is the same. Young people on the rampage. Fightin', drinkin', vomitin'. It's all over everywhere – not just here.'

Makes me sad to think of poor Barbara and Bet and Dolly hiding out in run-down pubs like the Journey's End – waiting for the ubiquitous 'Firkins' or 'Wetherspoons' to blunder in and transform the place into yet another generic binge-hole.

Most of the ladies here tonight have come to hear Keith play. Dolly's a long-time fan.

'He's smashing is Keith. You can't beat a bit a country music can you? It's so emotional. It can make you laugh one minute, cry the next. There's not a lot of pop music can do that.'

Bang on cue, Keith steps up to the mike.

'Good evening ladies and gentlemen. I have to warn you straight off that I've caught whatever bug it is that's going around at the moment so bear with me – I'm a bit husky I'm afraid.'

With the backing track on full, Keith launches into a rousing version of Buddy Holly's 'Goodbye Mary Lou.' Dolly, Bet and Barbara immediately jump down from their stools and start mouthing along to the lyrics and serenading each other. Three songs in and it's time for Keith to demonstrate his yodelling skills. Written down it looks something like this: yiddlooodlelllidllioddlediodleidoo.

After a couple of Orbison songs – 'Only the Lonely', 'Pretty Woman' (sans spangly outfit and wig) – it's time for Keith to rest his throat over a couple of pints. As he hops down from the tiny stage, I notice a scruffy piece of A4 stuck to the back wall:

if
you want two sing
on
karaoke please fill
a slip in if you don't
you WON'T

Keith isn't too keen on the whole karaoke craze.

'Ultimately it means less work for pros like me. Amateurs may have all the right equipment but they can't really sing. Trouble is venues hire them because they're cheap.'

By the end of the second half of Keith's set most of the ladies are up on their feet doing that old lady dance – arms in the air, gently swaying, a bit unsteady on the pins. For an encore Keith gives us another rousing blast of 'Hello Mary Lou'.

He may not have sold any CDs and the audience has been a bit thin on the ground but Keith seems remarkably upbeat. I'm reminded of something he said earlier in the day – 'the best thing about not being ambitious is that you stop worrying about 'making it. . .'

With the Manifold-mobile loaded and ready to go, Keith hands me the signed release form along with a contact number for *Big Timers* Roy and Jackie Toaduff who live just a few miles north of Matlock.

'We're all rooting for you James. I expect to see *Reach for the Big Time* back in the shops before the end of the month.'

End of the month. . . shit that's only two weeks away and I still only have about a third of my entertainers on board. . .

I have to decide what to do next. Kenny Cantor's other contact,

Bunny Lewis, is about thirty miles up the road in Manchester. But I only have an address, no number. Unfortunately Directory Enquiries has drawn a blank (Bunny Lewis is obviously a stage name). The question now is, do I risk turning up at Bunny's house unannounced with the possibility that she may not even live there any more, or do I head over to Roy and Jackie's and get them out of the way first?

Right now I'm in no fit state to drive anywhere. I've been drinking solidly and irresponsibly for several hours. I ask my new best friend Dolly if she knows of any B&Bs nearby – she rolls her eyes and points to the pub sign above the door – 'The Journey's End '.

'Talk to Tracy, she'll sort you out with a room.'

Tracy is pulling the last few pints of the evening and doesn't seem remotely interested in sorting me out with a room.

'We don't usually cater for single night occupancies' she mumbles.

'But I only need the room for one night. What difference does it make?'

'We can make an exception just this once but it'll be forty pounds for the single night. Normally we'd only charge thirty and that would include breakfast but seeing as it's Sunday tomorrow and you only want to stay for the one night, breakfast won't be included. Suppose you'll be wanting to see the room before you decide?'

How can I resist? She leads me down a gloomy corridor and into what is essentially a box-room containing a lumpy single bed. In the corner sits an ancient, teak-effect black and white TV with a coat hanger for an aerial. Forty quid does seem a bit steep but I'm too drunk to haggle. . .

'Do you accept credit cards?' I ask.

'Sorry duck, no. I'll need paying in cash up front.'

'But I only have fifteen pounds on me.'

'There's a bank in town. Five or ten minute drive away.'

Can she not see how pissed I am? The whole point of staying here is to avoid having to drive anywhere. 'How long will it take me to walk to the bank?' I ask through gritted teeth.

'No idea. You'll have to ask my husband, he's downstairs.'

Tracy's hubby scribbles down some directions on the back of a beer mat and tells me to watch my back as it can be dangerous round these parts on a Saturday night. I half expect him to add '. . . Beware the full moon my lad and whatever you do, don't stray from the path.' The old ladies at the bar have suddenly stopped cackling – they seem genuinely worried at the thought of me wandering the mean streets of Macclesfield at this time of night. Everyone watches in silence as I head out into the chilly night. Will

I make it back in one piece? I wonder. Do I want to make it back in one piece?

It isn't until I reach the concrete shopping precinct where the hole-in-the-wall is situated that the atmosphere turns decidedly Saturday-night-town-centre. Two inebriated girls in white mini skirts and six-inch heels are shouting abuse at each other. One of the girls is slumped against the cash dispenser in a puddle of vomit. The other is being pursued by two aggressive-looking lads in white shirts and blobby trainers.

'What ye fucking doin'? Eh, what the fuck do ye think ye doin'? Come here slag and give us some of them chips.'

One of the lads then shoves the girl with the chips, sending her and the bag of chips spilling across the car park. Another lad appears from the shadows and a non-specific scuffle breaks out. The girls try and run away but only manage to teeter a few yards in their stilettos before collapsing onto the cold pavement. From what I can make out, there seem to be three issues at stake here – the unfair apportioning of chips, jealous girlfriends and unfaithful boyfriends. The blokes poke and prod at each other while the girls stumble around yelling 'Slag!' and 'Bitch!' at passers by. One of the lads catches my eye and shouts 'Oi wanker!' as I scurry away with forty quid stuffed in my sock and a slick of vomit stuck to the soles of my shoes.

The door of the Journey's End is locked when I arrive back. Through a window I spot Tracy wiping down surfaces and putting chairs on tables.

'Thought you'd done a runner', she says, reluctantly letting me back in '. . . get into a fight did you?'

'Not exactly.'

I hand over the forty quid and limp off to my freezing, damp cell. The heating has been turned off despite the fact that it's even colder inside than it is out. As I crawl under the thin, greasy duvet, a broken toenail catches on the bobbly polyester cover. There's absolutely no warmth under here – I may as well be lying under a handkerchief.

I head back into the bar to ask Tracy if she'd be kind enough to turn the radiator on for an hour or so but she tells me the heating always goes off at 8pm whatever the weather. How very English.

Seeing as I'm never quite sure where my quest will take me next, I've cleverly brought along a rucksack containing several changes of clothes. Tonight, that extra clothing might just be enough to save me from hypothermia. I empty the contents onto the bed. Three pairs of socks should be enough to keep my feet from falling off. A fourth pair makes a handy set of mittens. A pair of M&S boxer shorts fit snugly over my head to form a protective balaclava (the button-fly acts as a useful breathing hole). Now all I have to do is lie very still and pray for sleep.

A couple of hours later I wake up in a contorted heap of layered laundry. The slidey duvet is lying stiffly on the floor and I can't work out why I'm being suffocated by a pair of my own pants (the button fly has somehow managed to work its way round to the back of my head).

I jump out of bed – mouth dry, head throbbing – and fling open the sheet-thin curtains, only to be greeted by what must be one of the most depressing views in Britain – a boarded up off-licence with the word BOOZE written in huge red letters above the door.

After a chilly shower (the hot water also seems to have been rationed) I attempt to dry myself on the stiff square of material hanging by the side of the basin. Tracy calls it a towel – I call it a small cloth.

Having denied her guests the basics of heat, hot running water and something big enough to dry your testicles on, Tracy completes the whole prison-like experience by making it virtually impossible to leave. Both the front and back doors are locked and bolted and because it's Sunday morning the prison warders are all still tucked up in bed. I eventually manage to convince a doddery old cleaner to let me out by threatening to call the police.

I suppose it could have been worse – I might have ended up at the 'Samaritan Fun Day'.

12. What a Drag

Bunny Lewis
Bunny Is Box Office
Bill stopper on all leading cabaret bills. A guaranteed money spinner and theatre packer. TV appearances all channels.
Current film now on general release –
A Couple of Beauties
Enquiries for first class dates only in 1975
Contact: Bunny Lewis Enterprises

Bunny looks like a real honey in her promotional photo – an old-school brassy blonde sprawling seductively across a bed of creamy satin sheets. My girlfriend however isn't so sure. All year long she's been trying to convince me that I've been making a terrible sex blunder – that the gorgeous looking Bunny isn't everything she's cracked up to be.

'Look at his hands. And those arm muscles. Bunny is so a bloke.'

'And the cleavage? How do you explain that?'

'Trust me, those old Playtex Cross-Your-Heart bras could work miracles.'

There's nothing on Bunny's flyer to suggest she's a man and I happen to know plenty of girls with bulging biceps and spade-like hands, so to settle the argument I've come up with a wager. If, in the unlikely event Bunny does turn out to be a man, I have agreed to dress as a woman for a week – if she's a woman then my girlfriend will become my boyfriend for the week.

As I head west towards Manchester, I try and imagine my girlfriend with a bushy moustache and trilby.

Directory Enquiries couldn't find a number for Bunny – the closest they could come up with was a Ronnie Lewis living in Crumpsall, just outside the city. I do have an address though. . .

It takes less than half-an-hour to reach the outskirts of Manchester but then it all gets a bit complicated. According to Kenny C, Bunny lives in Whalley Range, a suburb just to the north of the city, but it doesn't seem to be marked anywhere on the map and I'm beginning to wonder whether Kenny is getting his own back by sending me on a wild goose chase. Maybe he's trying to tell me that I am in fact the 'whalley' in all of this.

It's impossible to tell where one Manchester suburb ends and another begins and I seem to be going round in very small circles. Unlike most men however, I've never had a problem with asking strangers for directions – I mean is it really such a sign of weakness to admit being a bit lost? Maybe I go too far the other way – in the space of a mile I ask a surly teen, a young couple with twins and a tramp clutching a bony dog if they can help me out – but none of them has even heard of Whalley Range.

I decide the only thing to do is head for the centre of town, look for road signs – if there are any – and work my way backwards. After nearly an hour of meticulously following arrows to the city centre, I seem to be heading out into open country. Surely this can't be right. I pull up alongside a busy bus stop to ask for help.

'Excuse me, does anyone know where Manchester is?'

Ten miserable faces stare back at me. Eventually a small boy on a BMX skids over to the car.

'This is Manchester mate. Where you headin'?'

'I'm trying to find the centre.'

'Which bit – there's loads of centre?'

'Well I'm actually looking for Whalley Range but it doesn't seem to exist.'

'I'll ask me dad.' He cycles over to one of the bus-stop zombies and returns seconds later with some good news.

'Mi Dad says you're already in Whalley Range – this is it.'

'What? Oh. Really? Ah. Thanks very much.'

'By the way mi dad says did you know you had black smoke coming out your exhaust pipe?'

Shit – that's all I need. Luckily, what I thought was open countryside turns out to be a large expanse of brown wasteland dotted with light industrial units, one of which happens to be a garage with several wrecks rusting on the forecourt. I pull in for a check up.

'You're burning a lot of oil mate' the friendly mechanic tells me.

'Is it serious?' I ask.

'Depends what you mean by serious.'

'Well, does it need seeing to straight away?'

'Only if you want to avoid pissing off the environmentalists.'

'How much will it cost to fix?' I ask.

'Couple of hundred. I could have it done for you in about a week.'

Sod the environment, I have entertainers to see, a book to save and a bankruptcy order to avert. . .

The curtains of Bunny's grey 1930s semi are well and truly drawn and there's a definite feeling of 'gone-away' about the place. After ten minutes of wandering up and down the drive I slump back into Cabaret and start banging my head against the steering wheel. I'm tired, hung-over and grumpy. Not seeing Bunny today is really going to bugger up the schedule. I could be in Derbyshire now with Roy and Jackie Toaduff gathering some more leads. I need to catch them this week before they head off on their annual three-month round-the-world pleasure-cruise.

I somehow manage to fall asleep with my head resting against the hard plastic dashboard, but am suddenly awoken by a little man hammering on the windscreen.

'Excuse me, could you move your car please – it's blocking our drive.'

Two shambling figures with heavy shopping bags shuffle slowly up the driveway of 57 Appletree Road – Bunny's house. Unfortunately neither of them seems to be blonde, big-breasted or, more worryingly, female. . .

'Excuse me; I wonder if you could help me. I'm looking for Bunny Lewis – I believe she lives at this address?'

The smaller of the two men gives me a startled look.

'She? She is me. . . who are you?'

'I'm James. But hang on. . . are you sure you're she?'

'What do you mean – of course I'm sure.'

Oh dear, I think we may have got off to a bad start. If he says she's she, then she he must surely be. But the elderly man standing before me isn't quite the leggy glamour-puss from my book. This 'Bunny' looks more like a 'Brian'.

I fill him in on the reasons for my unexpected visit and as a gesture of reconciliation offer to help take in the shopping, which seems to consist almost entirely of family sized tins of 'Smash'.

'Sorry, I had no idea you were a transvestite. . . ' I tell him, hoping this will clear up the confusion. But he looks horrified.

'I'm not a transvestite – I'm a drag artist.'

'Oh, right – sorry.'

'Transvestites get a kick out of wearing women's clothing – I do it for a living.'

'I see. . . erm, where would you like me to put these tins of Smash?' I should probably just shut up now.

Bunny and his long-term partner manager Mike Parker are just like an old married couple – lots of finishing each other's sentences and reiterating what the other has just said. The first thing I notice as they lead me through their cluttered hall is a fantastically kitsch oil painting of Bunny in full regalia – all silver sequins, thick purple eye-shadow, lusciously long, spidery lashes and a massive blob of bleached blonde hair. We're talking Margaret Thatcher meets Mira Hindley via Danny La Rue. This is more like the Bunny I'd been hoping to meet.

I follow them through to the kitchen where several more giant tins of powdered potato are fighting for space on the dresser.

'This is where the monkeys used to play.' Mike tells me with a smile.

The monkeys? Does he mean *The Monkees*, as in 'Hey, hey we're the. . . '; if so, what the hell were a bunch of Californian mock-musicians doing playing in Bunny's kitchen?

'*The Monkees* you say?'

'Oh aye – chimps too.'

So that would be the simian variety of monkey then.

In the early '70s Bunny and Mike went completely bananas and bought themselves an entire zoo's-worth of primates. For several years they shared their small Manchester semi with four rhesus monkeys, three chimps, a brace of Barbary apes and Alvin Stardust's Spider monkey, Gwenan.

'Alvin Stardust's spider monkey you say?'

'Oh aye. . . Gwenan was our favourite – a special gift from Alvin.'

I don't know about you but Alvin Stardust used to scare me when I was a kid. Something about that black diamond-studded leather glove. And I still can't understand why he was cast as the road safety man in that public information film. . . The only reason I ever looked left and right before crossing the road was to make sure Alvin Stardust wasn't waiting to pounce.

Mr Stardust wasn't the only scary Glam Rocker to help us 'look left, look right. . . look left again.' Les Gray, the lead singer of Mud, was also on hand to remind us not to muck about on motorways.

Back in the '70s, late-night TV was awash with portentous public information films designed to put the fear of God into us. I used to dread going to sleep at night, not because of the ghouls living in the wardrobe but because I feared I might fall out of bed and electrocute myself on a loose cable. According to Charley the Cat – guru-of-death and star of many a public information film – serious injury lay around every corner. I even stopped playing in the local park in case a dirty old man offered to show me his 'puppies'. The 'Play Safe' campaign of the late '70s showed in graphic detail the terrible charred consequences of what would happen if you chose to ignore Charley's priggish paw wagging. Children who threw lighted fireworks didn't just end up in hospital, they were shown wandering the streets with empty eye-sockets. Naughty boys who played with electric cables saw their feet quite literally explode. Even something as soft and welcoming as a carpet had the potential to maim or even kill if trodden on incorrectly. Most terrifying of all was the 'What to do In the Event of a Nuclear Attack' film. The only practical piece of advice the government could offer in the event of a thousand suns unexpectedly going off in your back garden was to 'take shelter under a nearby table'. Failing that there was always the step-by-step guide on how to dig your own grave (seriously).

Maybe the C.O.I. should have made a public information film about the dangers of keeping Barbary apes locked in a small suburban kitchen – 'In the event of an ape attack hide inside a family-sized tin of Smash and wait until the threat has passed.'

Poor old Gwenan had obviously been so traumatised by her years with Alvin (this was the man, don't forget, who had a hit with 'It's Better to be Cruel than be Kind') that she used to insist on sleeping in Bunny's bed. The other monkeys could enter and leave the house at will via a giant cat flap fitted to the back door – provided they knocked first (Bunny is a stickler for good manners).

Now I'm no pet expert – my guinea pig Nora died less than a week after moving in with me – but a small semi in Whalley Range is surely not the place to rear primates. It's a little known fact that monkeys actually enjoy throwing their own faeces at each other – it's a kind of game to them. They also have a tendency to swing from things – and if there are no branches to hand, they'll swing from anything – light-fittings, wardrobes, glass cabinets. Life at 57, Appletree Road must have been a gas, which makes you wonder why the neighbours never complained about the smell.

'We eventually taught our youngest, Judy, how to use the toilet. But she enjoyed wiping her bottom so much we had to ration the loo paper. She'd often get through eleven or twelve rolls at one sitting.'

By the end of the '70s the Animal Rights movement was in full swing (unlike Bunny's apes) and shortly after the 1980 Dangerous Wild Animals Act was passed, Bunny returned home to find police marksmen on his roof and a court order to remove the monkeys.

'They were all eventually re-housed in Chester Zoo. I only ever visited once – it was too painful seeing them behind bars. They went mad when they saw me. . . '

Appletree Road is a lot quieter these days and not just because of the lack of monkeys.

'During the '70s this house used to be a riot of entertainers – we became a sort of boarding house for acts working at the local clubs. This kitchen once rang to the sound of comedians, magicians and singers, all sitting around, drinking, laughing and having a good time. We don't get that many visitors these days – the locals all think we're a bit strange.'

Looking at Bunny now, it's hard to imagine him in a full-length sequinned robe and false eyelashes – he seems so utterly male. But then I suppose drag has always been less about realism and more about grotesque caricature. And I should know – I have been that grotesque caricature. My first professional acting job saw me cast as an all-singing, all-dancing Judy Garland. The play was a gratuitously camp take on the 1969 Stonewall riots – a key turning point in the gay liberation movement. As a white, heterosexually stiff Englishman, I've never been much of a dancer – swaying awkwardly to 'Come on Eileen' at wedding receptions is about my limit. So you can imagine my horror when I discovered I would be shimmying across the stage of the Shaw Theatre in a pair of high-heeled ruby slippers, fishnet stockings and a pillbox hat. On some nights you could actually see the word 'embarrassment' oozing out of my face. As if this wasn't humiliating enough, the bastard director made me wear two pairs of extra thick American tan tights underneath the fishnets to try and conceal the thick spidery hairs on my legs. That summer had been one of the hottest on record, so by the end of each performance the rest of the cast were refusing point blank to stand anywhere near me. To put it bluntly, I ponged – I ponged bad. I take my pillbox hat off to Bunny – dressing up as a lady can seriously damage a man's health (. . .let's hope my girlfriend has forgotten about our silly wager).

'Would you like to see some of my outfits?' asks Bunny, unlocking the back door.

'Prepare to be stunned. . . ' adds Mike with a grin.

At the end of a narrow alley at the back of his house are three tatty lock-up garages containing a vast cornucopia of campery.

I've never seen so many frocks in one place. Some shimmer, others sparkle – all have that unmistakable whiff of '70s sauce. I trail my hand along rail after rail of full length lime green sequinned ball gowns, wedding dresses with veil and train attachments, purple jewel-encrusted robes, fairy costumes, frilly maids' and even frillier nurses' outfits, silver micro minis and God knows what else. Hanging at the back of the garage under several layers of protective plastic sheeting is Bunny's pride and joy – an immaculately laundered, full length gold sequinned dress worn in the 1973 British comedy caper movie *A Couple of Beauties*. No, I haven't seen or heard of it either – and nor has Google, Blockbusters or *Halliwell's Film Guide*. But considering the stellar cast of Pat Coombs, Bernard Manning and the spiv from Dad's Army, I'm surprised this low budget British take on *Some Like it Hot* hasn't become a cult classic. Bunny played the role of lead drag despite having never acted before in his life. After the film received an unlikely premier in Leicester Square, Bunny decided to set his sights on a career in movies. Ideally he would like to have joined the *Carry On* team but the show was already top heavy with camp entertainers and so it was never to be. After several unsuccessful attempts to break into film, Bunny returned to his day jobs – running Bunny Lewis Enterprises talent agency during the day and performing drag in the evening. His agency concentrated exclusively on booking strange speciality acts such as Igor Gridneff – a mad Dutchman whose act involved balancing on top of twelve-foot stepladders. And Tommy 'Toes' Jacobson – a man born without arms but whose incredibly dextrous feet could shoot rifles and even shave hirsute members of the audience. Although Bunny Lewis Enterprises is still officially in business, Bunny has found it increasingly difficult to find decent speciality acts and even harder to place them in work.

Because of the looming deadline I've vowed to spend less time with my entertainers but I can't resist an invitation to see Bunny perform that night. . .

We're on our way to the annual 'Tinsel and Turkey' bash at the Queen's Hotel in Blackpool where Bunny has been booked as the after dinner entertainment. The party had originally been planned for Christmas Eve but 'unforeseen circumstances' meant the festivities had to be cancelled until after the New Year. So tonight is a belated way of saying sorry to the coach loads of disappointed pensioners who missed out on their annual pre-Christmas bash.

Mike is quietly snoring in the back of Cabaret as we crawl through the seedy purlieus of northern Manchester. His head is resting on a pile of sparkly evening gowns and baby doll outfits. As we trawl along the M61 past the brutal tower blocks of nearby Horwich and

Chorley, Bunny tells me how much he would like to have become what he calls a 'true star'. Like Keith Manifold, Bunny feels his industry has been hi-jacked by karaoke kids and one-hit wonders.

'I saw this singer on stage the other night who only had two songs in his entire repertoire – one of them had been a hit, the other was the 'B' side of that same hit. He ended up singing variations of the same two songs all night. Today's disco divas or whatever you call them think show business is about instant fame. They seem to have forgotten about hard graft.'

Unfortunately Bunny has decided not to perform his Dolly Parton impression tonight – the fake bosoms he uses are so huge they restrict his ability to walk, let alone sing. These days he only ever brings them out on very special occasions. Sadly he won't be treating us to his comedy-Marlene-Dietricht drag routine either. No, tonight Bunny will be performing as his alter ego, 'Bunny'.

In a small ante-room of the hotel I help zip him into a spectacular gold lamé baby doll outfit and ask him to tell me more about his Bunny alter ego.

'Simple really – she's based on a more outrageous version of me. She's like everyone's favourite maiden aunt – a bit naughty but loveable – a tart with a heart.'

The real Bunny is a polite, rather subdued character so I'm looking forward to witnessing the transformation. I only wish he'd tell me his real name so I could separate the two characters.

We're at the back of the spectacular hotel ballroom, behind a makeshift curtain. Bunny seems nervous as he waits for his cue to go on. He keeps fiddling with his feather boa and peeping through a crack in the curtains to see if the audience have finished gobbling their turkey dinners. There doesn't seem to be any stage to speak of – just a clearing in between several large round tables. After a short drum roll, a little man in black tie introduces 'our very special guest Miss Bunny Lewis'.

I wish him luck as he flings back the curtain and teeters out across the shiny wooden floor, curtseying and air kissing as he goes. He certainly seems more at ease as his brassy alter ego. All the old ladies in the audience go wild as he struts his spangly stuff. The husbands meanwhile look on with a mixture of horror, confusion and delight. It's probably been quite a while since any of them were this close to such a spunky, high heeled 'lady'. Bunny remains oblivious to their lusty looks and much prefers flirting with the grannies, who shriek with joy every time he flicks his blonde wig or throws a mock look of disdain. Having calmed the riotous pensioners with a long withering stare, he introduces the resident two-piece band at the far end of the ballroom.

With microphone in hand, he launches into a butch rendition of the gay man's anthem 'I am What I am', stopping intermittently to tell a saucy aside. 'Once upon a time there were these two gays – now they're bloody everywhere. . . !' (Sings) 'I am what I am and what I am needs no excuses. . . ' The band is finding it hard to keep up with the sudden stops and starts. . . 'I met this woman the other week who swallowed her glass eye by mistake – now she has a "womb" with a view. . . !' (Sings) 'I beat my own drum, some call it noise – I think it's pretty. . . '

Apart from the odd innuendo, Bunny's act is surprisingly smut-free. And I thought drag artists were supposed to have the biggest potty mouths in the business. Gentle ribbing of the audience seems to be the order of the day as he marches up to an elderly lady dressed in a tartan skirt and starts having a go.

'That's a lovely skirt dear – surprising what you can do with an old sugar bag.'

I have no idea what an 'old sugar bag' is but the lady in the tartan skirt thinks it's hilarious. Bunny doesn't believe in prolonged humiliation and quickly moves on to find out more about his audience.

'So where are you lot over here from then?' he asks, pointing at no one in particular.

'Southport' replies a group of respectable looking ladies in bright blouses. Bunny curtseys low, revealing a pair of stubby ankles – 'Ooohh, you're dead posh in Southport – I've heard you even get out of the bath to pee. . . What about this side of the room – where are you lot from?'

'The Wirral' – yells an even livelier crowd of wispy blue-rinsers.

'Oh the Wirral, I know the Wirral – been there many times. Very nice. . . where is it again?' More hysterical laughter. . .

'And what about you lot?'

'Chester – hooraaaaaaaaaay!'

'I'll tell you one thing about Chester – you've got a bloody good zoo there.'

A certain chimp comes to mind. . .

It's hardly the biting wit of Bill Hicks but who needs insightful observations into the human condition when dressing up in a gold lamé baby-doll gets you just as many laughs? In the middle of a noisy musical number, he marches up to three stern looking ladies with downturned mouths, hard-set perms and a refusal to enter into the spirit of things.

'Look at these three nuns over here. . . ' he says, making sure everyone has a good stare – '. . . Just look at 'em – the three "nuns": never had none; doesn't want none and never likely to get none.' The ladies' mouths remain firmly hump-back-bridged – I suspect Bunny may have touched a nerve. . .

Just when you think he's said something outrageously smutty you realise it's all in the body language – a raised eyebrow here, a well-timed flick of the feather boa there – far naughtier in a way than boring old knob gags. 'Wanker' is the only vaguely rude word he uses and even that is spoken in a hushed Les Dawson-style whisper.

Bunny started out in the bad old days when the Lord Chamberlain would censor anything remotely lewd or 'inappropriate', which I guess would explain why his humour has remained relatively free of smut. (The term 'blue comic' I later discover refers to the blue felt-tipped pen used by the Lord Chamberlain's office to censor scripts.) Even if you were lucky enough to escape the dreaded blue ink there was still the 'Watch Committee' to worry about. This self-appointed bunch of do-gooders would flinch at the merest suggestion of a nipple. Cross-dressing and gay references were a complete no-no. But comics and dragsters soon found a way to out-fox the miserly moralists. For camp comics such as Bunny's mate 'Rubber-Necked' Nat Jackley, the smut was all in the delivery. So it wasn't until he actually got up on stage and started speaking that the real meaning of the words became apparent – by which time of course the Lord Chamberlain's Office and Watch Committee had already passed the material as clean.

The Watch Committee would only ever attend Monday night performances to check for filth, so the first performance of the week was always kept clean. For the rest of the week you could be as crude and as lewd as you liked although sex wasn't the only thing to get up Big Brother's nose. The 'Lord's Day Observance Society' was on constant lookout for blasphemous performances. Right up until the-mid '70s Sundays were still considered sacred, and it was illegal for performers to wear outrageous outfits or even to use certain props. Dressing up in ladies' clothes was seen as sacrilegious. To get round the problem, Bunny would perform his drag act in a solemn pinstripe suit, which kind of defeated the whole object of the show. Fellow drag artist Jack Storry's speciality was to dress up as a Blackpool landlady – complete with pinny, curlers and a rolling pin. But on Sunday nights he'd simply leave the pinny backstage, put on a shirt and tie and come on as the Blackpool Landlord. He didn't get many laughs but at least he wasn't arrested for indecency.

It's audience participation time at the Queen's ballroom and Bunny is casting around for volunteers to join him in an impromptu performance of *Cinderella.* A paunchy man and his even paunchier

TOP: Tony Tadman – Mr Sexique
BOTTOM: 'Now you see them...' Mark Raffles and his amazing disappearing poodles.

The Shades of Harmony – '...a facility and correctness that attests their great sensibility' it says here.

Victor Seaforth after being lowered into his specially adapted 'Toulouse Shoes'.

One of these men stood in for Michael Jackson on *Top of the Pops*...

A bundle of Ken Joy.

Bunny Lewis – definitely a bloke.

'Mr' BUNNY LEWIS

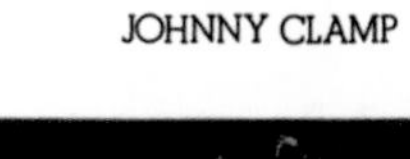

'Did you hear the one about the gag on any subject?'

Chris Smith – he's a puppet-man-possessed.

Terry Burgess will 'amaze and amuse'.

Country music – Midlands style.
Keith Manifold - Available at all good East Midlands record stores.

Bobby Knutt – he's from Yorkshire you know.

Dottie Wayne – just put your lips together and blow.

James and Tony Peers outside Tony's entertainment empire in Scarborough.

Leslie Melville a.k.a Percy Pie-Crust (sans Charmaine the psychic hen).

The 'Almost Famous' Jack Mayes - 'Everyone loves my Hairy Harry.'

R2-D2 and a very bad Chewbacca look-a-like.

Tony Peers a.k.a 'plus support'.

Bobby Bennett – also makes a damn fine dame.

Terry Seabrooke – 'I found this in the attic'.

Des Owen – 'free pink wafers available in the foyer'.

James and Kenny Cantor - it's make or break time in Lowestoft.

'Oi Chubby, where's my copy of *Reach for the Big Time?*'

Roy and Jackie Toaduff – cruising the world.

Victor Seaforth's kitchen – the perfect setting for a spot of James Cagney.

TOP: My ever faithful Ford Capri Cabaret - definitely worth 'making a song and dance about'.

BOTTOM: Johnny Clamp trumpeting Ford Motors' crowning achievement.

friend have reluctantly agreed to play the ugly sisters while an older man with a stick and bad knees has volunteered to play an unlikely Prince Charming. It's all become very *Generation Game*, with Bunny doing his best Brucie-in-a frock impersonation.

After much 'oo-ing' and 'ahh-ing' and general mucking about, Prince Charming eventually forces Bunny's chubby foot into a suitably sized sequinned stiletto, much to the delight and relief of the audience.

Three encores and several dozen curtsies later the brash, grinning, ludicrously attired Bunny teeters back behind the makeshift curtain and immediately returns to his quiet, rather unassuming self. He's relieved that the show has gone so well and hurriedly changes back into his old grey civvies. Mike's waiting for us in the bar with a well-deserved pint.

Back in Whalley Range, Bunny is only able to offer me one lead – his old mate Kenny Baker who I've already seen. . . I'd been hoping Bunny Lewis Enterprises might have come up with something, but unfortunately not one of his clients appears in my book.

I shouldn't think Bunny's act has changed much since the 1970s. But then I doubt his audience has either. I hope he doesn't decide to hang up his frock and boa any time soon – he wears them so well. He even manages to make walking in stilettos look easy. I ask him for some tips, seeing as I too may well have to don the old ankle-breakers if my girlfriend holds me to my word. His advice is simple. . .

'Keep practising and don't worry if you make a tit of yourself.'

13. Everything's Coming Up Roses

Reach for the Deadline: eleven days to go...
Legend has it that shortly after the parish church at Chesterfield was built, an evil witch – no doubt cackling and cursing the while – circled the newly completed spire on her broomstick causing it to bend and buckle in a really quite creepy way.

As an eleven-year-old horror fanatic, I easily convinced myself that this bizarre legend was true and so whenever we were up in this part of Derbyshire I'd pester my parents for a detour. As we'd approach the menacing spire I would try and imagine what ghastly occurrence could have driven the gnarled old hag to bring such a bizarre curse on the town. How disappointing to discover that the crookedification of the wooden steeple had nothing to do with warty old witches and everything to do with the warping effects of drizzle.

As I skirt the walls of the church, heading north to Dronfield, I can still feel a residue of fear in my neck.

There's a real sense of northern machismo about this part of the Midlands – once the heart of a proud mining community. Most of the pits are long gone, leaving behind a scarred landscape hewn from the bleak edges of the Peak District National Park.

Cabaret's heating system has decided to pack up on one of the coldest days of the year so I've just bought myself a pair of old-fashioned leatherette driving gloves from a nearby garage. This is a worry – in the past I would never have been seen dead in a pair of driving gloves but now I seem to be entering the realms of the terminally nostalgic: Ford Capri; brown leatherette driving gloves; Hammond organ classics on the tape deck. All I need now is a pipe, some matching leatherette elbow patches and a gorgeous 'honey' at my side.

I've somehow managed to drive straight through the nondescript town of Dronfield and out the other side without even noticing. An old man in a tartan cap gives me directions back to The Chantry, a hotel belonging to my next Big-Timers Roy and Jackie Toaduff.

The imposing, if slightly bleak Victorian red-brick building has huge bay windows and an 'Addams Family' style front door. The cemetery of the nearby church backs onto the hotel garden. Cheery ornaments – stone frogs, grinning gnomes – rub shoulders with mournful Victorian gravestones: 'Beloved husband Stanley – committed back to the soils 1885'.

I make my way across a large empty car park and ring on one of those old fashioned bell-pulls, half expecting Bela Lugosi to answer. The place seems deserted.

'Hello? Anybody home?' I tiptoe across the chilly reception area looking for a desk with one of those pingy bells on it. But my attention is suddenly drawn to a large wall covered in faded photographs of old movie stars and TV personalities.

'What do you think of my wall of fame?' asks a ghostly, disembodied voice. Suddenly a protective grill in front of the hotel bar clanks into action, slowly rising into itself to reveal an immaculately suited man in his seventies clutching a glass of whisky.

'Is that really you with Paul Newman?' I ask incredulously.

'Oh yes – that photo was taken in the very doorway you're standing in now.'

'But what was he doing here?' I ask.

'He'd been visiting some nearby caves and needed somewhere to stay the night. You can imagine my surprise to find the most beautiful man in the world standing on my doorstep. By the way, I'm Jackie. You must be James.'

Roy and Jackie Toaduff
International Entertainers
Six Royal Performances, major theatre and cabaret circuits on four continents
'Professional polish of a dazzling duo.'
'Britain's right royal ambassadors at large.'
No sole agent.

'Come and meet the rest of my dear friends' he whispers, guiding me over to the wall with a well-laundered cuff.

Virtually the whole of the reception area has been turned into a floor to ceiling shrine to the many stars Jackie and his professional partner Roy have entertained over the years. Golden era Hollywood greats rub frames with cheesy '70s game show hosts and nearly-forgotten soap stars. A grinning Leslie Crowther sits uneasily next to a signed photo of Bette Davies. Vincent Price and Bet Lynch stare at each other across a beaming mugshot of Bob Monkhouse. Look carefully and you can spot Roy and Jackie in nearly every shot – either leaning into view or standing respectfully to one side as the stars take centre frame.

Jackie is in awe of old-fashioned glamour and has recreated a little piece of Hollywood glitz right here in the rather shabby surroundings of the Chantry Hotel. The sky outside may be dishcloth grey and the drizzle constant, but here in celebrity corner, Jackie can lose himself in a world of sunny people with sunny lives, sipping sunny cocktails under sunny skies.

Tears well as he holds up a photo of a fragile looking Ginger Rogers – 'she asked me to marry her twice you know but it didn't feel right – what with me being an ex-coal miner and she being a big Hollywood star. She remained one of my closest friends though.'

I'm nervous about showing Jackie *Reach for the Big Time* – with all that hob-nobbing with the stars, maybe he doesn't see himself as a light entertainer anymore. This after all is the man who spent twenty years onboard the *QE2* entertaining the likes of Sammy Davies Junior, Jimmy Stewart and John Craven.

When I do eventually pluck up the courage to show him the book he does seem somewhat surprised to have been included – he and Roy never really felt part of 'that world' as he puts it. And unfortunately he doesn't recognise a single act. This is serious – I need more leads but Jackie is more interested in telling me about his unfinished autobiography *From Coal-dust to Stardust.*

'I've had a lot of interest from publishers but none have bitten yet. But they will. . . I know they will.'

Roy suddenly appears from the garden. He looks quite a bit older than Jackie and seems flustered.

'We're all waiting for you Jackie. . . everyone's asking where you are.'

Roy has invited some friends round for tea and has asked Jackie and me to join them. But much as I'd love to stay, the clock is ticking and I really should be heading over to Scarborough to see Tony Peers who has promised me some new leads. But I feel terrible leaving so soon – they've only just signed the release. So I decide to take Roy up on his offer and stay for tea.

I'm confused about Roy and Jackie's relationship. Although they're both called Toaduff, Roy doesn't seem old enough to be Jackie's father and they certainly don't look like brothers. Roy lives just across the car park in an old converted garage while Jackie has set up home in a small flat in the hotel. I ask Roy to explain.

'I'm not really called Toaduff. . . my real name is Roland Roy, I only adopted Jackie's surname because it seemed like a good idea at the time. He'd received so much publicity in the local press after dancing with Princess Margaret at a charity ball that he became a bit of a celebrity in South Yorkshire. So it seemed like a good idea to take on the mantle of his success.'

They may not be related, but the Toaduffs seem much more than just professional song and dance partners – they sound alike, dress alike and have spent so much time at sea cruising together, I wonder if there's something they're not telling me but I guess it's cheeky to ask.

One thing's for sure – both men are sticklers for smartness and are appalled by my slovenly appearance. I try to explain that one of the hazards of being on the road is that you tend to let personal grooming slide. But Jackie's not convinced.

'We've always maintained the very highest standards of attire wherever we are. And we only ever use the finest tailors. I can't bear this modern fashion for scruffiness and ripped jeans. Even when I worked down the mines I maintained certain standards.'

Jackie comes from a long line of coal miners and is convinced the film *Billy Elliot* is based on his life.

'The similarities are uncanny. My dad forced me down the mines and used to beat me up for wanting to be a dancer. Mum just thought I was a sissy and worried about what the neighbours would think.'

But young Jackie was determined to follow his dream. Although he continued working down the mines until he was fifteen, he still managed to find time to hone his considerable clog dancing skills. Although a little shaky on his pins these days, Jackie can still perform many of the old moves and is keen to give me a demonstration. He takes me through to the main hotel dining room – a kitsch paradise of pink walls, ruched curtains and plastic pot-plants. The room is divided in two by a handy proscenium-style arch – perfect for giving an impromptu performance. 'Roy and I often put on our top hat and tails and give the diners a blast of the old routine.'

Jackie dims the red lamps and breaks into a silent clog dancing routine (the dining room is heavily carpeted).

Roy and Jackie's old-fashioned style of hoofing kept them in continual work throughout most of the fifties. But by the mid '60s, the world of entertainment had been hijacked by a bunch of scruffy urchins with long hair, leather jackets and surly attitudes. Roy and Jackie were about to be consigned to the bin marked 'square'.

'Pop stars were just a joke to us – none of them could sing or play their instruments and they all looked terrible – the so called 'music' made no sense to us – it just sounded like a horrible noise.'

The boys battled on with the pink lounge suits, fake tans and perma-grins but by the late '60s their keep-smiling-through, life-is-a-cabaret routine was looking decidedly cheesy. Almost overnight the work dried up as clubs and theatres across the land became enamoured by a new breed of rough and ready singer. In an attempt to compete, the boys even tried adding a couple of Beatles songs to their repertoire. . .

'We decided to take the mickey out of The Beatles by shaking our heads and screaming into the microphones in an exaggerated way. We assumed the audience would realise how silly it all was, but in the end they actually preferred The Beatles songs, so it all became a bit embarrassing.'

And so in 1970 – the very same year The Beatles broke up – Roy and Jackie hung up their dress-shirts and bought the Chantry Hotel as a retirement project. But then came the call from their manager, Colin: the QE2 were keen to hire them for a two-week gig round Australia. Two weeks turned into twenty years. Jackie's eyes mist over as he recalls the sheer luxury of it all.

'We were treated like royalty. First class all the way – as much free food as we could eat and all the glamour we could ever wish for. They even gave us our own suite. Can you imagine that?'

Before heading over to Roy's for tea, Jackie gives me a whirlwind tour of his beloved hotel. He leads me down a long chilly corridor, past another wall of fame where a yellowing photograph of John Craven cavorting about in a pair of yellow swimming trunks jumps out at me.

Next to John Craven is a photo of a stern looking Michael Caine leaning against the Chantry bar with a G&T in one hand, his daughter in the other and a smiling Jackie lurking in the background. Amazed, I check for signs of scissor-cuts and dried glue but the photo of Jackie dancing with the queen's sister seems to be genuine enough. Hanging above the fireplace next to Princess Madge is a framed review of one of Roy and Jackie's last shows on the QE2, written by the captain of the ship himself.

. . . Their immaculate song and dance routine would in my biased opinion have swept them to TV stardom long ago if they hadn't spent so many years treating the passengers of the QE2 to nightly exhibitions of their glittering talents. But the Toaduffs aren't totally dependent on stage work since they own the busy Chantry Hotel which keeps them busy outside the calls of cruising.

Jackie is in reflective mood as we wander over to Roy's house.

'Our friend Bob Monkhouse was furious that we were never given our own TV show. He even put in a good word for us at the BBC but it never came to anything. Such a shame.'

Roy is busy handing round beef sandwiches to his guests when we arrive. He has no fewer than six television sets dotted around his small cottage – from a tiny portable in the downstairs loo to a brand-new fifty-five inch mega-plasma in the sitting room. For a man in his eighties, Roy seems pretty clued up about all the latest advances in digital technology – giant surround sound speakers fill every corner of the room.

Although they were never offered their own TV show, Roy and Jackie did once appear on the box as guests of Michael Barrymore in 1992 (Barrymore had seen them perform on the QE2). The purpose of this afternoon's tea party is to give his friends and me a special screening. . .

I squeeze on to the three-piece suite next to Jackie. After a dramatic build up – curtains drawn, lights dimmed, drum roll from Jackie – Roy seems to be having a few problems working the fancy new DVD player (he recently had the Barrymore show transferred). Several remote controls are bandied about, random buttons pressed and batteries needlessly changed. But the screen remains blank apart from some flecks of snow and a low humming sound.

'I just don't get it – I'm pressing AV1 and it's coming up as AV2. What does it mean? Jackie, do you know how to work the damn DVD?'

Jackie gives a little shrug and wanders off to the kitchen, biting into a custard cream.

Roy's guests have gathered round the TV to offer advice.

'Try kicking it' suggests Cyril, a charming man with bow legs.

Roy is rapidly losing his patience and throws one of the remotes to the floor.

'Are you sure you've got it on the right format?' asks another whiskery man tucking into a potted-meat sandwich.

'I don't know what you mean Ted. What format?'

'Try pressing channel zero,' suggests a tubby lady in a crocheted shawl. . . 'usually works on my old set.'

'I'm with Cyril. . . ', bellows Jackie from the kitchen. '. . . Kick the bloody thing!'

'Shut up Jackie. You don't know what you're talking about. . . ' Roy is utterly exasperated.

After several more minutes of random poking, Roy eventually manages to find BBC One. But now the volume control is stuck on full and we have to endure several deafening minutes of *Blue Peter*.

'. . . and make sure you cut the cardboard wide enough to draw on the rabbit's face, and don't forget scissors can be dangerous, so always get help from a grown-up.'

As the camera pulls back from the hastily constructed cardboard rabbit, I half expect to see a bushy-haired Peter Purvis grinning back at me from the enormous screen. But the fresh-faced scissor-wielding presenter is barely out of his teens. Weren't John Noakes and Valerie Singleton well into middle-age when they presented the show?

Roy has finally discovered how to work the DVD and the volume is back to normal. Time for Roy and Jackie's big moment. Jackie does another drum roll on the coffee table as Barrymore welcomes the boys to the studio. Jackie shakes his head as he remembers the terror of that day.

'We'd been forty years in showbiz; this was our very first time in a TV studio and we were given less than an hour to rehearse. I mean really. . . '

'Ladies and gentlemen, they've been in show business forty years, they've been all over the world and always with each other – here they are – put your hands together for Roy and Jackie Toaduff!'

What an entrance – the boys sweep down a circular staircase – all teeth, bow ties and 'only the finest tailored suits'. They've been given two numbers to sing – Bette Midler's 'Wherever We Go' followed by their signature tune – 'Everything's Coming Up Roses' from the musical *Gypsy*.

It's touching to hear the boys sing along with themselves – voices slightly more tremulous now:

. . .You'll be swell! You'll be great!
Gonna have the whole world on the plate!
Starting here, starting now,
Honey, everything's coming up roses!

Clear the decks! Clear the tracks!
You've got nothing to do but relax.
Blow a kiss. Take a bow.
Honey, everything's coming up roses!

Now's your inning. Stand the world on its ear!
Set it spinning! That'll be just the beginning!
Curtain up! Light the lights!
You got nothing to hit but the heights!
You'll be swell. You'll be great.
I can tell. Just you wait.
That lucky star I talk about is due!
Honey, everything's coming up roses for me and for you!

Although they must have watched this clip a hundred times, they still seem to get a real kick out of seeing themselves on screen. Every moment is lovingly relived, re-sung and remembered – 'Not bad for a couple of old fools,' says Roy as the credits roll. '. . . what a nice man that Barrymore is – so kind'.

As the years pass and memories of a long working life together begin to fade, here imprinted onto this strange, digitally encoded piece of twenty-first-century plastic is proof that Roy and Jackie 'made it'. It seems twenty years onboard the QE2 doesn't even come close to twenty minutes on Barrymore. . .

14. Tony Peers

Tony has booked me in to the impressive-sounding Grand Hotel on a high bluff overlooking the seaside town of Scarborough. His twice-weekly show at the hotel's Cabaret Ballroom means he's able to get me a hefty discount.

The Grand is just a big old show-off of a place – all mock Gothic majesty on the outside, shabby fug on the inside. My room is dank and smells of old Lambert and Butler, so I head downstairs to the Cabaret Ballroom for a pint. Tony's *Showstoppers* song-and-dance spectacular is in full swing. Described by producer Tony as 'tits, teeth and feathers', the show features a troupe of tightly trousered young men and enormously feathered women belting out a medley of popular musical numbers. A young Filipino boy dressed in a sailor suit is in the middle of an impassioned rendition of 'Some Enchanted Evening' as I take my seat at the back. I wish the Toaduffs were here – they'd love all this.

The audience – a few stony-faced old ladies sipping halves of light ale – seem singularly unimpressed by all the soaring plumage and plunging leotards.

Two teetering singers sporting enormous feathered mushroom-clouds try to get us all to sing along to 'Life is a Cabaret' but no one can really be bothered. After the final encore, one of the dancers, still dressed in a pair of magnificently camp angel wings, appears from behind the curtain and tells us to check out the 'in-house shopping opportunities' now available in the foyer gift shop – 'Various knitwear now up to half-price'. She then goes on to tell us all about tomorrow night's exciting line-up of entertainment, which includes a panel of racing experts giving essential tips on how to back the right horse. I'm tempted to go along just in case I'm presented with that bill for £25,000. Under two weeks to go and I still have loads of entertainers to find. . . I feel increasingly unable to relax, worrying about where I'm going to find my next lot of Big-Timers. To take my mind off things I head into town for something to eat.

I'd always imagined Scarborough to be one of those sleepy little seaside towns full of mousy Alan Bennett-types tiptoeing through teashops, but it seems the place has gone the way of all provincial seaside towns, with retail clones such as Dixons and Carphone Warehouse dominating the high street. Apart from the vague smell of seaweed, I might just as well be in Northampton, Coventry or Peterborough. This being a Friday night the town centre is full of rowdy youths spilling out of mega-sports-bars, hurling the contents of their stomachs over each other.

I pause outside the exotic-sounding 'Privilege Tableside Dancing Club' – a cheerfully uninhibited strip joint just across the road from Dixons. Several lads in blinding white shirts hover outside. Once upon a time places like this would have been hidden away down dingy back alleys or in rancid basements with only a scratched name on the doorbell. They'd have been filled with spluttery old geezers with bladder problems and unresponsive wives. Now of course, shame itself has become shameful, and so the basement has risen to the sunny high street and the biro sign is now in pink neon. You can even spend your lunch hour here, leering at gyrating bottoms as you gobble down your Chicken Caesar – 'You'll find us between the "Scarborough Tandoori" and "Carpetland"'. I weigh up my needs and opt for a lamb bhuna at the Scarborough Tandoori.

Three youths sitting opposite me have just ordered a 'Scarborough Special Tandoori' and are in the middle of a heated debate about the merits of English food verses that of the subcontinent. The youngest of the three is extolling the culinary virtues of a plate of baked beans with grated cheese on top. His friends dare him to place an order with the waiter. Their jolly banter is making me feel lonely. If I thought the 'Privilege Tableside Dancing' club next door would help ease the pain I'd consider going along. Instead, I abandon the rest of my bhuna and head back to the hotel. All that sea air and fried ghee has made me sleepy.

I'm in an unusually perky mood the next morning as I race across town for my meeting with Tony Peers. But when I arrive at 'Tony Peers Productions Ltd' there doesn't seem to be any sign of the man himself.

'I'm afraid he's had to go into hospital this morning at very short notice' his assistant tells me.

'Nothing serious I hope?'

'No, he'll be back shortly.'

'Tony Peers Productions' specialises in provincial pantos and 'summer spectaculars' in seaside theatres up and down the East Coast. Everyone in the office seems a little nervous of their boss. The fax machine has just broken down and the staff have been drawing straws to decide who's going to be the one to break the bad news.

A large 4x4 suddenly skids across the gravel car park and pulls up next to Cabaret. Everyone rushes back to their desks and tries to look busy. A small rotund man with a stoop hops down from the 4x4 and starts checking out my wheels.

'Whose is the heap of junk?' he asks, shuffling through the front door with an armful of photos and CVs.

I'm assuming this is Tony and that he's referring to my Capri. I don't recognise him at all and had been expecting a tall, rather distinguished looking man, like the bloke in my book.

Tony Peers
Comedian
. . . is a very funny man

Tony doesn't hold with ceremony – he's abrupt and to the point.

'Actually I'm a huge fan of Ford Capris. I've owned four in total – bought my first one when I was on tour in Leicester – 1600, GTX LR cherry red with a jet-black bonnet – the dog's bollocks. I then bought myself a limited edition black John Player Special two-litre jobbie with gold trim. But best of all was my massive three-litre monster – what a beauty. So yes, I like Capris. . . but not yours.'

He shakes my hand and goes straight to the fax machine. Everyone remains hidden behind their computer screens, waiting for an explosion that thankfully never happens.

'So this book of yours – just a bunch of old failures and has-beens isn't it?'

I laugh nervously but Tony seems quite relaxed about his quip.

'Don't get me wrong, I think the book's bloody hilarious. People are still ringing me up about it. But let's be honest, none of us really made it in the business and surely that's what makes it funny right? Our time as entertainers has been and gone. We are the flotsam and jetsam of the entertainment world. For Kenny Cantor to make such a fuss – well it's just daft.'

Tony has no delusions of grandeur when it comes to his career. He's fully aware of how absurd it all is – 'I used to call myself Tony 'Plus-Support' Peers because that's how I was always billed – they very rarely used my name on posters.'

The phone hasn't stop ringing since I arrived – agents and actors mainly, trying to get in early for the annual panto at the Spa Theatre which Tony also runs.

Behind his desk is a poster advertising another 'tits, teeth and feathers' extravaganza happening over at the Spa. This particular show also features a couple of comedians, one of whom immediately jumps out at me. I recognise the droopy moustache and National Health specs. He's quite a bit puffier now than in his 1980 flyer but the face is unmistakably that of Big-Timer Bobby Knutt.

'Is that who I think it is?' I ask excitedly. Tony nods and gives me a broad, satisfied grin. Mr Peers it seems is as keen as I am to save *Reach for the Big Time* and has become quite the local celebrity since his face appeared in the national press.

'I'll take you to meet Bobby after the matinee if you like' he says, bashing the side of the fax machine with his fist.

Bobby is one of the few entertainers in my book not to have included any details about what he does. Could this be because back in 1980 he had a small part in *Coronation Street* and so didn't feel it necessary to remind anyone of who he was? This puts me in mind of some of the movie stars still advertising in *Spotlight* – an annual directory for actors. I've been advertising with them for over ten years but haven't had a single job or even an interview as a result. But because I'm a relative unknown I keep sending in a large cheque and my black and white head-shot, just in case Spike Lee should one day happen upon Volume Seven, page 1,263 and think, 'hey, this is just the skinny white guy I've been looking for.' The thing I don't understand is why international movie stars like Anthony Hopkins and Jeremy Irons keep on advertising each year. Surely everyone in the business knows what these guys look like by now.

With an hour to kill before Bobby's matinee, Tony offers to take me to his favourite Italian restaurant for lunch. As we make our way along the high street, past the now busy-looking 'Privilege Tableside Dancing' club, several locals spot Tony and head over for a chat.

'People round here call me 'Mr Scarborough' he tells me proudly. 'Everyone knows me – I'm thought of as a bit of a character.'

The owner of Angelo's greets us with open arms and a free bottle of Chianti. During lunch Tony notices a look of growing panic on my face; panic that I'm never going to find everyone in time. I show him the long list of acts still unaccounted for. He pours me a glass of Chianti, and works his way down the list. Of the twenty or so entertainers, Tony has definite phone numbers for song and dance man Des Owen; magician Mark Raffles and singer Dottie Wayne. My aim now is to try and get as many approvals as possible by phone and then have them send me the release by post. I take out the mobile and start dialling – all three of Tony's contacts are intrigued but won't sign up until they've seen the actual book, which means a trip to Blackpool to meet Des and Mark and a hike over to Peterborough to see Dottie. So what might have been a short trip to the letter box is going to be another two-day job. And I still need to find another eighteen acts. Tony suggests I try calling his mate John Adrian at the Water Rats. I don't know why I haven't asked Adrian for help before now – that Water Rats boat trip really came up trumps. With the added confidence of a second large glass of Chianti I call John and immediately throw myself at his mercy. The good news is he's happy to help and has asked me to email him the list. But there's a hitch – he doesn't feel comfortable about handing out contact details to me over the phone – so instead he's going to pass on my message and have them call me direct. This is far from ideal but Tony is optimistic – 'Adrian knows everyone – and they all trust his judgement – you'll be fine.'

As we pull into the Spa Theatre car park, Tony lets out a little yelp of horror. Someone has parked in his exclusive 'Producer' parking space. And it doesn't take a genius to work out who that naughty person is – the registration number of the offending vehicle reads 'NUTT 10'.

I feel for Bobby Knutt. The glory days of *Coronation Street* must seem a long time ago as he grapples with a typically unresponsive matinee audience. I can imagine how he must be feeling. I still shudder at the memory of all those dire *Pride and Prejudice* matinees. In retirement towns like Eastbourne and Torquay, the audience would be made up entirely of old people's homes. All you could hear from on stage was the irritating click-click of boiled sweets tapping against false teeth. During the interval, trays of tea and biscuits would be handed round the auditorium. So by the time it came to Darcy's romantic interlude with Lizzie at the end of Act III, I'd be competing against a background of slurping, burping and the inevitable slow dash to the loo. Pensioners seem to forget that theatre is a live experience and that actors have ears – 'why doesn't he just get on and kiss her?' cried one old lady sitting in the front row. 'Not very manly is he?' commented another.

School kids are just as irritating. At least old people pretend to be interested in theatre, whereas kids on school outings simply use the darkened auditorium as an excuse to misbehave. I've had everything from chewing gum to 10p pieces hurled at my head. But it's the constant crackling of sweet wrappers and the singing along to iPods that leads many an actor to consider infanticide. You're never allowed to react of course because that would mean coming out of character and 'breaking the fourth wall'. . . The kids are well aware of this, which is why actors make such irresistible targets. It's the teasing-the-guards-outside-Buckingham-Palace syndrome – the more you keep a straight face the more the little buggers love to taunt. But the hell of the matinee doesn't end with the performance. I've never met an actor whose heart doesn't fall out of his bottom at the prospect of the dreaded question-and-answer sessions held after the show. Children use these as a way of exacting revenge for the two hours of torment they've just had to endure. Humiliation is the usual weapon of choice. For instance Darcy became known as 'Arsey' as in: 'What's Arsey like in bed' and 'why has Arsey got chewing gum in his hair?'.

Bobby Knutt plays the professional Yorkshireman to a tee; his act involves poking fun at poncy southerners, pointing out how stupid people from neighbouring Derbyshire are and complaining about how crap the rest of the world is for not being from Yorkshire. It appears these views are deeply held as he continues his rant with me in the bar afterwards. Even though he's dismayed to hear about my Derbyshire connections, he agrees to sign the release and wishes me luck.

After several more pints, Tony and I head back to his office so that I can email my 'still missing' list to John Adrian. Top of the list is comedian Dick Pleasant. Of all the acts in *Reach for the Big Time*, Dick holds an extra special place in my heart. Not only did he star on the cover of the book, I also managed to include three different versions of his flyer from the early, mid and late '70s. Dick seems to capture the very essence of light entertainment. Apart from the wonderfully silly name, there's the cheesy grin, the greased down hair, the carefully applied pencil moustache and the big fat cigar held firmly between stubby fingers. I'm disappointed that so far no one has been able to give me any clues as to his whereabouts. Tony only vaguely remembers the name.

As the deadline looms, I feel an added sense of urgency about finding Dick. For all I know he may be furious that I featured him on the cover without his permission. Finding him must now become a priority – after all it is Dick's comely face that will be staring out from the shelves of Books Etc (God willing).

As well as Dick, my most-wanted list reads like a very odd entertainers' roll call:

- *Brother Dominic – The Merry Monk of Magic*
- *The Gay Duo*
- Vince Eager – '*A Tower of Entertainment*'
- *Lips*
- Tony '*Shades*' Valance
- *The Harlequeens*
- Caroline Blue
- Ken Baines
- *Kat Mandu*
- Jon Marshall – '*The Man With the X Ray Eyes*'

So many of my favourite acts are still on the list. I'm now desperate for any clues on the whereabouts of 'John Marshall – *The man with the X Ray eyes*' whose act included '*the amazing Blindfold Drive – a sensational outdoor attraction*.' John looks like one of those baddies from *The Avengers* – all raffish moustache and skinny-rib polo-neck. The flyer goes on to tell us that John is:

> *. . . guaranteed to keep the crowds on the edge of their seats with excitement. He provides a thrilling display of driving skill after his eyes have been sealed and hooded. £500 challenge.*

One of the reviewers goes on to say that:

> *. . . an eye surgeon who bandaged his eyes said, 'it's perfectly true that there was no fooling, no devices, nothing. It was a fact that he did this completely blindfolded and with no external aid. The whole thing was perfectly thrilling and very fascinating. I think it is the most original stunt I have seen for many years both here and in America.*

Mr Marshall, if you're out there, take off the blinds and make yourself known to me.

I'm also still no closer to finding:

The Amazing Kat Mandu
The world's most famous parastuntologist
Specialises in:
Human suspension
Walking on a ladder of razor blades
Five foot leap onto broken glass
Human hanging and strangulation
Lying on broken glass with persons on his chest
Smashing bottles across bare throat
And many other amazing feats
Contact Baker Artiste Promotions

Then of course there's the Gay Duo. Someone out there in entertainment-land must know where they are now. . .
I've decided to also send my list to the journalist over at the *Birmingham Echo* in the hope that he might be able to put out another appeal.

Whilst on Tony's computer I check my emails to find one piece of good news waiting for me. Chubby Oates has sent me a message to let me know he'll be in London tomorrow visiting his club in Covent Garden. His mate Terry Seabrooke has told him all about the book and he'd very much like to meet up for an early afternoon drink. So that's tomorrow afternoon taken care of.

I've enjoyed my visit to the seaside – Tony's been so enthusiastic about the book and is a real spur.

Cabaret's back-end rattle seems to be getting worse but I'm too scared to take her in for a check-up in case it's something serious – I'm not sure I could continue my journey without her – she's become such a loyal companion.

During a rest stop at Leicester Forest East service station I receive a breathless call from Tony. He's had a brilliant idea and is so excited he can hardly speak.

'James, let's put on a show featuring all the acts from your book. I'll provide the venue and some free publicity. All you have to do is convince the old troopers to appear in a one off variety show at the Spa – we could make it a charity gig in aid of the Water Rats if you like.'

I tell him I think it's a great idea – a 'last hurrah', a for-one-night-only, all-singing, all-dancing all-round-light-entertaining Spa-spectacular.

I'm in buoyant mood as I cross the M25 heading back into London – as well as Tony's Big-Time Variety Extravaganza, I'm really looking forward to meeting 'Fat and Funny' Chubby Oates.

Thirty-three years on, I wonder if his description of himself still holds true. . .

15. Shades of Disharmony

Reach for the Deadline: nine days to go...

Only minutes after speaking to Tony and feeling great about the world, I receive an unexpected call from Spain. Seems Victor Seaforth has been in touch with his ex-clients *The Shades of Harmony* and they're none too pleased to hear that I've used their promotional material without asking. I try reasoning with them over the phone but there's a delay on the line and we end up talking at cross-purposes. I eventually persuade them to let me come out to Spain to meet them but they seem pretty adamant about not allowing me to include them in the book. I suggest meeting at their house outside Malaga but Felicity prefers more neutral territory – so we agree to meet at a bar in nearby Torremolinos.

Because of the sudden need to fly to Spain, my meeting with Chubby Oates is going to have to be a flying one.

Chubby (like Bunny, he refuses to tell me his real name) is waiting for me outside the 'Club for Acts and Actors', an ancient light entertainers' drinking den just off Covent Garden piazza. Chubby doesn't seem very chubby at all these days but he has acquired a particularly fine pair of mutton-chops. He's been in the bar most of the morning, which is why he can't remember who I am or why I'm here. I show him his page in *Reach for the Big Time* but it takes a while to register...

Chubby Oates

Fat and Funny

Contact: P.A. College Road, London

He stares at his 1972 photo for a moment before suddenly dissolving into peels of hysterical laughter. 'Fuck me, I was fat!' he bellows. But why does he sound so surprised?

We head upstairs to the bar where a couple of toothy old entertainers are boozing and bantering at each other. They shout something incomprehensible at us as we settle down at a nearby table. I recognise the barman as the actor who played Friar Tuck in TV's *Robin of Sherwood* back in the 1980s.

Every wall is covered in framed photographs of vaguely familiar faces from the hazy days of '70s showbiz. Having your mugshot on display here at the CAA is considered quite an honour, although positioning is everything. Behind the bar seems to be the plum position although the decision as to where your image will be hung rests entirely with the CAA committee, who can demote you to the landing outside the ladies' loo if you're caught misbehaving too many times. Chubby's photo is still in its rightful place behind the bar.

The CAA is caught in a delightful '70s time warp. The swirly carpets are covered in old fag burns and there's a definite whiff of fuggy provincial theatre about the place: a mix of stale dressing room and dusty wardrobe. I doubt the walls have seen a lick of paint in decades. Hard to believe such an archaic establishment can survive these corporate times – Firkin's must be salivating at the prospect of turning what is quite a substantial piece of prime Central London real-estate into yet another vast binge-den. Chubby takes me out onto the landing and shows me the amazing floor to ceiling collage of faded light entertainment posters leading from the hallway all the way up the stairs. Did people really only have to pay £1.75 to see Larry Grayson's twice-nightly show at the Wellington Theatre in Great Yarmouth back in 1973? And what was so funny about Don Maclean and Leslie Crowther's 'Laughter Show' at the Bird's Nest in Lowestoft? And I wonder how many times little Don Estelle had to sing 'Whispering Grass' at the Lido Theatre in Margate back in the summer of '77?

The bar is rapidly filling up with pint-swigging, anecdote-swapping entertainers. Chubby shambles over to the bar and starts haranguing a group of comics for not buying him a drink – don't they realise he's just finished filming a new Channel Four reality show about life in a '60s holiday camp? Chubby had originally been cast as the resident comic – a role he has played for real for most of his life – but at the last minute, the producers of the show decided he wasn't 'authentically "'60s"' enough. So he ended up playing one of the 'holidaymakers' sent to endure two weeks of hell in a chilly 1960s-style holiday camp complete with dank chalets, potty chalet maids, processed peas and ugly knee competitions.

Chubby insists on buying me a whisky as he tells me all about himself. I really shouldn't be drinking as I have a plane to catch, but it seems churlish to refuse. Ten minutes later I return the favour. Unprompted, Chubby then orders me another double. Well, it would be rude to leave it at that so I get the next round. Friar Tuck is so enjoying Chubby's anecdotes that he throws in a couple of doubles on the house and – well – you can see where this is heading. Sure enough I start to lose the ability to construct sentences. While Chubby remains sweatily avuncular, I begin to sway dangerously. Neither of us is making much sense but we seem to be making each other giggle a lot. He reminds me of a cockney version of that upper class buffer character played by Paul Whitehouse in *The Fast Show*. There's something deliciously infectious about Chubby's chortle. He's just about the jolliest man I've ever met and a dead ringer for Father Christmas – all plum-red cheeks, ho-ho-ho laugh and snowy white chops.

The bar is now heaving. I vaguely recognise some of the punters and should really be in there, handing round the book, trying to jog a few memories but Chubby has beaten me to it and is already holding forth at the bar with *Reach for the Big Time* in one hand and a glass of whisky in the other. The crowd is in rapture as he shares anecdotes about some of the acts from the book. Occasionally someone joins in and embellishes a story.

I check the time. Two hours to go before my flight leaves – I should be checking in by now. Luckily I have my passport with me but there's definitely no time to go home and pack. I'll just have to buy a change of underpants when I get to Malaga.

Rather than interrupt Chubby in mid flow I decide to creep off without saying goodbye. Stumbling out across a rainy Covent Garden, I manage to trip over a couple of Norwegian tourists before eventually jumping on a bus bound for Victoria.

The Gatwick Express isn't running due to a 'security alert' so I have to take the slow train via Purley and New Cross. I'm never going to make it at this rate – I need another drink – no, no. . . must resist the urge to buy a can of McEwans.

At check-in I have to plead with a member of staff to let me through – the gate is now officially closed even though there's still half an hour at least before the plane is due to leave. The surly girl at the desk becomes less aggressive when she sees the look of panic in my eyes. She waves me through although she can't guarantee they'll allow me on at the other end. Luckily an old lady with a gammy leg has also left it to the last minute and is hobbling down the easyJet gangplank as I arrive.

I haven't eaten all day and am desperate to soak up the whisky sloshing about in my stomach. But all the cabin crew can offer me is a no-frills cheese roll, which at £4.50 isn't so much a cheese roll as a lump of chilly dough that smells a bit cheesy.

The arrivals hall at Malaga Airport is like a giant, seething real-estate agency offering a little slice of sunshine to drizzle-soaked Brits. Whole mountainsides seem to have disappeared under ribbons of white condos. These vast, faceless developments, proudly displayed on giant billboards, have been built to cater for the recent mass exodus from Britain. The promise of a 'bargain in the sun' has pushed property prices round here up by eighty percent in the last five years and this Andalucian feeding-frenzy shows no signs of abating. On the way to the car-rental desk I count twenty different realtors all plying the same bland lifestyle of featureless boxes 'within easy reach of the golf course'.

The space-age car Avis have given me isn't doing my hangover any good. It takes ten minutes to work out how to open the lethal electric doors that slowly glide out and along the side of the car. All very fancy but utterly useless if like me you're in a hurry to get somewhere.

With ex-pat radio station 'Spectrum' blaring out 'non-stop '80s classics' I head out towards the coast. With 'What is Love?' by Howard Jones ringing in my ears I park up next to a vast swathe of beach.

Torremolinos was the first of the Costa Del Sol mega-resort developments of the late 1960s. This once spectacular stretch of coastline went from quaint fishing village to grotty suburb of Birmingham in less than two years. Recently however, 'Torre' has been trying to smarten up its image by actively discouraging the very people who have kept the town in business for the last three decades – namely the 18–35 booze-hounding Brits. The tourist board is attempting to attract young families, but as I wander along the immaculate beach, the only kids seem to be the thirty-year-old beer-bellied variety clutching bottles of San Miguel.

It's low season right now but you'd never know it. While the locals are all wrapped in thick cardies, the ever optimistic bare-chested Brits seem blissfully unaware of the chilly north-easterly blowing in from the sea.

Because of the usual delays at the airport I've had to move my meeting with *The Shades of Harmony* over to tomorrow morning. So now I can nurse my hangover in peace with a jug of sangria.

After a remarkably cheap but restless night at the Alamo, the best of a rather grotty bunch of concrete hotels, I head down to the Cat and Newt pub on 'Hawaii Beach' – one of Torres' many themed beaches.

I hope I recognise Ian and Felicity – they look about thirty in the *Reach for the Big Time* photo, which means they must be pushing sixty by now.

I wait at the bar, nervously swigging a bottle of lager, keeping a watchful eye out for anyone with steam coming out of their ears. A middle-aged couple come striding towards me – I immediately recognise Felicity by her moon face and crescent eyes. Ian seems to have turned from a hairy guitar playing folkster into a small shrew-like figure.

Ian catches my eye first – although he has no idea what I look like he can obviously smell fear.

'So where's this book then?' he asks.

'Ah yes of course' I reply, rifling through my duty-free bag containing two new pairs of Spanish underpants, a toothbrush and a slice of tortilla nicked from the Alamo's breakfast buffet. So that's pants, toothbrush and some congealed omelette. . . but no sign of the book. Right, okay, don't panic. Maybe it's fallen under the table. I get down on all fours and start scrabbling about amongst the fag butts. If Ian and Felicity thought I was dodgy before, what the hell are they going to think now? Must stay calm.

'Sorry about this – must have left the book back at the hotel – silly me. I'll be right back.'

I order them a couple of beers and skulk back to the Alamo. Please God let it be under the bed. I feel another Lost Key moment coming on as I rush into last night's room and start searching in all the most unlikely places: behind the sink, under the mattress, and below the 'Please to be avoiding emptying the used tampons down the toilet' sign next to the loo.

I run out into the corridor and accost a moustachioed cleaner doing a spot of vacuuming. Unable to speak a word of Spanish I start miming frantically – 'me lost book in room – pink book about this big!' I draw a smallish oblong in the air with my fingers 'The book is about light entertainers – me need to find fast.' He shakes his head and looks a bit scared at my sudden, mad gesticulations. I feel like Basil Fawlty as I continue haranguing the poor bloke. 'My balls (clutch testicles) are on the line if no find book. . . okay? You understand? Comprende? Very Important!'

He shrugs. I continue, 'You sure you no find book in room, under duvet maybe? Man on cover with cigar and big smiley face.' I pull what I think is a big smiley face but judging by his reaction is probably more like a big scary face. He grins nervously, starts fiddling with his vacuum bag and then slopes off down the corridor muttering under his breath.

This is getting serious. I need to find that book – it's my only copy. I try retracing the last couple of days in my head. Maybe I dropped it during the mad dash to the airport or while I was buying underpants. The thing is I don't remember seeing the book at all since I arrived in Spain. . . and then suddenly I remember why. Three words: Oates, Chubby and whisky. I left the damn thing with Chubby. I knew I shouldn't have had that last double scotch. My trip to Spain has been a complete waste of time and money.

Ian and Felicity are not amused when I eventually arrive back at the Cat and Newt empty handed – I've kept them waiting for over half an hour.

'It seems I've temporarily mislaid the book. Stupid old me. Erm, anyway, look, you know how important this is to me. Is there anything, anything at all I can do to convince you to sign the release and remain in the book?'

But short of magically conjuring up another copy from somewhere, I'm simply not going to convince them.

This is absurd. I'm meant to be in Blackpool tomorrow with Tony Peers' contacts. But I can't leave Spain now, not until Ian and Felicity have signed up. I could phone Chubby I suppose and ask him to send me the book. Trouble is I don't have his phone number on me and I doubt there are many 'Chubbys' listed in Directory Enquiries. I even think about calling the publishers to ask them to send me a copy – but all the stock is supposedly under lock and key. . .

I need to think about this over a plate of calamari. Unfortunately, none of the restaurants near the beach seem to be serving anything resembling Spanish food, so I settle for a plate of sausage, egg, chips and beans. My next line of attack is to phone round a few friends back home – see if any of them managed to buy a copy before it was shelved. I try Nick who can't believe I've been such an idiot.

'For God's sake man, what are you playing at? Just declare yourself bankrupt and forget this ridiculous folly. You're becoming an embarrassment. Come home immediately.'

Thanks for the encouragement Nick. My girlfriend is slightly more sympathetic: 'I did try and buy a copy but Waterstone's had sent them all back to the publisher by the time I got there.'

Then I remember – my new best friend Keith Manifold has three copies. Maybe he could FedEx one to the Alamo. I even have his number in my phone. I call him up but there's no answer. I leave a message, telling him about my predicament. I feel terrible about putting him to so much trouble but I'm determined to make it up to him when I get home.

Later that afternoon Keith rings back to tell me he's happy to FedEx me a copy – all he needs is the address of the hotel.

Miraculously, the parcel arrives first thing the following morning with a note from Keith – 'Keep at it James!! Don't give up!!'

I immediately call Ian and Felicity and arrange to meet them at the magnificent baroque cathedral square in the centre of Malaga. All being well I should make the last flight back to London.

After a couple of lattes, the two of them seem to have warmed to me a bit. . . They've had a good look at the book and are satisfied I'm not out to take advantage. But what's really baffling them is why I bothered in the first place. Why would anyone want to look at a book about a bunch of old performers nobody's ever heard of? 'What on earth is it for?' asks a bemused Ian. And I really don't know how to answer – I mean what is the book 'for' exactly? Some see it as a poignant snapshot of a more innocent world; others just see a bunch of grinning buffoons with silly haircuts. When Nick asked me the same question all those months ago it seemed so clear in my mind but now I'm not so sure. . . just what is *Reach for the Big Time* actually about?

Thankfully, Ian and Felicity aren't about to scupper my quest by refusing to sign the release. Actually I think they feel a bit sorry for me – as though I have nothing better to do with my life than chase around after long-forgotten performers.

Felicity seems particularly puzzled by my odd obsession with *The Shades of Harmony* promotional blurb on the old flyer.

'Victor insisted on writing it,' she tells me with a giggle 'you see, he believed passionately that there was a right and a wrong way to behave on stage. We were ordinary folk singers but he wanted us to sound all posh when we sang. He taught us to enunciate every word.' (So that's what he meant by '. . .a facility and correctness which attests their great sensibility.')

Victor spent hours teaching Felicity how to enter and leave a stage.

'He liked big, sweeping, over the top entrances and would make me wear huge, glittery ball-gowns. These would have been fine for places like the Café Royal but were totally unsuitable for the tough northern club scene.'

Whereas most entertainers worked their way up through the

grubby northern club circuit to the more salubrious theatres and cabaret clubs in London, *The Shades of Harmony* did the reverse.

'It was a rude awakening – Victor had got us some great gigs early on in our careers but then the phone stopped ringing and we were forced to hit the road, which meant touring the tough mining clubs of the north-east. We weren't used to living in damp digs and performing to such rough audiences. Adding jokes and impressions between songs seemed to help but we still had it tough.'

And what about the name? Why 'Shades' of harmony, I wonder? Felicity raises an eyebrow.

'To be honest we weren't the greatest harmony group in the world. . . I can't actually remember who came up with the name but we thought it was apt. . . '

But surely a 'shade of harmony' is no harmony at all? Felicity is keen to demonstrate what she means. With Ian on melody and Felicity on 'harmony' they give me a blast of John Denver's 'Country Road'. Shades of harmony echo round the square, causing pedestrians to stop in their tracks and dogs to cock their heads in surprise. The harmony is ever so slightly off so I suppose she's right – they really do perform in shades of harmony. . .

Felicity would one day love to have a good old singsong inside Malaga cathedral. Maybe after a few beers. . .

Despite becoming reasonably well known in the Thanet area of Kent where they lived before moving to Spain, the duo decided to call it a day in the late '80s. 'We'd had enough of touring and were sick of England. So much rudeness, aggression and drizzle.'

And so they upped sticks and moved to sunny Montemar, a new-ish town, just up the coast from Torre. From there they ran an 'entertainment bar' for ex-pat talent – Freddie Starr was a frequent visitor. But the bar wasn't attracting enough punters and began to lose money – 'there's no profit in entertainment out here' Felicity laments. And so the couple retired to a small condo in one of the sprawling new developments above Malaga – 'if only we'd gone into the property business instead of entertainment we'd be millionaires by now'.

Felicity is keen to remind me how great life can be out here in ex-pat land – 'Every time we see a bunch of lager louts on the beach it reminds us of why we left England.'

Apart from the sunny weather and the cheap fags, I'm still not sure what attracts so many Brits to this part of Spain. It must be something to do with the leisurely pace of life. Ian now helps run his son's Jacuzzi business ('Everyone in Spain wants a Jacuzzi – it's become a real status symbol'), while Felicity enjoys pottering in the garden. She describes this part of Southern Spain as 'like England forty years ago' – which they both agree is a good thing.

As we wander back across a sun-dappled cathedral square, Felicity does admit that life out here can be pretty boring. But she and Ian have managed to retain a healthy sense of humour and are able to cope with whatever life throws at them.

'Well, I mean you just have to, right?' they repeat in unison.

16. Hotel Famous

Everyone should visit Blackpool at least once. Even posh people who only ever holiday on remote flooded islands in the Caribbean should allow themselves the experience.

Recently the whole country has been banging on about a loss of British identity. But Blackpool is surely British-ness personified – rude, brash, melancholic, slightly depraved and with an utterly bleak outlook (try visiting the Golden Mile on a wet Wednesday in February).

I reckon, as a nation, we're not nearly as sophisticated as we like to think. We may pretend to have gone off bingo, Findus Crispy Pancakes, pick-n-mix and jumble sales, but that's like the French pretending not to like baguettes, terrible pop music and ladies with hairy armpits. Imagine if Italians suddenly began looking down their Roman noses at tiramisu, terrible pop music, spaghetti and exotic fountains? They never would of course, because they love being Italian and the French adore being French. Unlike the Brits, they don't feel the need to apologise. Somewhere down the line we decided that being British was – well – ever so slightly naff. We became paranoid that the rest of Europe was laughing at us and so set about trying to become more like them. But there's a reason why we don't have a café culture in Britain – and it's the same reason why we don't promenade through our city centres at dusk eating ice creams and smiling at each other, and why we choose instead to get rat-arsed and fight. We find it hard to admit that deep down we are a brutish nation. So why can't we just be relaxed about it?

Well, because we're not very good at that either. The truth is, you can stick as many continental-style café tables on the pavement as you like but we're still more likely to start throwing them at each other than sit at them. Chairs and tables are simply inanimate objects on a pavement unless there's a culture behind them: style, ritual, long lunches, a sense of place, of joy; you know, that whole bonhomie thing the rest of Europe does so well. In Britain we worry that if you allow tables and chairs outside one café, they'll all start wanting them and before you know it there'll be pavement anarchy and the council will have to bring in new by-laws.

This will be my second proper visit to Blackpool (not counting the brief 'Turkey and Tinsel' sojourn with Bunny). When I was twelve my mother dragged me here on a 'Derby and Joan' pensioners' 'coach' trip. I had cunningly wheedled my way out of the Skegness excursion the year before, so she made a special effort to include me this time around. My mother, a dedicated helper of the aged, would use me as a useful pair of un-arthritic hands. She cleverly managed to rope me into everything from whist-drives to delivering meals-on-wheels, a task I found particularly depressing. Handing out inedible ordure to helpless old ladies in bungalows wasn't high on my list of cool things to do as a teenager. I'll never forget the feeling of shame as I'd reluctantly lift the hospital-style metal lid to reveal a slop of tepid, overcooked stew – more 'muck-on-a-truck' than meals-on-wheels.

The 'Derby and Joan' Blackpool trip involved fourteen hellish hours on a coach followed by an hour of sitting about on deckchairs in a bitterly cold north easterly. No time for the Pleasure Beach, or donkey rides or a trip up the Tower. When you hit seventy-five, licking Mr Whippy ice creams with a rug over your knees is quite exhausting enough.

I seem to have spent so much of my youth and early career sharing tea and custard creams with the elderly and incontinent. When I started out as an actor you needed to have an Equity card to work professionally, but in order to work professionally you needed to have an Equity card. To get round this silly conundrum, young actors would sucker old people's homes into letting them perform for free on the condition that the home provide them with written proof of a 'paid' contract. Equity insisted on at least twenty-four of these 'professional' contracts before issuing a card, but I reckon this was simply a pernicious way of putting would-be actors off entering the profession – instead, of course, it made us all the more determined. And so for six weeks I travelled the country with my fellow Equity-card-seekers Tony and Emma in a show we imaginatively entitled 'The Olde Tyme Music Hall Cabaret'. It was a hastily flung together affair – our hearts weren't really in it – featuring hoary old cockney songs such as 'Maybe It's Because I'm a Londoner'. The act was specifically targeted at the senile, the blind and the hard of hearing – a demographic I was only too familiar with from my days as a muck-on-a-trucker. It took us precisely one afternoon to rehearse all the songs before hitting the road in Tony's clapped out Morris Ital. The act itself lasted less than an hour and included a short quiz to test everyone's knowledge of music hall. First prize was a bottle of apple Schloer (the closest thing to champagne that we could afford) while the lucky runner up received a tin of Extra Soft Fruit Jellies (sorry, but we weren't even getting travel expenses despite what was written on the 'contract').

Tony and I were okay singers but Emma was as flat as a sheet. None of us was into the whole music hall vibe and found it all a bit embarrassing. But nursing homes across the land were only too pleased to give their inmates a bit of free entertainment at our expense, so we were soon able to secure the required number of contracts. But boy, were we rubbish. . . Tony couldn't stop giggling the entire time and Emma's singing deteriorated rapidly the longer we were on the road. I meanwhile fell into a deep depression brought on by the heavy smell of infirmity. Trouble was, we'd never know what to expect when we arrived at a venue – and nor it seemed did the venue. Sometimes we'd be greeted by a great fanfare and find ourselves being regally escorted to a nearby town hall with an unnecessarily large stage, professional microphones and several hundred excitable old folk shipped in from nearby nursing homes. Poor dears were probably expecting Roy Hudd and June Whitfield in full Victorian garb. What they got were three talentless layabouts in jeans and scruffy attitudes. At other times we'd show up at some small, privately run establishment called something like 'Homedean' or 'Ferndean' where three old ladies would be gently snoozing under several feet of crocheted blanket. Being sung to by three opportunistic actors was probably the last thing they needed. One old lady ended up cacking herself right in the middle of Emma's appalling rendition of 'Pack Up Your Troubles In Your Old Kit Bag'. Six weeks later though, we were legally allowed to call ourselves 'professional' actors, despite the fact that none of us had received a penny for all our hard work.

Blackpool Tower suddenly looms into view like some ghostly Eiffel

Tower caught in quicksand. Traffic on the Golden Mile is backed up all the way from the Pleasure Beach at one end to the Tower at the other. Who says English seaside resorts are in decline? It's a typically rainy day but the place is heaving. Groups of rat-faced lads in hoodies dart in and out of young families pushing twin-berthed prams; the wide sandy beach is dotted with groups of huddled old ladies clutching ice cream cornets. I park up in a side street and go for a wander.

The first thing that hits you as you approach the Golden Mile is the fetid stench of horse-shit emanating from the gutter. Pony and trap rides have become a popular pastime for tourists, but the resulting deposits mean that this stretch of road should immediately be renamed The Goldung Mile. The chilly wind whistling in from the sea only helps to whip up the smell and carry it inland.

The seafront is just as gaudy as I remember from my youth, but these days it also feels rundown and sleazy. I pass one of those scam 'auction rooms' hastily set up in a deserted shop that would probably once have sold toffee apples. It's run by the usual gang of petty shaven-headed criminals trading in dodgy electrical goods – punters are lured in with the promise of a cheap DVD player but leave with empty pockets. And this is where people come to have a good time?

Depressed by the grubbiness of the seafront, I head back to the car to find a grizzled man with a ginger handlebar moustache nosing about under the front wing.

'G'day,' he says tipping his Crocodile Dundee hat '. . . nice car mate.'

'Thanks. . . she's old but I love her.' I'm used to passers-by giving Cabaret admiring glances but why is he on all fours inspecting the sills?

'Don't worry mate, I'm a mechanic. Just checking for rust. Got my own garage back in Perth, Australia – I specialise in old Capris – got several of me own.'

Rob – a dead ringer for hippie legend David Crosby – is in Blackpool visiting a cousin. He's also here to ride Blackpool's latest rollercoaster attraction, the aptly named 'Big One'. Rob is a rollercoaster fanatic but right now he's more interested in getting under Cabaret's bonnet.

'Could you split the hoodie for me? – I'd love to take a Captain Cook at the engine.'

I open up the bonnet and watch Rob's head disappear inside. He starts tweaking and pulling at various wires before popping back up to announce that I'm in dire need of a new carburettor. His hands and face are caked in oil and there are flecks of the black stuff all over his clothes and in his hair. I offer to fetch him some tissues and a beer.

'You're all right mate, nothing wrong with a bit of 'crude'.

He stands back for a final admiring look at the car.

'What are the chances eh mate? I mean what are the chances? You, me and the car meeting like this? Something in the stars I guess. Anyway, take care of her mate, she's a little beauty.'

And with that he heads off in the direction of a very large, very scary looking rollercoaster. I, meanwhile, have a date with the first of Tony Peer's contacts.

Des Owen

An experienced entertainer whose act is composed of comedy with an excellent presentation of song and dance. A very experienced compère with strong personality. So successful in 1972 season at the Summerland Entertainment Centre Isle of Man, has been rebooked to Star in and also to Produce his own shows in the Summerland Showbar in 1973 season.

All Enquiries Devon Road, Blackpool

Des is busy sorting through a pile of programmes for this afternoon's matinee performance of the World War Two nostalgia show We'll Meet Again. He's been working front of house at the Pavilion Theatre ever since he retired from showbiz.

While he's busying himself for this afternoon's show, I take the opportunity to have a nose around the famous Winter Gardens complex. The foyer is a riot of competing posters for forthcoming shows. I particularly like the sound of 'Trevor Chance's Legends – live on stage look-and-sound-alike versions of all your favourite pop stars including Robbie Williams, Neil Diamond, Ronan Keating and Rod Stewart'. I could probably live without the Chuckle Brothers' show 'Pirates of the River Rother' over at the Central Pier. If only I had time to stick around for 'Emu's Clowntime Circus', opening shortly at the Tower Arena. Unfortunately Rod Hull, Emu's original arm-buddy, died several years ago after falling off his roof, but his son Toby has taken over bird-duties and is valiantly keeping the Emu legend alive.

I wander back to the foyer of the Pavilion Theatre and am greeted by an elderly man in thick stage make-up and full RAF uniform. He introduces himself as Frank, one of the performers from We'll Meet Again.

'So you're a friend of Des' – thanks for coming, we need all the audience we can get at the moment. Numbers have been terrible. I blame David Essex – we just can't compete. . . ' (David Essex is starring in '*Boogie Nights 2 – This Time it's the '80s'* next door at the Opera House).

Frank suddenly notices *Reach for the Big Time* tucked under my arm.

'Good heavens, is that Dickie Pleasant on the cover of your book?'

'Yes, do you know him?' I ask excitedly.

'Well, I knew him once – long time ago. Haven't seen Dickie for years. I always wondered what happened to him. He was a real one off. . .' This is the first snippet of information I've had about my elusive cover star – so now I know he actually existed. . .

Des reappears in his smart front-of-house uniform, name badge proudly on display. He's brought someone over for me to meet.

'James this is Douggie Chapman – Douggie is our producer and may be able to give you some more leads – he's been in showbiz forever, haven't you Douggie?'

Douggie is your archetypal small-time impresario – fat cigar in one hand, several gold rings on the other. He wears a rainbow-coloured tie and huge Kenny Cantor-style blue rimmed spectacles. A gust of thin orange hair hovers precariously above his shiny forehead. Part comedian, part pantomime dame, part summer season comic, Douggie is able to offer me another five leads, all of whom live in Blackpool: *Crick's Canine Wonders*, Clive Webb, Mark Raffles, Bobby Bennettt and Leslie Melville. Unfortunately he hasn't seen Veronica Crick of *Crick's Canine Wonders* for several years but he does have an ancient number for her.

Crick's Canine Wonders

The only act of its kind to feature a boxing match with dogs.
An animal act with a difference – suitable for all ages.

Canines in a
Really
Indescribably
Clever
Knock-out
Speciality

He also remembers working with Veronica back in the late 1970s.

'Wonderful act. The dogs wore proper boxing gloves and everything – after the boxing match they'd play five-a-side football on stage – marvellous.'

Douggie has more up-to-date contact details for comedian Bobby Bennett, ex-*Tiswas* regular Clive Webb, and Leslie Melville – 'the man with the psychic hen'. For a glorious moment it also looks as though he's about to give me details for one of the most intriguing acts of all – Gay Duo.

Gay Duo

Sophisticated cabaret – with an unusual repertoire of original point numbers and tempo songs to piano accompaniment – mostly about the gay way of life. From 'Goblin Man' to 'Not in the Mood' to 'Invitation to an Orgy' and 'My Guy's Gone Straight' – these numbers provide a professional and amusing act for Gay and mixed audiences alike.

But sadly he's mistaken them for another camp '70s turn – The Gay Edwardians – a double act from Sunderland.

The foyer is beginning to fill up with elderly punters. Douggie takes me over to meet Blackpool stalwart Derek Yelding, a local performer who's come to see this afternoon's show. Derek used to perform with a yodelling crow before he had a stroke earlier in the year. Frustratingly, that's about all I can tell you about Derek because Des has just told us to take our seats as the show's about to begin.

Before checking their tickets, Des likes to greet each punter with a broad smile and a chat.

'Hello Sheila, you well?' Sheila, slumped in a wheelchair, looks anything but well.

'Not too bad Des.' She croaks.

'Good – well done love. Enjoy the show and don't forget, free tea and biscuits in the foyer afterwards.'

This is Des' favourite part of the job – communing with the audience as they file in.

'I always try and find out how everyone is' he tells me 'you know, have a little chat. Well it makes the whole experience nicer for everyone doesn't it?'

I'm not sure if I'm in the mood for two hours of wartime song and dance routines, but Des has gone to the trouble of reserving me a free ticket so I can't very well refuse. And anyway I still haven't managed to talk to him yet about the book.

Looking around at the elderly audience, I wonder how long a theatre like The Pavilion can continue in its present state. The auditorium is barely a third full and I fear Wetherspoons may be waiting in the tatty wings, ready to pounce. The once vast stage area has already been lost to the 'Theatre Bistro' where light lunches have replaced light comedies. The current stage is a small, temporary looking structure jutting out from the bricked-up proscenium arch.

Des nods to the stage manager to let him know that the punters have all been seated. A three piece band strikes up a jaunty version of *Ain't 'Alf Hot Mum*'s 'Meet the Gang' song:

'Meet the gang 'cos the Boys are here, the Boys to entertain you. . . '

Des plonks himself down in the seat next to me and starts shaking his head – 'Dear oh dear – even less audience than yesterday.'

We stay in '70s sitcom-land for a jolly rendition of 'Who Do You Think You Are Kidding Mr Hitler?' from *Dad's Army*, sung by my friend in the khaki jacket.

Next up is a bald bloke doing a passable Kenneth Williams impression ('Oooh, shut ye mouth'), followed swiftly by a 'wacky' comedian dressed in a nappy running around the stage with a pram. The show climaxes with a sing-along tribute to that bastion of political correctness *The Black and White Minstrel Show*. It's as though rock 'n' roll and the civil rights movement never happened. . .

'If we leave now we can get to the tea and biscuits before everyone else' Des whispers as the band strikes up the big finale. We tiptoe out into the lobby where a long trestle table has been set up with one of those military-style metal tea-urns. Douggie has beaten us to it and is already tucking into a plate of pink wafer biscuits.

'Did you enjoy the show?' he asks, showering me with pink crumbs.

'Oh yes. I especially liked the man with the pram' I reply, filling a flimsy plastic cup with heavily stewed tea.

'Evening shows are even less well attended than the matinees – seems old people don't really like to go out much after about 7pm.'

'Oh well' I reply 'at least everyone seemed to be enjoying themselves.'

Des wanders over with a mouthful of biscuit.

'So where are you staying tonight?' he asks.

Good question and one I haven't even thought about yet.

'Can you recommend anywhere?' I ask, pouring myself some more tea.

'There are hundreds of cheap places round here. You shouldn't have a problem finding somewhere. In the meantime why don't we go next door to the Bistro for a drink – talk about your book? By the way, I've managed to get you a free ticket for tonight's performance of *Boogie Nights 2*.

Aggggh! From wartime nostalgia to David Essex – the mind

boggles.

'That's very kind but I really need to find somewhere to stay', I tell him with an added sense of urgency.

'Oh, you'll be fine. I thought as you'd come all this way to see me, it was the least I could do.'

I don't have the heart to tell him I'd rather sit in a bath of acid than watch David Essex sing '80s 'classics'.

It feels odd drinking beer and eating crisps on what used to be The Pavilion stage. Frank Sinatra and Judy Garland once performed here, right about where the sandwich counter is today.

Des doesn't do much song and dance these days, not since his knee started giving him gyp. It's been a long time since he was tap dancing his way across the ballrooms of Butlins.

'I once shared digs with Jimmy Tarbuck and Jimmy Cricket' he says proudly. Since officially retiring from the business, Des has spent several years working as a TV extra – he even had a line of dialogue in episode thirty-two of *Born and Bred*. These days Des is happy to be a showbiz observer, handing out programmes at the theatre door.

I show him his entry in *Reach for the Big Time* over a packet of pork-scratchings. He giggles and brings out a carrier bag full of old black and white publicity shots of him in action – all smiles and raffishly angled boater.

He signs the release and tells me it feels great to be so appreciated.

As we stroll over to the Opera House, I ask Des if Blackpool has changed much over the last thirty years.

'I hardly recognise the place anymore' he tells me with a sigh. 'Us old-timers are a dying breed and there doesn't seem to be anyone to take our place. The town has been going downhill rapidly over the past few years. When I first did the 'Non-stop Cabaret' show at the Dixieland Bar in 1967, people would queue round the block for a seat. That's all changed now; all the shows are struggling – and that includes the big Jim Davidson, Cannon and Ball type shows.'

These days few big TV names are prepared to spend a whole season in Blackpool when they can earn just as much from three days on *EastEnders*.

'We still get the occasional ex-star coming up here for a couple of weeks – you know, the faded ones – but they never stay for long.' Des lowers his voice as we enter the cavernous three-thousand seat auditorium. 'Even David Essex isn't much of a draw these days – look, the place is virtually empty.'

He's right – there can't be more than a hundred people in the audience. I still think of David Essex as the housewives' crumpet of choice but I guess these days his core audience are more likely to be next door enjoying 'We'll Meet Again' and a free pink wafer.

I thank Des for the ticket and wish him well with his front-of-house duties. Twenty minutes into the show it becomes clear why the theatre is so empty. *Boogie Nights 2* is rubbish – just a lame excuse to cobble together a few cheesy '80s cover versions. What little story there is seems to revolve around two rival gangs fighting over a garishly futuristic bar, made of cheap plastic and a few strip lights. Half an hour in and there's still no sign of David Essex. Maybe he's off sick – maybe he's too depressed to leave his dressing room. During a noisy rendition of Madonna's 'Holiday' I creep back out into the foyer to make some more calls. Veronica Crick's number is out of service and there's no answer from either Leslie Melville or Bobby Bennett. But I do manage to speak to Clive Webb, who tells me he's working at a circus in Great Yarmouth but would be more than happy to meet up – 'I do two shows a day so I'm always around.'

I step out into the chilly night and stumble upon a strange coincidence. Opposite the Winter Gardens is a hotel called. . . The Melville – I wonder if it might have some connection with my man Leslie?

Leslie Melville

'A Bird's best friend'

Leslie Melville who features Madame Charmaine, the world's greatest Clairvoyant Hen – presents a fast moving comedy and mystery act playing for astonishment and laughs. He gets plenty of both!!

Not 'Cod' but definitely tongue in beak!

Cabaret successes include: Stockton Fiestas, Talk of the Midlands, Wooky Hollow, Cresta Solihull.

No sole agent

I approach the fierce-looking receptionist. . .

'Excuse me, do you have a Leslie Melville working here by any chance?'

'Leslie Melville? You sure you don't mean Dave Melville, the owner? Or John, his brother?'

No, no, definitely Leslie – used to tour the country with a psychic hen. . . ' She stares at me blankly.

'I've been working here for twenty years. If there'd been a Leslie Melville or a psychic hen on the premises I'd have known about it.'

'Pity, I really needed to talk to him about that hen. You're absolutely sure there are no other Melville relations nearby?'

'Positive.'

'Oh well I had to ask. By the way do you have any rooms available?'

'Just for tonight is it?'

'Yep.'

'Just for yourself?'

'Yep – unless I get lucky of course. . . '

She's not amused by my rather asinine quip.

'Sorry, we're fully booked' she says abruptly.

'But why did you ask. . . oh never mind. Can you recommend anywhere else?'

'This time of night? I doubt it. You'll have to knock on doors.'

'Which doors?'

She points me in the direction of a couple of nearby streets, which are apparently heaving with cheap guesthouses.

As I make my way to the first of the two streets, I shudder at the distant sound of Michael Jackson's 'Beat It' emanating from the walls of the Winter Garden.

Virtually every house along street number one has a sign in the window offering 'tea and coffee making facilities' and 'hot and cold water' – some even offer 'optional evening meal' and 'TV in all rooms'. Riotous window boxes spew blood red chrysanthemums down grey pebble-dash walls. Brightly painted front doors compete for passing trade, like flowers competing for bees.

I decide to work my way methodically up one side of the street and down the other. First up is The Greendale Guesthouse, which looks welcoming enough until I notice the large NO VACANCY sign hanging in the window. Next door is the Tudor Rose B&B, a half-derelict, creepy looking place with boarded up windows. So far, so closed.

I guess there must be a difference between a guesthouse, a B&B and a hotel but from the outside they all look pretty much the same. The grandly named 'Chatsworth Guesthouse' isn't quite your stately Derbyshire pile, more a pile that's in a bit of a state – battered old sign, dead flowers in the window box and a drunk man muttering on the doorstep. But the lights are on and the sign in the window definitely says VACANCIES so I tiptoe up the path to take a closer look. The owner suddenly appears in the doorway and starts prodding the drunk with a broom handle.

'Excuse me,' I ask 'do you have a single room for tonight?'

'Just for yourself is it?'

I'm tempted to reply '. . . well no actually, I'd like a single room with a bed big enough for me, the drunk and a couple of dancing girls.' But I'm tired so I just nod instead.

'Sorry mate. I've no singles left.'

'Do you have any doubles?' I ask.

'Yeah. Three.'

'So could I take a double instead?'

'Sorry mate. Two or more people in a double only.'

'But I'll pay the extra. . . '

''Fraid not – I might get a late run of couples, you never know.'

Late run of couples, at this time of night, is he mad? He should be biting my hand off.

'Glendeans', 'The Derby', 'Greenglens', 'The Rookery', 'Homemead' and 'Rosemeads' are all out of single rooms too and, like The Chatsworth, have refused to offer me the option of a double. Blackpool it seems does not cater well for the single traveller. The landlady of the Albion, a more upmarket looking B&B at the far end of the street, suggests I try the fabulous-sounding 'Hotel Famous' down on the seafront, which apparently has plenty of singles. I would love to be able to tell you that I stayed at the Hotel Famous but unfortunately the manager has a strict no-backpackers policy.

'But I'm not a backpacker' I tell him, adjusting the straps of my backpack. 'I drove here – in a car.'

'So what's that on your back?'

'This? Oh this is a rucksack – completely different.'

'Sorry mate – no backpackers, no rucksackers. You'll have to find somewhere else.'

This is ridiculous, I'm in Blackpool – B&B capital of the world – and here I am seriously considering having to spend the night in my car. I try The Alain Hotel next door where a tight-bodied gay man in a figure-hugging T shirt welcomes me in. He's not exactly your stereotypical rolling-pin-and-curlers type of Blackpool landlady but he seems friendly enough.

'I have one single left but I have to warn you it's on the small side. Sixteen pounds a night including breakfast – would you like to see it?'

Sixteen pounds including breakfast? What's he offering me here, the urinal? Well, he may as well have been. The room is truly grim – the smell of damp is overpowering and the bed is. . . well it's just horrid. The nearest shower (reeking of mildew) is three floors up and there's one of those noisy industrial air conditioners just outside the bedroom window. Quite honestly I'd rather sleep in the car. I make my feeble excuses and leave.

In desperation I head back over to the second of the B&B streets.

I've decided to try three more places and then call it a Capri. First up is a large Indian restaurant that also doubles as a hotel. There are no singles left (obviously) but the landlord is willing to let me have a double – but at a price. He leads me down to a poky room that smells of stale lime pickle.

'You can have it for a hundred quid.'

A hundred quid? He's having a laugh.

'I'll get back to you' I tell him, catching my rucksack in the revolving doors as I leave.

Okay, Highbury Hotel, make my day. Looks fine from the outside – clean front door and a tasteful window box. The smell on the inside isn't bad either – a bit heavy on the old air-freshener perhaps. Andy, the chirpy landlord, is only too pleased for the late custom and has no problem with the sack on my back.

'How does eighteen pound a night sound – with full English?'

'Full English – what's that?' I ask. (Sounds a bit saucy.)

'Breakfast mate, full English breakfast – fried egg, sausage, bacon, Frosties – the works.'

Bacon and Frosties. . . sounds interesting. Andy hails from Basildon and has a voice like a machine gun.

'Sounds too good to be true' I reply dragging my rucksack in from the cold.

'Biggest-bloody-bargain-in-Blackpool-mate. By the way which part of South Africa you from?'

'South Africa? No, no – I'm from Derbyshire.'

'No you're not. I know a South African accent when I hear one. Come on, whereabouts?'

'No really, I'm the 'full English.'

'No way. Let me see. . . I reckon. . . Durban. Am I right?'

'I'm from just outside Derby in the East Midlands. I've never been to South Africa.'

'I know you're bullshitting me mate, but you shouldn't be ashamed – apartheid wasn't your fault – or was it?'

I laugh awkwardly.

'Could I have a look at the room?' I ask, trying to change the subject.

'Follow me bushman.'

He takes me up a narrow flight of stairs and into a back room, which I fully expect to be the usual damp single-bedded cell. Right now though, I'm so tired I'll take anything, even if it means sleeping under a rug with Andy.

The room is actually quite pleasant, despite a cacophony of chintz – massively flowered wallpaper clashing noisily with a heavy mauve and brown carpet. There are the ubiquitous doilies on every surface and some china figurines displayed along the mantlepiece. The en suite bathroom is surprisingly fragrant, if a little cramped. The loo roll has been discreetly hidden beneath the skirts of a bashful doll and there's even one of those useless miniature bars of soap that refuse to lather however hard you rub.

I hand over my eighteen pounds, fall back onto a surprisingly springy mattress and immediately drift into a deep coma. Eight hours later I wake exactly where I fell, still fully clothed but a bit smellier.

As I stumble out of the shower, the mobile starts ringing and I answer it with soaking hands. It's 'International Mr Pickpocket' Mark Raffles's wife, Joan. She's concerned about my planned visit this afternoon. Funny, when I spoke to Mark earlier he seemed quite excited about seeing me.

'Are you saying we can't meet up this afternoon?' I ask.

'Well, it's just that Mark hasn't been too well recently – he's eighty-six you know. What exactly was it you wanted to see him about again?'

I thought we'd been through all this. Turns out Mark has to go into hospital for some tests early afternoon and so could I call back in a week or so to rearrange our meeting.

'But I've come to Blackpool especially' I tell her. 'Look, I promise I won't take up much of his time; I've been so looking forward to meeting Mark.'

'I'll see how he feels when we get back from hospital and then give you a ring.'

She sounds doubtful. In the meantime I try calling Leslie Melville and Bobby Bennett again but maddeningly neither of them is answering. . . and Veronica Crick's number is still dead. I ring Douggie to check I haven't written the numbers down wrong.

'I'm afraid the details may be a bit out of date – I haven't seen Bobby for a while – I don't even have an address for him but I'm pretty sure he still lives in Lytham St Anne's.'

Lytham is only a couple of miles down the coast so I decide to head over there after my full English to see what I can find.

Andy doesn't just own the Highbury – he cleans the rooms, changes the sheets and cooks several full English breakfasts every morning. Dressed in a wipeable plastic pinny with a large labrador face on the front, he shows me to my table where a large lady in a flowery blouse is tucking into several slices of soggy white toast. Sitting opposite is her grown up son, an equally large, sullen looking man in his early forties. Why has Andy put us all at the same table when we seem to be the only people staying here? The three of us sit in awkward silence. Andy suddenly reappears with three enormous plates of fried cholesterol. He tells us to 'enjoy' and disappears back into the kitchen. The terrible silence is only broken by the occasional sound of scraping forks. Andy's full English is obscenely huge – two eggs, two fried bread, two bacon, two sausages and a slick of something that might once have been button mushrooms. Andy pops his head round the door.

'Everything alright. . . ?' he asks jauntily '. . . would you like fruit juice or cereal for afters? We've got Frosties, Rice Krispies or Coco Pops.'

I opt for the Frosties while my table companions plump for another rack of Mother's Pride. After several large mouthfuls of sausage, the lady looks at her empty plate and sighs.

'We've both been on Weight Watchers diets – Gary here has lost two stone, haven't you Gary?'

Gary ignores his mother and carries on chewing the fat.

'And now we've just gone and ruined everything – this is our third full English of the week.'

'Are you here for long?' I ask, relieved that the silence has at last been broken.

'We're up from Crawley for the week.'

'Oh nice. Good luck with the diet.'

'Yeah, we'll need it.'

Gary remains resolutely sullen as he mops up the last of his gooey fried egg. I knock back another mug of industrial strength tea, wish my weight-watching friends a pleasant stay and head out into the day.

As I speed along the coast towards Lytham I pass a sign for 'Pontin's Holiday Camp – next right'. I wonder how many of my entertainers have performed here over the years? I decide to take a closer look.

The 1960s style complex is completely cut off from the nearby beach by an almighty sand dune running the entire length of the coast road. I pull into the enormous empty car park next to a ribbon of corrugated chalets, each with its own little garden. The security man on the main gate won't allow me into the complex proper without a room key so I stroll nosily up and down outside the chalets. An old lady and her husband are sipping tea together, gazing out across the bleak car park to the mountainous dune beyond. A few doors down an overweight man with white varicose-veined legs stands forlornly in his slippers, swigging from a two-litre bottle of Woodpecker cider. I head out across the busy road and make an unsuccessful attempt to scale the precipitous dune. How frustrating to be so close and yet so impossibly far from the beach – the nearest gap in the dune is a good mile and a half down the road at Lytham.

The respectable resort of Lytham is so desperate not to be associated with its gaudy neighbour that the town seems to have eschewed anything even remotely seasidey. No bingo halls, candyfloss sellers, noisy amusement arcades or rip-off auctioneers here – just a pleasant row of grand Victorian houses fronting a wide sweep of dog-shit-free beach dotted with healthy young mums and their well-behaved children. Even the pensioners striding up and down the front seem unnaturally wholesome with their over-sized khaki shorts, black knee-length socks and wide brimmed hats.

I don't know what I hope to achieve by coming here. I probably wouldn't recognise Bobby Bennett if he came up to me, shook my hand and said 'Hello, my name's Bobby Bennett'; unless of course he still had the same bushy 1973 bowl haircut. But like most of the entertainers I've met so far, Bobby's hair has probably thinned to a grey wisp.

The local library seems like a good place to do a bit of research – maybe they have a record of Bobby on microfiche. But the librarian is nonplussed by my request. Maybe she thinks microfiche is something you have with micro-chips.

'We've got internet but you need to book in advance.'

All of the computers are taken and everyone seems settled in for an afternoon of surfing. Suddenly my phone rings and a dozen faces scowl back at me.

It's the journalist from the *Birmingham Post*. 'Just thought you'd like to know I have a couple of contacts for you' he says excitedly. 'Paul Carpenter, a.k.a. *The Judge*, and ex-impressionist Tony Tadman. They sounded intrigued by your quest so I gave them your number. Hope that's okay.'

Okay? This is fantastic news. Sure enough, ten minutes later *The Judge* rings to tell me he'd like to see the book but doesn't think they'll be any problem with me using his image. Paul lives in Yorkshire so if I leg it I could, at a pinch, drop by on my way to Dottie Wayne who is based in Peterborough.

My search for Bobby Bennett is leading me precisely nowhere. I suppose I could start knocking on random doors but Lytham is a big town – it could take me weeks to get round everyone. Maybe Leslie Melville can help – if only he'd ring me back. . .

After a short paddle in the freezing North Sea I head back into Blackpool for some lunch. Unless you enjoy a non-stop diet of fish and chips, saveloy and chips, chicken nugget and chips, peas and chips or kebab and chips (with curry sauce), eating out in Blackpool is somewhat limited. I drive around in the vain hope of stumbling across a charming, rustic neighbourhood café but the closest thing to 'rustic' is the giant Harvester style restaurant stuck out on a grim retail park. So I head back to the seafront for saveloy and chips.

Sitting down at a table to eat doesn't seem to be the done thing in Blackpool, so, like everyone else, I wander over to the nearest stretch of beach and plonk myself down on the damp sand. I'm about to experience my very first Blackpool sausage when the mobile rings. In my struggle to find the bloody thing (bottom of an impenetrably deep pocket) I manage to drop the entire contents of my lunch onto the sticky, wet sand.

'Hello, it's Joan Raffles here. Good news – Mark is feeling much better and would be happy to see you this afternoon. Would one o'clock be okay?'

'Absolutely' I reply, wiping the sand from my sausage. If I spend an hour with Mark I could be with *The Judge* in Yorkshire by late afternoon and then on to Peterborough in time for supper with Dottie Wayne.

I throw the rest of my lunch to the hungry gulls and check my 'Mapquest' directions. From the printout it looks as though Mark's street is bang in the centre of town but in fact he's a good half-hour drive away in the sprawling suburb of Bispham. Mark and his wife are waiting patiently for me in the driveway of their house when I eventually roll up.

Mark Raffles

International Mr Pickpocket

Recently toured with The New Seekers

Has just completed work on the remake of The Corn is Green *starring Katherine Hepburn as consultant, adviser on pick-pocket sequences.*

'With his nimble fingers and amazing illusions Mark was slick, polished and totally professional. His endearing personality made him the firm favourite.'

– Gazette June 1978

Enquiries for Summer 1979

Now booking all venues for the winter season 1978-79

'We thought you'd forgotten about us' Mark says tremulously. 'Come on in – would you like some sandwiches? We've just made a fresh batch.'

'Yes please – I had to donate my lunch to the seagulls.'

Mark leads me into the hall.

'You may find these of interest' he points to dozens of variety posters covering the walls. Mark has supported some impressive entertainers in his time – I'd love to have seen him in *The Rolf Harris Show* starring Rolf Harris; Scotland's top comedy duo *Cheeky Bee* and the sensational Mark Raffles'.

'All the posters are in chronological order – so feel free to have a wander.'

Mark is proud to have appeared on the same bill as legendary music hall star Max Miller. Music hall was still a big inspiration for many acts in the 1970s, and to appear on the same bill as Max was every light entertainer's dream.

'On some of the advertising, I used to be referred to as the 'wines and spirits' because of my proximity to the alcoholic beverage adverts featured at the bottom of the posters.'

You have to look carefully to spot Mark's name – he's just below The Sensational Karloffs, Alfred Thripp and Nixon and Dixon.

Joan hands me a plate of fish-paste sandwiches with the crusts taken off. I grab a greedy handful and continue up the staircase.

Mark, although frail, is tall and dapper and dressed in a smart blue blazer with silk neckerchief. His wig is curlier than the one worn in his old publicity photos but it's a good fit.

Early on in his career, Mark decided he needed a more memorable name and so changed it to the Austin Powers-sounding 'Frank Verity St. Clair – *Mayfair's Mystery Man'*.

'Being a Manchester lad, I'd never actually been to Mayfair but I thought the name sounded suitably sophisticated and it seemed to go well with my top hat, opera cloak and white gloves. I suppose I got a bit above myself in those days.'

Mark had been honing his skills as a magician for several years before deciding to specialise in the art of pickpocketing.

'The act just took off and I became known as 'International Mr Pickpocket' – would you like to see me in action?'

And before I can say 'Hey, where's my watch. . . ' Mark is dangling it in front of my face.

'How did you do that. . . ?' I ask.

'Aha, you need to be on your guard when I'm around' he says with a wicked glint. 'If you were a professional magician, I'd be able to sell you a copy of my limited edition DVD *The Legacy*, which reveals all my secrets.'

'But couldn't I buy one anyway?' I ask, fancying myself as a bit of a latter day Artful Dodger.

'Not unless you're a member of the Magic Circle – I'm not allowed to give away the tricks of the trade to just anyone.'

He saunters over to an old bureau, unlocks the top drawer and brings out a large hardback book entitled *Pickpocket Secrets of Mark Raffles*. Sadly this too is only available to people within the profession. Anyone wanting to buy a copy (only five hundred were ever printed) had to prove their credentials by signing a condition of sale certificate, stating:

. . .The purchaser will not divulge any of the secrets or specialised information contained in this book to a third party. For a period of five years from the date of publication of this book the purchaser undertakes not to sell or give away the book to any third party unless with the prior written permission of the author and publisher. Under no circumstances must the book be sold or given to anyone who has not a bona fide interest in magic. The author and publisher reserves the right to institute such proceedings as are necessary to protect his interests.

Heavy stuff. Mark hands me his glossy promotional brochure containing some information about the book along with several reviews, including one that describes Mark as 'the best pick-pocketer outside of prison'.

Although I'm not allowed to look inside, the book apparently reveals all the secrets of good pickpocketing, including how to steal from various sizes of pocket, (a device known as 'dipping') and the best method of surreptitiously removing braces, neckties and jewellery without being caught. Mark's skill as a pickpocket has taken years of dedication and practice. But he owes it all to his trusty assistant JR.

'Would you like to meet him? I keep him locked up in the garage.'

I feel increasingly inquisitive as he leads me across the drive. Why is JR being held prisoner in Mark's garage, and shouldn't I be calling the police?

The garage door creaks open to reveal a dark and cobwebby place. I look around for signs of life, or should that be death? Suddenly I spot a tall motionless figure standing in the shadows. This must be JR – but he looks so stiff. . . Mark beckons me over for a closer look, but trepidation has suddenly turned to fear. Maybe I should run away now while I still have a chance – I don't want to end up like JR, bound and gagged in a corner of Mark's garage. Mark reaches across and yanks open a dusty curtain – sunlight floods in to reveal a six-foot man dressed in a '70s style brown terylene suit. His eyes are glassy and he has a fixed, maniacal grin on his face. He appears to be made entirely of moulded plastic.

'I bought him from a mannequin shop and adapted him myself'. Without thinking I go to shake 'his' chipped plastic hand.

'What's he for?' I ask.

'Back in Charles Dickens' time, pickpockets would practise their craft by attaching bells to a stooge's inside coat pocket. The aim would be to remove various items without ringing the bell.'

Mark took this practice a stage further by attaching electronic pads to the inside of JR's pockets. Good pickpocketing is all about stealth and careful handling – reach too roughly inside JR's suit pocket and you activate an alarm. JR is simply a giant version of that popular children's board game 'Operation' but with wallets and biros instead of spleens and hearts. JR short-circuited in 1983 and has remained out of action ever since, although he did once appear on *The Russell Harty Show*, when Mark was asked to give a TV demonstration of his pickpocketing skills.

Although Mark is the acknowledged king of pickpocketing, even he admits to sometimes stealing more than he bargained for.

'I once performed at an after dinner function and decided to target an old gentleman sitting in the front row. I slipped my hand inside his jacket pocket and whipped out a pair of false teeth by accident. It was horribly embarrassing for both of us; the teeth were still moist with spittle and bits of chewed food. I once stole a packet of Durex. . . by mistake of course. They are usually kept in inside jacket pockets and I tend to just grab whatever I can and hope for the best. . . '

I ask him what the secrets of a good pickpocket are.

'Well it's all about misdirection and distraction and you need to have plenty of nerve. . . '

Just then his wife bursts in with another plate of sandwiches. It seems Mark doesn't only steal from pockets. He's somehow managed to remove both *Reach for the Big Time* and a release form (which he has dutifully signed) from my bag without me even noticing.

I'd heard about Mark's remarkable disappearing poodle act through Tony Peers, but so far there's been no mention of poodles, and certainly no sign of any.

'Gracie Fields was the last to go. . . ' Joan tells me mournfully 'she died in 1989. Sweet little dog she was. . . '

All twelve poodles were named after the couple's favourite music hall turns – there was Mr Tilly, Flory Ford, Little Tich, Elsie and Doris Waters, Renee and Billy Houston, Gracie Fields and Eartha Kitt. Walking in the park with that lot must have been a scream.

To make up for the disappointment of not seeing his poodle act in the flesh, Mark puts on an ancient video recording from the early 1970s of them performing at a theatre in Jersey. The act is introduced by none other than Kenny Cantor's showbiz chum, Val Doonican.

And onto the stage skips a youthful looking Mark, with the ever-faithful Joan at his side. She's like a Debbie McGee to his Paul Daniels. After a cheesy organ build-up Mark gets down to business, plucking a dozen young poodles out of thin air. The Jersey audience is in rapture and so am I. . . Why don't they show stuff like this on TV anymore? Mark should definitely have been given his own show.

'But how do you make them disappear?' I ask, determined to break his code of secrecy. 'Were they secreted about your person?'

'Aha, that would be telling. . . ' he replies.

In true magician style, Mark has no intention of telling me anything other than that training poodles takes a long time and involves patience, repetition and of course plenty of choc drops.

After the video, he takes me down to the end of the garden to show me where the poodles used to play.

'When we were on the road the dogs would travel with us in the back of the van. Incredibly, they always seemed to know when we were approaching a new venue as all the tails would start wagging and they'd become terribly excited.'

When the dogs began dying off, Mark considered replacing them but by then the industry was changing rapidly and poodle acts just weren't in fashion anymore. Of course Mark wasn't the only person to include performing dogs in his act – I ask if he's heard of Crick's Canine Wonders?

'Oh yes of course – very amusing act – I saw them many times over the years. No idea what happened to Veronica. She may be dead of course. . . '

I really hope not. . .

Unlike Des, Mark is optimistic about Blackpool's future and is particularly excited about plans to turn the town into a mini-style Vegas gambling resort.

'The town is in desperate need of regeneration – the new mega casinos will bring wealth and jobs and create more work opportunities for people like me.'

I love his optimism. Here is a man rapidly approaching his ninetieth year, seriously considering future work possibilities. Of course he has no intention of retiring and is still out there plugging away and working as hard as ever. These days he performs mainly at company functions. You'd think after sixty-six years of poodling and pilfering, Mark would be ready to slow down but International Mr Pickpocket prefers to look to the future, and is constantly thinking up ever more devious ways of alleviating people of their possessions.

As I leave he's keen to remind me that he only ever uses his thieving skills for fun – and to prove it, he hands me back my wallet.

17. The Judge

The small Yorkshire village of Catterick is situated bang in the middle of a war zone. Behind a tidy ribbon of cottages lies the largest army camp in Europe. Young men carrying sub-machine guns lurk on virtually every street corner. As I drive through the village some of them seem to be eyeing me up as a possible terrorist threat – although I'm not sure a suicide bomber would actively choose a 1983 Ford Capri Cabaret as his weapon of mass self-destruction.

A monstrous tank rumbles towards me, suddenly veering off the road and up a wide dirt track towards a pretend killing-field. You wouldn't want to be caught misbehaving on the streets of Catterick that's for sure – mind you, I haven't seen a single civilian yet – probably too scared to leave the house, what with all that military hardware on show. I wouldn't be surprised if the soldier pacing up and down outside the post office had orders to shoot any pensioner caught queue-jumping.

The Judge
International Disc Jockey and Compere
Available for cruises, radio, hotel, discos, restaurants, cabaret
(Without equipment or with my own)
My own equipment consists of stereo unit of high quality with my own radio mic, ideal for compering competitions and large light and effects roadshow
Successes: Summer Season Butlins Holiday Centre
'Downtown' night spot, Trondheim, Norway.
Also appeared at hotels
NO VENUE TOO SMALL OR TOO LARGE
One of the largest road shows on the South Coast
'Judge Manor', Brighton

Ex-travelling DJ Paul Carpenter, a.k.a. The Judge, lives in a small cul-de-sac just off the main street. When he eventually answers his front door, I'm shocked by the dramatic change in his appearance – the svelte young man sipping from a cocktail glass in *Reach for the Big Time* has certainly bulked out in the intervening years.

Although he hasn't DJ'd for many years, Paul has kindly brought down his original High Court Judge outfit for me to look at. But why *The Judge* moniker?

'I'd originally been hired to dress up as Father Christmas for a works disco back in the summer of '73 but the costume shop had run out of Santa Claus outfits. The nearest thing they had left was a high court judge costume so I took that instead and the name stuck.'

Paul's early ambition was to follow in the footsteps of his then next door neighbour, legendary DJ Alan 'Fluff' Freeman. But after a few failed attempts to break into local radio he settled for the rough and tumble of the travelling disco scene, driving up and down the M1 in his hand-painted psychedelic Transit van and spinning Suzi Quatro 'discs' at wedding receptions. But being a one-man mobile discotheque didn't come cheap, what with the lighting rig, turntables and all the latest Gary Glitter LPs to buy. Soon Paul found himself in serious debt and had to sell his beloved van along with all the disco equipment. To tide him over he took a part-time job at a local Butlin's holiday camp as the Hi de Hi wake-up man.

'I was a real-life Ruth Madoc. I even had to do the three-note ding-dong-ding sound on the vibraphone every morning and yes we really did have to say 'Hi de Hi campers!'

But being a part-time Ruth Madoc wasn't really for him, and in desperation he turned to the meat trade, starting out as a tripe-dresser.

'I had to wash and bleach bucket loads of raw cow intestine and then transport it all by lorry from the abattoir to various butchers' shops in Birmingham.'

These were gruesome times for Paul – slaughter-houses back then were dangerous, unhealthy places to work.

'My abiding memory is of having to load lorries with buckets of cow hooves. The buckets were so heavy with hoof that I'd collapse under the weight and end up covered in maggot-infested cow-legs.'

As well as the horrendous hoof-hauling, Paul's job also involved carrying huge frozen sides of beef on his back.

'The abattoir manager made me carry three at a time, hence the severe arthritis in my back. I really didn't choose to work with meat, I was just desperate for the money – I should have made the move to radio when I had the chance but I missed the boat. . . '

His next job as a shop assistant at Courts furniture store must have seemed like a paid holiday after all the blood and maggots.

I'm about to show him *Reach for the Big Time* when suddenly, from out of nowhere comes the most terrifyingly loud noise I've ever heard. At first I think a nuclear bomb has gone off in Paul's back garden but then through a window I see the tail-end of a Tornado jet fighter tearing across the sky, just a few feet above the houses opposite. I never realised sound could be so visceral. Paul doesn't even flinch.

'If you're standing in the garden you can actually see the pilot's face – that's how low they fly. Anyway you think that's bad – you should try waking up in the middle of the night with the sound of a .50 calibre machine gun going off at full tilt. Now that's really scary.'

It seems operation-let's-scare-the-shit-out-of-James has begun in earnest – fierce gunfire can be heard coming from the other side of Paul's garden fence and the air is filled with a low, threatening rumble.

'That's the jet-engines firing up at the airport.' He tells me nonchalantly.

'You have an airport here too?'

'Not exactly – it's fourteen miles away. . . '

'But it sounds so close. . . '

'That's jet engines for you.'

When the time comes to leave I'm actually too scared to step out of the house for fear of another Tornado attack or a possible carpet-bombing of Paul's front lawn. My nerves are in tatters but Paul assures me that these fly-pasts only usually happen about three or four times a day. Three or four times a day? Surely no man can be expected to put up with that level of torture. I'd be a dribbling wreck after a single afternoon. But Paul seems resigned.

With a signed release safely tucked in my pocket, I poke my head out of the front door, check if the coast is clear and make a dash for the relative safety of my Ford Panzer-Division Capri.

I can't say I'm going to miss this corner of a Yorkshire field that is forever Bosnia.

Dottie Wayne has just phoned to invite me for a steak supper – I tell her I would be delighted but could she please crack open the brandy as my nerves need calming. It's after midnight when I finally arrive at Dottie's house in the delightfully named Gracious Street on the outskirts of Peterborough.

'Good heavens! A Ford Capri!' she says, greeting me at the door with a large glass of Courvoisier. 'I used to have one of those, before I upgraded to a Probe. . . '

As a professional 'siffleuse', Dottie Wayne has turned the humble act of whistling into an art form. Handel's 'Entry of the Queen of Sheba' is apparently the hardest tune of all to whistle – 'It's so complicated that I usually forget to breathe, which can be a problem.' But not this evening – the sound emanating from her lips is pitch-perfect. Who needs a thirty-piece orchestra when you can hire Dottie?

Over a delicious plate of sirloin steak we chat and drink long into the night. I was hoping to be in Great Yarmouth this evening but after all that brandy I'm going to have to take up Dottie's kind offer and stay the night in her spare room.

Before heading off to bed I hand her *Reach for the Big Time* for some bedtime reading. As I'm cleaning my teeth, I can hear her cackling next door.

This is the first decent night's sleep I've had in ages. Dottie's luxury divan has left me feeling invigorated and ready for my trip to Great Yarmouth.

Waiting for me on the kitchen table the next morning is a note: 'Here are four more leads for you. Hope they're useful!! *The Webb Twins* (Hi de Hi!) and *Twice as Nice* both live in Essex, just down the coast from Great Yarmouth, so you could visit them on your way back to London. I'll call ahead and let them know you'll be getting in touch. GOOD LUCK JAMES XX DOTTIE.'

Less than a week to go before the deadline and I still have

another six entertainers to visit and several more unaccounted for. And now I have two more to add to my still-to-see list. I call John Marshall of *Twice as Nice* first but he's in the middle of a family crisis and won't be able to see me, unfortunately. However, he has given me permission to use his image and has asked me to send a release. David Webb of *The Webb Twins* is happy for me to drop by on my way back to London. As a long-time fan of *Hi de Hi!* I'm particularly looking forward to meeting him.

As I speed across the flatlands of Norfolk on my way to Great Yarmouth, I receive a call from the publishers. They need an update on my progress so far. Keeping 35 000 copies of *Reach for the Big Time* in storage doesn't come cheap and they're obviously keen to know whether their investment is going to pay off. I try and sound upbeat – 'Everything's on course and I'm really looking forward to seeing the book back in the shops', I tell them. But whilst it's true I've been making good progress over the last few days, I still have a horribly long way to go.

As I approach the outskirts of Great Yarmouth, the knot in my stomach has become noticeably tighter. Maybe I should have come clean – told my publisher the truth – that I am nowhere near completing the task. At least then they'd be prepared for the worst. I need a slice of Little Chef cheesecake and some time to think.

The remaining acts on my list are ones that haven't used their real names, meaning they will be that much harder to track down. Where, for instance, does one begin looking for:

Brother Dominic
The Merry Monk of Magic
Something really different in magical entertainment
A truly international act performed in first class mime.
Two other non-monk acts also available.
Stage, cabaret, and all types of functions

I doubt there's a single monastery in the country that can point me in the right direction. And what about my self-strangulating nutcase *Kat Mandu*? Apart from not including his real name on the flyer, it's hard to tell what he looks like as his head is buried in a pile of broken glass. And of course *The Gay Duo* remain a tantalising mystery.

In a last ditch attempt I place an advert in the wanted section of Loot. With a mouthful of cheesecake I dictate my ad over the phone:

'Help! Has anyone seen or heard of *The Gay Duo*, an all singing all gay double act who performed in clubs around Britain in the mid to late 1970s? I'm also trying to track down a number of other performers including a parastuntologist called *Kat Mandu* who performed headstands on broken glass; *The Merry Monk of Magic* (who wore a full monk's habit during his performance) and a northern comic named Dick Pleasant. Several other acts still to find. . . if you have any info please call – '

So now that my most-wanted list is out there in the public arena, all I can do is keep buggering on. . .

On the outskirts of Great Yarmouth I receive two excellent phone calls in quick succession. Both Bobby Bennett and Leslie Melville have called to say they've had a word with Douggie and appreciate the urgency of my quest. Because of this they are prepared to sign the release without seeing the book. I feel as though I'm cheating by not actually going to see them but at least now I don't have to drive all the way back to Blackpool. And I've had a good chat with both of them which is good. Bobby tells me he used to present *Junior Showtime*, the popular kids' talent show from the '70s, but is now playing panto dames – this year he's doing his Widow Twanky at Wolverhampton. Sadly, Leslie Melville's remarkable clairvoyant hen, Charmaine, was laid to rest in the late '70s. . . Since then Leslie has concentrated on being an award-winning children's entertainer. His clown character Percy Piecrust won him the 'Children's Entertainer of the Year' award back in 1997. I ask him if he knows anything about my other bird-obsessed performer, impressionist Tony Durant.

Tony Durant – The Birdman
The best birdman in the business. Authentic bird sounds – recognised by the RSPB
Bird, Animal and Sound impressionist supreme!
Sound effects man extraordinary!
Radio, Theatre, Cabaret
Personal Manager: Miss Polly Pinkerton

Leslie remembers seeing Tony's act but has no idea what became of him. 'He did a brilliant skylark if I remember rightly.'

Great Yarmouth feels even more rundown than Blackpool. An

atmosphere of postwar gloom hangs over the narrow streets that cluster round the seafront. Backstage at the beautifully preserved Hippodrome Circus (the last remaining permanent circus in Britain), Clive Webb is practising a tricky stunt involving a retractable knife and a foam pigeon.

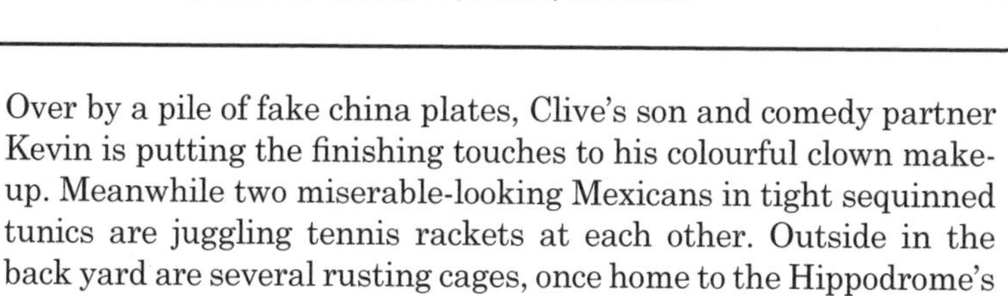

Over by a pile of fake china plates, Clive's son and comedy partner Kevin is putting the finishing touches to his colourful clown make-up. Meanwhile two miserable-looking Mexicans in tight sequinned tunics are juggling tennis rackets at each other. Outside in the back yard are several rusting cages, once home to the Hippodrome's resident lions and tigers.

'They won't allow us to keep wild animals anymore – it's considered politically incorrect' Clive tells me as we head down a dark corridor past a group of svelte African men in loincloths practising some back-breaking limbo moves.

On the back of his dressing-room door Clive has pinned a hand-written note sent in by a disgruntled member of the audience:

Dear Hippodrome
I didn't like your show.
The clown was nasty.
From Sam aged 5

Clive looks back at me from his dressing room mirror: – 'You can't please everyone', he says gloomily. A thin cloud of melancholy hangs over Mr Webb. He doesn't seem at all 'barmy' these days. I want to ask him about his time on *Tiswas* but he seems reluctant to talk about the glory days.

'It was all so long ago. I spent most of the time dressed in silly costumes hurling custard pies at Chris Tarrant.'

Clive has had to come in early today to take part in a local newspaper photo shoot with some schoolchildren. But as he buttons up his ringmaster's tunic and adjusts his highly polished top hat I get the feeling he's not really in the mood. He shuffles out across the brightly lit auditorium and takes his place amongst a large group of excitable ten-year-olds. As the cameras start to flash though, Clive switches effortlessly to 'barmy' mode, grinning and gurning on cue.

Back in his dressing room, Clive readies himself for the matinee performance, pacing his scruffy dressing room and going over some lines in the mirror – 'Good afternoon boys and girls – are we all having fun?' He then checks that all his props are in place – comedy car-horn, wobbly cricket bat, retractable knife, foam pigeon – before heading over to the stage entrance where his boss, the owner of the Hippodrome, Peter Jay, is waiting to wish him luck.

With his carefully arranged mullet, weather-beaten features and tight black jeans, Peter is your archetypal ageing rocker. As drummer with '60s combo *Peter Jay and The Jaywalkers*, he once toured with *The Beatles.* With his rock and roll lifestyle firmly behind him, Peter now runs pretty much all the entertainment venues in town. He has promised to give me a tour of his empire after the show.

The last time I went to a circus was back in 1982. The main attraction back then were the animals, especially the ones that could bite a man's head off. Forget juggling trapeze artists, all we wanted to see were elephants on beach balls, man-eating tigers and dogs on horseback.

Although Peter is still sore about having to part with his animals, the Hippodrome show has retained much of the old fashioned slapstick and audience participation of a traditional circus.

As well as holding the whole show together, Clive's job as ringmaster includes regularly spraying the audience with water and encouraging his son to smash china plates over his head. The second half of the show is more spectacular, with those Mexican jugglers and a daredevil high-wire act.

When I catch up with Clive afterwards, he's already reapplying his make-up, polishing his scuffed shoes and removing bits of broken china from his hair in preparation for this evening's show.

He remembers reading about *Reach for the Big Time* in the papers and even has a copy of the *Telegraph* article pinned to his fridge back home, so it came as quite a shock to discover that he was actually in the book. But now he's determined to get his hands on a copy, and if signing the release helps, then he's in.

Peter is waiting for me in the foyer, chatting animatedly to members of the audience as they file out. He seems a popular figure, joking and laughing with some of the older regulars.

The first stop on our whirlwind tour of the Jay empire is the old Windmill Theatre on the seafront. Originally built in 1908 as the country's first 'electric picture house', Peter's father Jack converted the building into a theatre back in 1965. At the time, Jack specialised in adapting popular films and TV shows. In 1976 he staged 'The cast of *Crossroads* plus Julie Ege in the hilarious comedy *The Mating*

Game (as seen on ITV)' – tickets for this extravaganza were a mere £1.20. For an even more paltry 65p you could have witnessed 'For the first time EVER, live on stage – *Planet of the Apes* featuring Galen, Urco, Dr Zaius and a full supporting cast of gorillas and astronauts.' I'd have paid £65.00 to see that. . . !

The Windmill is now home to one of Peter's more eccentric ventures, 'The Hollywood Indoor Crazy Golf Course'. The theme is gothic horror, but because of strict planning laws the course had to be built without making any alterations to the fabric of the ornate interior. Playing a round of crazy golf inside a Grade II listed theatre with a man who once toured with 'The Beatles' has to be one of my more surreal experiences.

These days kids don't seem interested in playing indoor crazy golf so Peter is planning to convert the building yet again, this time into 'The Hollywood Night Club' – I for one will be sorry to see the old golf course go.

In the foyer of the theatre Peter has erected a small shrine in honour of his time with The Beatles. On display in a glass cabinet are a couple of Peter Jay LPs next to a faded black and white photo of The Fab Four and an original poster from The Odeon Theatre Leeds, proclaiming twice nightly performances (5.15 and 7.45) by 'The Exciting! The Dynamic! The Fabulous! *Beatles* supported by The Dynamic! *Peter Jay and the Jaywalkers*! Also Britain's Top Disc Double *The Brooks Brothers*, The Glamorous *Vernon Girls*, the ace vocal group *The Kestrals* and your favourite Canadian compere Frank Berry.'

Frank, where are you now? Please get in touch.

The sun is beginning to set over the 'Las Vegas Amusement Arcade' as we continue along the seafront to the splendid neo-classical Empire Theatre, now a rather brash Moroccan theme bar called ZEN ('I'm thinking of changing the theme to Egyptian – Morocco is so last year'). Peter's other behemoth The Grand Theatre, situated at the far end of the seafront, is now a multi-screen cinema. And it is here that I felt I must take my leave of the charming Mr Jay – he has kindly given me a free ticket to see the latest Bruce Willis movie in Screen One.

My night at the Treetops guest house a couple of blocks from the Hippodrome is not a happy one – the landlord is a large, psychotic looking man who fires great globules of phlegm at me whenever he speaks. His Thai wife seems nervous as she hands over the keys to my room and with good reason – the stench of cat wee keeps me awake for most of the night. By 6am I'm back on the A1 heading south to Manningtree in Essex.

Hi de Hi!

18. Go, Go, Go to the Holiday Rock!

Reach for the Deadline: six days to go. . .

Unfortunately there's only one Webb twin waiting for me in Manningtree. David's brother Tony is out of town on business, but judging by all the publicity material laid out on David's coffee table, I would never have been able to tell them apart anyway. In a spare bedroom that also doubles up as a tiny recording studio, David is busy editing a radio documentary about his beloved Essex cricket club.

'I'm hoping it might be aired on Radio Suffolk.'

There's something of the John Major about David – the soft nasal voice, the mild-mannered courteousness – he comes across as a solid, thoroughly decent, cricket-on-the-green, real-ale type of Englishman – the sort you don't see very often these days. You certainly wouldn't describe him as showbizzy.

Although David seems pretty relaxed about being out of the whole *Hi de Hi!* spotlight, he admits he wouldn't have minded a few more TV offers after the show ended in 1987.

'It all went a bit quiet – I'd been hoping for another series to come along but all I was offered was a walk on part in *'Allo 'Allo*. After living the high life with *Hi de Hi!* I just couldn't face going back to working the live club circuit again. Too depressing.'

So he retired to Manningtree and built himself a little studio and has been twiddling the edit suite knobs ever since. All very different from the heady days of the late '60s when young David wanted desperately to break into variety.

'I made the decision early on never to say that I was a singer or a performer – just that I was *available*. Always be available – that's been my motto.' And it paid off – after a stint at Butlins in Clacton, David and his brother gave up a career in close-harmony singing for a job on *Top of the Pops*, working as stand-ins during technical rehearsals.

'I've played everyone from Cliff Richard to Donny Osmond to one of the Pointer Sisters. I even stood in for Michael Jackson once. It didn't seem to matter to the producer that Michael was a little black kid and I was a tall white man from Essex. . . '

But the twins didn't just stand in, they also doubled up as audience members during the recording of the programme. Their job was to look like regular punters while at the same time clearing a path for the heavy camera equipment – not an easy job when faced with a wall of hysterical Donny Osmond fans.

It was during their time at *Top of the Pops* that the twins heard that producer David Croft was on the lookout for experienced Butlins performers to appear in his new sitcom set in a 1950s holiday camp.

'We appeared in fifty-seven of the fifty-eight episodes but hardly said a word. The money was good though and the royalty cheques are still coming in twenty years later. The series is always being shown somewhere in the world.'

Although David's brother isn't here to sign the release, David is sure he'll be happy to help out so I leave an extra copy of the release for him to pass on. The bad news is that David, the last of my known contacts, doesn't have a single lead for me.

'Are you absolutely, positively, one hundred percent sure you don't know anyone from the book?' I ask for a third time.

'Positive. . . I'm really sorry.'

'But you're my last hope. Could you go through the book just one more time to make sure. . . '

David obligingly works his way through the book yet again but each turn of the page elicits the same slow shake of the head.

'I'm so sorry but I've been out of the loop for so long', he says handing me back the book.

'But what about Dick Pleasant, surely you've heard of him – big cigar, pencil moustache, strange hair? Look at him. . . !'

David seems a bit startled by my rising hysteria.

'No, sorry – I don't know him at all.'

'What about *The Merry Monk of Magic* – fat clergyman in a hessian habit? Come on, think. . . '

But it's no good, the more manic I become the more he closes up. I apologise for my sudden loss of control and head back to the car feeling guilty. I'll make it up to him by buying all the *Hi de Hi!*s on DVD.

During the drive back to London I'm overcome by a gnawing sense of futility, as though the last three weeks has been nothing more than a pointless exercise in hope over adversity. I mean, what have I actually achieved apart from raising everyone's hopes? Yes, I've had an adventure but what about my trusting entertainers, what are they going to get out of all this? I can't bear the thought of having to disappoint them. All I can do now though is wait for *Loot* and John Adrian to uncover the last of my most-wanted list.

The International Capri Club's annual get-together starts tomorrow. Maybe I should put my worries on hold for a day. . . I know that Cabaret has been looking forward to meeting up with some old pals. . .

19. Keeping the Legend Alive

Reach for the Deadline: four days to go...

Geoff Watkins has over a thousand Ford Capris in his attic – many of them still in their original boxes. But only a fraction of his collection is on sale here today.

'How much is this one?' asks a bald Capri-head pointing at a battered three-inch model of a Mark Two.

'You can have it for seven quid mate. Quite a rare model is that.'

The man shakes his hairless head and ambles off.

'Ok four quid'.

Another deal is made.

'I only paid a pound for it' whispers Geoff once he's sure the purchaser is out of earshot.

As an avid buyer and seller of model Ford Capris, Geoff spends most of his weekends at conventions. But the International Capri Club's annual get-together here on Badger's Hill in Gloucestershire is the highlight of his year.

As with most outdoor events in the UK, this one has turned into a bit of a mud bath. Although officially an international get-together, most of the enthusiasts I've met so far hail from just outside Birmingham. Geoff is a native of Solihull. He tells me these occasions are '. . . a great opportunity to meet up with old friends – both people and cars. . . '

Next door to Geoff's stand is the 'South Hampshire Capri Club', housed in one of those grand marquees with the gothic-style windows. Parked outside is a row of beautifully restored Mark Ones.

Over at the other end of the field, a group of burly-bottomed blokes from the 'Luton and District Capri Club' are busy polishing half-a-dozen dazzling Mark Threes. All the cars are for sale and come with a set of furry dice as standard. Over in an adjoining field, members of the 'Coastal Capri Club' are having difficulty assembling their marquee – only two pairs of hands and a lot of tent-pegs.

The three football-pitch sized fields are packed with every conceivable model of Capri, from immaculately restored late '60s Mark Ones through to rusty mid period Mark Twos and souped-up, fire-breathing Mark Threes with gurgling engines and massive, intimidating spoilers jutting from the boot.

Each car has a tent pitched up alongside where proud wives prepare sausages on disposable barbecues. Their tipsy husbands meanwhile stand around discussing paint-jobs over warm tins of Carling.

Against my better judgement I've decided to spend the night here and have managed to borrow an ancient orange tent with a tear down one of the panels. I've never been one for sleeping under canvas, not since my geography teacher made me organise a disastrous outward-bound school trip to the Peak District. For some inexplicable reason, probably to do with cruelty, I'd been assigned the job of team-leader, much to the amusement of my fellow classmates, who knew perfectly well that I was about as outdoorsy as a carpet. Mr Hat the geography teacher hoped the assignment might toughen me up a bit or at least improve my appalling organisational skills. But the truth is I was born a wuss and will remain a wuss, and no amount of sitting about in chilly fields is ever going to change that.

Geoff has kindly offered to help me assemble my decrepit tent. He's just given Cabaret the once over and is amazed by her lack of rust.

'Some models have survived better than others,' he says, hammering in a muddy peg '. . . all depends on the year really. For some reason you don't see many 'V' reg Mark Twos or 'A' reg Mark Threes on the road. There are still plenty of 'B' and 'C' reg Mark Threes and 'M' reg Mark Twos around. Mark Ones are the most durable because they used better quality steel back in the '60s.'

Geoff is a walking *Hayes Manual* when it comes to Capris. As well as all the matchbox versions in his loft he also has five life-size models on his drive, and is part of a growing number of younger fans.

'Capris are wicked man – and so cheap to run. You can have loads of fun adapting the bodywork.'

Steel dashboards, ostentatious spoilers and massive sound

systems seem to be the most popular additions, much to the horror of older purists who strive to maintain original features at all costs. Geoff though is into the whole retro motoring experience.

'You can't have fun with modern cars – they're so rigidly put together and generic looking – a bit like modern pop stars. I mean when did you last see a proper bumper on a new car? They're all moulded into the bodywork these days and therefore impossible to remove or adapt. Capris are like toy cars – you can take them apart and bolt them back together again really easily. And the engines are reliable too. Did you know Stephen Fry's dad helped design the gearbox for the Mark One?'

That's very reassuring to know but seriously, is there anything those blasted Frys can't put their over-educated minds to? Most of the Capri-heads stumbling around Badger's Hill are in the ruddy spread of middle age (a bit like Stephen). For them, this weekend is all about wallowing in nostalgia – for many the Capri was the first car they ever owned, while others remember being driven to school in dad's precious three-litre Ghia. Twenty years on, deep resentments still remain about Ford's decision to end production. Geoff reckons it was the biggest mistake the company ever made. 'They still haven't come up with a decent replacement. Their last attempt was abandoned after only two years.'

Most Capri fans are united in their hatred of The Probe, the official follow-up which didn't appear for almost a decade after Capri production had ended. The name alone was enough to put most drivers off (although it doesn't seem to worry Dottie Wayne). There was something sophisticated – almost cosmopolitan about the name 'Capri' with images of yachting millionaires lounging about in the Med. In reality of course, the car was about as sophisticated as a bottle of Babycham but at least the name gave an illusion of grandeur, whereas the 'Probe' merely conjured up images of gruesomely manipulated orifices. Buying one must have been excruciatingly embarrassing: 'Hello Mr Car Salesperson, I'd like a top of the range Probe please. . . '

So far I've only spotted one rather embarrassed-looking Probe, hidden away in a corner of the top field. I'm surprised the owner had the gall to show its ugly face here. Earlier in the day I saw a couple of Brummie lads giving the car a surreptitious V sign as they hurried by.

'The Capri Grill' may sound like a swanky Italian restaurant but is in fact a rusty 1978 Mark Two with a barbecue where the engine should be. I'm with several hungry Capri-heads watching a shrivelled sausage turn to charcoal. 'Maybe we should come back later?' suggests a pale man in a cagoule. We all nod and move on.

Next to the Grill is a hand-painted leopard-skin Mark Two with a poster in the window advertising 'Capri – The Musical, 8pm Saturday 25th August 2001.' Damn, missed it. Also making a spectacular appearance in front of the main events tent is a bright pink stretch Capri belonging to Capri Club International head honcho John Hall. I particularly like the Rolls Royce grille and sliding passenger door.

On the way back to my tent I see a 'Y' reg, dark-over-pale blue Capri Cabaret come speeding round the corner. My immediate thought is that some bastard has just nicked my precious motor – so I give chase.

'Oi, give me back my Cabaret!' I bellow.

The car skids to a halt, spraying me with globules of mud.

'You okay?' asks the worried-looking girl at the wheel.

On closer inspection I notice that this particular Cabaret has much cleaner windows than mine and is altogether a bit nicer.

'Yes I'm fine.' I reply awkwardly 'Sorry about that – got a bit over excited – thought you were stealing my car. Seems we have the same model. Huh! Coincidence or what?'

'Eh?'

'You and me – same model of car.'

'What year is yours?'

''83 Cabaret.'

'First or second edition?'

'Erm – dunno. Didn't realise there were two editions.'

'I thought everybody knew that. Both models came out in 1983 but my second edition has nicer upholstery.'

'Right. . . I think mine's probably a first edition in that case.'

'Why don't you bring it over – I'm at the Dorset Club tent down the bottom end of the first field – we could compare notes.'

'Right. See you there then.'

Janey and her husband Bob run the Dorset Capri Club from their home in Poole but unlike Geoff, these Capri obsessives really do spend every weekend of the year attending Capri events.

'Last weekend was our only non-Capri weekend of the year and we hated every minute of it. We've been to over twenty so far, not just here but in America and Australia too. Last week we were in Denver, next week we'll be up in Derbyshire. But this is the most enjoyable of all the conventions.'

The word 'convention' suggests worthy lectures, furrowed brows and serious discussion. Here at Capri Camp the only discussion taking place is whether or not to attend tonight's concert given by heavy metal covers band *The Crappies* (An affectionate anagram of Capri.)

'Oh yeah, *The Crappies* – they're really crap' says Janey, who's seen them play live many times.

Apart from the number '2' after the word 'Cabaret', both our cars are pretty much identical on the outside. Inside, however, is a different story. Whereas Janey has kept her beloved interior spotlessly clean and tidy, mine is starting to look as though a tramp has taken up residence. Several squares of Dairy Milk have melted into the dashboard and an oversized road atlas with half the pages missing lies scattered across the back seat next to a single brown sock. The floor is covered in crushed Coke tins, Little Chef cheesecake crumbs and broken cassettes. There's also a faint smell of something rotten – an apple core caught under the seat perhaps, or a forgotten bit of pasty left in the glove compartment 'for later'.

'Look at that, only 43 000 genuine miles on the clock – she's a real beauty isn't she?'

Janey seems genuinely smitten by her second edition Cabaret and hardly even notices my boring old first.

'What I love most about Betty (I've yet to meet a male Capri) is her two-tone paint job. During the daytime you can't really notice it but come the evening you can really see the contrast. I love the sporty shape too.'

Janey's husband, a mechanic, is underneath his Mark 3, fiddling with the exhaust pipe. I interrupt his tinkering to ask if he can tell me why my Cabaret keeps making strange noises.

'Hmm, errrm. . . well, it could be anything really.'

'I see. Thanks for your help Bob.'

Bob's love affair with Capris began after his father bought him a 1972 Mark One for his seventeenth birthday. He's now the proud owner of five newly restored Mark Ones.

'Come and look at this' he takes my arm and gives me a guided tour of his 1972 2.8 turbo. 'I call her the Hell-Beast.'

'What's her top speed?' I ask.

'Off the clock mate – off the clock. Put it this way, the fuzz have a job keeping up. . . '

Janey interrupts.

'You know what's so great about these cars? The looks you get from other road users. Makes you feel kind of special. I'm always being cheered and hooted at.'

'That's 'cos you drive like a layyydy' jokes Bob.

Janey wants to know if I'll be attending tonight's festivities.

'What festivities?' I ask.

'Oh there's all sorts happening tonight. Some of the events are quite 'blue' if you know what I mean. The wet T-shirt competition is always a goody. Then there's the wet Y-fronts competition for the lads. Maybe you should enter that one?'

'Sounds exciting but I think I'll pass. What time does it all get going?'

'Proceedings start about 9pm. Let's hope the rain stops in time for the frozen T-shirt competition.'

'Hello?'

'Oh yeah! A group of topless girls are given a frozen T-shirt each – the first girl to defrost it and put it on wins a prize.'

'What time does that happen?' I ask rather too enthusiastically.

Bob calls out from under his Capri.

'The frozen T-shirt competition only happens at the Milton Keynes convention silly – never at Capri Camp.'

'Oh yeah sorry, I forgot – every meeting has its own unique events. Our branch is based near the coast in Dorset so we try and give our annual convention a nautical theme. Last year we ran a 'guess-the-fish' competition where blindfolded competitors were given a raw fish each and had to guess what it was. Disgusting really, but a lot of fun.'

Fun maybe, but what does feeling fish and the putting on of frozen T-shirts have to do with Ford Capris exactly?

'Well you know, it keeps everyone amused in between the judging events which, let's face it, can go on a bit sometimes. By the way, do you want to enter our raffle? You could win a 'C' reg Mark Three.'

She hands me a couple of raffle tickets along with a schedule for today's events. Most of the day seems to be taken up with judging competitions. There are umpteen different categories, including 'Best Personalised Bodywork', 'Loudest In-Car Entertainment', 'Best Engine Bay', 'Loudest Exhaust' and 'Best Overseas Model' (apparently there are some Scandinavians amongst us.) There's also a prize for 'Best Under Car Light Display' and '"Sexiest" Paint Job'. The Crappies are then due to hit the stage at around 10pm followed by a disco and of course copious amounts of drinking.

I've set my tent up in a corner of field number one – dangerously close to the main stage. The Capri Grill is back in action with several fat sausages and a couple of Findus frozen burgers blackening nicely. A young couple from the East London Capri Club and a gangly member of the King's Lynn branch are huddled round the grill exchanging Capri stories.

'Have you ever seen "ARK666Y"?'

'I thought it had been ritually burnt. . . '

'That's not what I've heard. Apparently you can hire it out for weddings and events. You can even spend the night in it – if you're feeling brave enough.'

Intrigued, I edge in for a closer listen. Turns out 'ARK666Y' is the registration number of – wait for it – the world's only haunted Capri. Several more people gather round the Grill to exchange tales of the so-called Devil-Car. According to Richard – a small bearded man from the 'Potteries Capri Appreciation Club' – some past owners have campaigned to have the car either burnt, buried or blown up. But it seems the present owner is milking the legend for all it's worth. He's even set up the Haunted-Capri website. Dave, a paid up member of the 'Wakefield and District' branch is the only person here to have actually seen the car up close.

'It didn't look particularly haunted to me, although I did feel a bit creeped-out in its presence.'

'So no bats flapping round the windscreen then?' I scoff.

'I wouldn't laugh about it if I were you mate,' warns Dave 'awful things happen to people who mock. . . ' (I didn't realise Capris had such good hearing. Oh no there I go again – double damnation.) '. . . Apparently some bloke with a brand new 4x4 went to visit the Devil-Car once and treated the whole thing as a big joke. The very next day the exhaust fell of his 4x4 and he started having nasty headaches.'

There seems to be some confusion as to whether it's the car or the number-plate that's actually haunted.

'I've heard the car can destroy relationships', announces Rich, as he takes a bite of burger. 'Apparently several owners have had failed marriages after buying the car. Some believe it's the reincarnation of Alistair Crowley – apparently he destroyed a lot of relationships too with all his philandering.'

Gangly man suddenly butts in. 'Well I heard that a Satanist couple from America hired the car for a weekend so they could fornicate in it. Apparently they were hoping to spawn the Devil's child. . . '

This is rapidly turning into one of those cheesy horror film moments when a group of teenagers gather round the camp-fire to tell tales of 'Old Gnarled Willy' – the local loon living in the forest. I can't believe they're all taking this so seriously. Sounds like a lot of hokum to me. Oh dear, I hope 'ARK666' isn't reading this. . .

John Hall is trying unsuccessfully to gather everyone together for the 'In Car Sound Off' competition. Seems he's having a few problems with the stage microphone, which keeps cutting out.

'Please. . . your. . . main tent. . . the. . . in . . . entertainment. . . petition. . . about. . . start. Would. . . wanting. . . enter. . . plea. . . in front. . . boots up. . . Bollocks. . . mike keeps cut. . . out.'

He eventually abandons the dodgy mike and starts bellowing instructions instead. It seems to be working – five fancy-looking

Mark Threes pull into a neat circle in front of the main stage. Proud owners make last-minute checks and adjustments to enormous woofers and tweeters. This particular event seems to be all about out-voluming your competitors. All five sound systems have been turned up to eleven, with each one blasting out a different track. *Queen's* 'Radio Ga Ga' seems to be the clear winner so far, easily drowning out Gloria Gaynor's 'I Will Survive' and *Motorhead's* 'Ace of Spades'. Meanwhile *Pink Floyd's* 'Us and Them' is having trouble keeping up with the high pitched squealing of *The Bee Gees'* 'Tragedy'. How anyone is supposed to give a valued judgement on such a cacophony is a mystery but the three judges seem to be listening intently. Suddenly all five sound systems burst into visual life – speakers flash red and green, fairy lights dance in time with the music and furry mascots glow rhythmically from the tops of speakers.

But what's this? 'Radio Ga Ga' is suddenly being out-decibelled by a late arrival; a bright yellow Mark Two with red and orange go-faster flames along each door has just roared into first place with Yes' 'Owner of a Lonely Heart' pounding out of the yawning boot. Everyone looks on in astonishment as the flashy owner (of the car, not the lonely heart) swaggers round to the back of his outrageously souped-up vehicle and flicks a magic switch. The crowd gasps in wonder as bursts of tesla coil lightning bolts flicker across the specially adapted plasma speaker heads and a magical under-floor neon light-show puts everyone else's efforts to shame.

As I move in for a closer look someone taps me on the shoulder. I turn round to see Geoff shaking his head and rolling his eyes. He has to bellow in my ear to make himself heard above Jon Anderson's high pitched warblings.

'What you're hearing now is like a whisper compared with my Sony mega-bass hyper system.'

I have no idea what he's talking about but it sounds competitive.

'Put it this way' he continues, 'I'll be happy to go head-to-head with this guy any day of the week.'

I think he means he's got louder speakers.

The rain is coming down again, turning everything to mud. But the really distressing news is that the wet T-shirt competition has been cancelled due to lack of interest. The organisers have decided instead to put on a play. (Now I'd love to be able to tell you what this so called 'play' was about but I'm afraid I was too pissed – as were most of the cast members stumbling about on stage. All I can remember is a podgy girl in suspenders getting it on in the back of the pink stretch-Capri with a bloke from Wolverhampton. Oh yes, and there was some fat bloke in a wacky costume dancing around like a tit. Nobody in the audience seemed to have a clue what was going on.)

It's now well after midnight and still no sign of *The Crappies*. John has just announced that the final competition of the evening will shortly be taking place, so could all competitors for 'Best Interior' please bring their cars over to the main stage area. Why anyone would want to start judging upholstery at this ungodly hour I can't imagine.

I'm beginning to wonder whether The Crappies actually exist. Apart from a tatty old drum kit and a torn black curtain with the Rolling Stones lips logo painted on it, the stage seems hopelessly ill equipped for a rock concert.

Soaked to the marrow, I decide to give up and go back to my tent. An earlier attempt to patch up the large tear in the canvas, using an old T-shirt and a single clothes peg, has failed miserably. The T-shirt is now lying in an adjoining field, dangerously close to a freshly laid cow-pat. Because of the recent downpour, the floor of the tent is now a series of shallow puddles and my hatred of camping has just deepened. Just as I'm finally dropping off into an uncomfortably damp slumber, the opening chords of 'Stairway to Heaven' suddenly suck me back into the land of the living.

'There's a lady who's sure all that glitters is gold and she's buying a stairway to heav. . . when she . . . there she . . . all th.. glitt. . . is gold and sh. . . ..ying a stair. . . . . . ven. . . Shit is this ..ucking mike workin' or wha'?'

So they made it at last. . . five hours late but here they are tearing through a barely audible rendition of 'Stairway to Heaven' in a broad Brummie accent. According to Geoff it's always hit and miss as to whether the band actually bother to show up to events like this. Apparently they don't like performing outdoors, especially in the rain.

'Ladies and Gentle. . . we're avin' a few . . . lems with the mike as you can . . bably 'ear. Any. . . this one's by Dee. .urple – it's 'alled 'Smoke on the Wart.'

'Dur dur durrr, dur dur de durrr, dur dur durrr, dur de de. . . '

And so begins the greatest air-guitar riff of all time. I should know, I must have played it a hundred times on my 'Fender Tennis Racquet'. Sadly, I had to give up my career as an air guitarist after an embarrassing incident at my girlfriend's parents' house. I'd been entrusted to look after the place for a couple of days and so took the opportunity to practise a few power chords while everyone was away. I didn't have my trusty Slazenger Stratocaster with me at the time so had to resort to a Gibson Umbrella hanging in the hall. Having carefully positioned myself in front of a full-length mirror, I began strumming along to The Who's 'Won't Get Fooled Again'. So there I was giving it the full Pete Townsend – legs apart, arms wind-milling furiously – when suddenly my girlfriend's upstanding army officer father appeared from nowhere. He'd had to cut his weekend short because of work commitments.

Now, I've always found playing air guitar in the nude a much more satisfying experience, and that day had been no exception (although for some reason I was still wearing socks).

'TURN THAT REVOLTING NOISE OFF!' bellowed the colonel, trying hard not to look down at my spinning testicles. I stood there in the deafening silence, buttocks clenched to bursting. Standing before me, in all his suited respectability, was the father of the woman I loved. I felt naked and exposed – hell, I *was* naked and exposed. In a rash moment of not-knowing-what-to-do-next I pressed the 'erect' button on the tightly folded umbrella-guitar. Out it popped, nearly removing – but usefully concealing – what was left of my shrivelled dignity.

Needless to say relations have been strained ever since.

The Crappies play on into the night, becoming steadily more pissed with each song.

'Are we allowed to fucking swear?' screams the lead singer, 'It's just that someone told us to mind our fucking language because there might be fucking kids in the audience.'

After a muted encore of 'Born to be Wild' everyone starts trudging back to their respective tents. John tries to keep the party going but for most of the middle-aged crowd the only thing 'born to be wild' round here are the screaming kids causing havoc back at the tent.

The following morning I wake with a stiff neck, a sore throat and a wet ass. This camping lark really is the pits. As I try and work out how to disassemble the torn remnants of tent, my mobile starts buzzing. Please God let this be John Adrian with some new contacts.

'Hello James. . . this is Alice Manifold – I'm ringing about Keith. . . I'm afraid he passed away suddenly last night of a heart attack. I thought you should know seeing as he was so excited about being in your book.'

This is devastating news. Keith, dead? But I hadn't even thanked him properly for helping me out over the Malaga fiasco. And I still owe him for the FedEx delivery. He can't be dead... not just like that.

Geoff suddenly appears and asks if I'd like to visit him next time I'm in the West Midlands. I wish he'd go away. My thoughts are with Alice and the children and the promise I made to Keith that *Reach for the Big Time* would be back in the shops by the end of the month...

A low mist hangs across the valley as I speed along the narrow Cotswold lanes. Every now and then I pass a Capri heading in the direction of Badger's Hill. It's customary when passing fellow Capri drivers to give a friendly toot and an appreciative wave, but on this sad morning such jollity seems inappropriate.

The mad camaraderie of last night's festivities had left me feeling refreshed and ready to face the uncertainties of the week ahead. But now there's an added sense of poignancy about the rest of my trip.

The International Capri Club bears a proud motto – it boasts of 'Keeping the Legend Alive' and as I sit at my desk, Keith's eager face staring back at me from the pages of *Reach for the Big Time*, those simple words seem especially fitting...

20. Mr Sexique

Although the news of Keith's death has left me feeling deflated and miserable, I have a renewed vigour to see this thing through. However, there's still been no word back from John Adrian or any response from the *Loot* ad. There is one piece of good news though – Tony Tadman, the compere from page nineteen of *Reach for the Big Time*, has left an email wanting to know more about the book. He sounds nervous when I call. Seems he and his wife are worried that I might be a reporter – I don't ask why at this stage. Tony hasn't seen the book but tells me he knows quite a few old timers in the business. After some gentle persuasion he agrees to meet up and go through the book with me.

'You're definitely not a reporter, are you. . . ?' asks Tony, mouth pressed against the glass panel of his front door. '. . . Because they sometimes just turn up on my doorstep. I've promised the wife I'd make sure.'

I'm in Stoney Stanton, a village just outside Nuneaton on the borders of Leicestershire, Derbyshire, Nottinghamshire and Warwickshire.

TONY TADMAN

Comedian – Impressionist – Compère

'There is no doubt that TONY TADMAN has the gift that all funny comedians possess; a cheeky warmth and a raw brashness, without losing that quality and style which has been acquired the hard way.

No stranger to the 'hard way,' Tony is an ex-international Racing Cyclist, who changed from turning fast wheels to fast impressions, and is proving a popular support and compere for top names at home and abroad with his friendly image.

With today's undervalued use of the word 'Star', this likeable lad from the Lake District reckons he aims to be a busy comedian, but laughing audiences around the country are tipping Tony Tadman to be a top funny man of the future.

Because of Tony's jitteriness, I initially suggested we hook up at a local pub, but he's insisted we meet at his place away from prying eyes.

I hold the pale pink cover of *Reach for the Big Time* against the glass panel to prove I am who I say I am. Once he's satisfied I'm not a meddling hack, he beckons me in and hurries me through to the privacy of a back room.

My original search for Tony had led me to a Midlands-based talent agency called 'Hollywood Promotions' in Nottingham, a company specialising in 'adult comedians ranging from naughty to saucy to blue'. They promised to pass on a message that sadly never reached Tony. I then Googled his name and discovered he was also listed on the books of another Midlands talent agency called 'Simply the Best Entertainment' but when I spoke to the boss there, he told me he hadn't represented Tony for many years and had no idea where he was. So it's great to have found him at last.

'I'm afraid you can't stay long; I don't want my wife to worry. She's still concerned you might be a reporter. . . '

'Are you in trouble with the law?' I ask.

'No, no, nothing like that. . . anyway let's have a look at this book of yours. . .'

The brilliant news is he immediately recognises cover-star Dick Pleasant and even remembers seeing him perform. . .

'Where is he now?' I ask excitedly.

'Oh now you're asking. I haven't seen him for years.'

Damn it – same old story. . .

'So what was he like?' I ask.

'Good old standard comedian was Dickie – always wore pancake makeup and a pencil moustache just like the old Victorian comics – in later years he looked a bit like Bernard Manning but thinner. I remember he always stood dead still on stage – never moved an inch. Someone could have let off a bomb and he'd have kept on going with his act. Supremely "professional" was Dickie.'

Describing a fellow performer as 'professional' seems to be one of the biggest compliments you can give. He goes on to tell me that Dickie, like many comedians of the day, had his own catchphrase that he would sprinkle liberally throughout his act – 'Ten more minutes and the money's mine' – he'd say grumpily, glaring at his watch.

Sadly Dickie began to lose his bottle towards the end of the '70s; as the industry began to change, he found it hard to adapt.

'When the northern pits closed down, live entertainment virtually disappeared overnight. The cabaret and social clubs all shut up shop and comedians like Dickie and I had to turn to stag parties to make a living – but the audiences for those sorts of gigs are notoriously unforgiving. Dick wasn't really up to it.'

Of all the entertainers I've met so far, Tony seems the most anguished about the way the industry has evolved over the last twenty-five years. He particularly mourns the passing of old-fashioned variety on TV.

'There doesn't seem to be much call for old impressionists like me anymore.'

Tony spent much of his early career imitating TV personalities and cartoon characters.

'I can give you a demonstration if you like.' And so with his beloved Bichon Frise dogs pirouetting round his ankles he takes me though the old routine – Ken Dodd, Frank Spencer, David Frost – all the old suspects. It's like the Mike Yarwood show all over again. Tony's ear for cartoon characters is remarkable and his Officer Dibble from *Top Cat* is spot on.

'Remember the theme tune?' He asks, face beaming.

'Certainly do.'

'Fancy a sing-song?'

If someone had told me a month ago that I'd be in Nuneaton singing the *Top Cat* theme tune with a man called Tony Tadman, I'd have told them to 'get out of here' but after everything that's happened, it all seems quite normal.

I find my ability to retain useless information, like the *Top Cat* theme tune, slightly disturbing. I used to be able to recite Shakespeare and Philip Larkin but not anymore. My subconscious decided long ago to chuck out all the useful, cultural stuff and replace it with trivia. . .

Altogether now:

Top Cat!
The most effec-tu-al Top Cat!
Who's intellectual, close friends get to call him T. C.
Providing it's with dignity
Top Cat!
The indisputable leader of the gang
He's the boss
He's the VIP
He's a championship
He's the most tip top – Top Cat!

Yes he's the chief
He's the king, but above everything
He's the most tip-top – Top Cat!

TC, if you really were the tops (and as a ten-year-old I certainly thought so) why are you never repeated? Maybe TC is no longer considered PC – what with the fascistic Dibble harassing all those poor destitute cats. Or maybe it was The Brain's unsympathetic portrayal of someone with learning difficulties.

While Tony's Top Cat impression is impressive, his Bugs Bunny could do with some work and never really gets beyond the 'What's up doc?' rabbity teeth noise that anyone with a half-decent set of gnashers can do.

Midway through his Popeye impersonation, Tony's wife calls to tell him his tea's ready. I think this may be a sign that she wants me to leave.

'Just out of interest Tony, why are you so nervous of reporters?'

'Didn't I tell you? I'm an adult entertainer now. . . some members of the press have had a problem with it in the past.'

Over the last thirty years, Tony has gone from Bugs Bunny impersonator and teller of old-fashioned mother-in-law gags to a late night adult entertainer and travelling strip show owner.

'I'd already started telling blue gags in my act so the whole stripping thing was simply an extension of that.'

As alternative comedy took a hold, Tony felt he needed to follow the trend and so he started peppering his act with rude words and sexual references, in order to get a laugh.

'I always felt it was a shame that so many of us had to resort to bad language. Adding a couple of naughty words at the end of a gag is a great way of emphasising the punch-line but if you use them all the time they become meaningless. And I think that's what's happened now, we've become desensitised to obscenity. But to me it's a lazy form of comedy.'

Although the alternative comedians of the early 1980s like to claim responsibility for the 'anything goes' style of comedy, it was actually the bêtes noirs of the alternative scene – comedians like Bernard Manning and Chubby Brown – who began the whole potty-mouthed revolution.

Tony initially got a job as the resident adult comic at a strip club in Leicester but he soon became restless and decided to set up his own company.

'The Tony Tadman Stag Show Exotica' featured 'sensational girls and superb sound and light system' and was an instant success throughout the Midlands.

He hands me a bunch of old promotional material including an early publicity flyer showing a young bright-eyed Tony dressed in a lacy lounge suit and black tie. The sleeves of his jacket have been rolled up to reveal a chunky stainless steel digital watch – no doubt featuring thirty-seven utterly useless functions.

He's leaning nonchalantly against the bar of a '70s style 'Palm Court' cocktail-lounge – all fake rubber-plants and crazy brick-inlays. By his side are two delectable semi-clad, bubble-permed ladies named 'Debs' and 'Angel' – both are dressed in red polyester baby-dolls and sensible sandals but neither seems particularly comfortable about having to display their bosoms to the world. Tony looks cheerful enough though, judging by the 'Aren't-I-the-lucky-one' grin on his face.

He has plenty more publicity material where that came from, including a handmade promotional calling card outlining his many talents. On the cover is a black and white photo of Tony in full '70s perm – inside are various reviews from unspecified sources:

- *Tony is in great demand for 'Stag Shows' and always makes a great impact with his specially prepared material for those gentlemen-only occasions.*
- *Tony's cartoon voices and crazy noises are an ideal choice for radio commercials and TV voice-overs.*
- *Or if you require a compère/commentator or humorous break during your trade, sports, business conference, after dinner, exhibition, promotion show etc. then Tony Tadman has the ability to change his style to suit most tastes, easy and relaxed or quick and witty. Don't allow your hard work for your show to be wasted, use a professional who takes pride in his hard work.*

All enquiries to: FOXY INTERNATIONAL PROMOTIONS. Address: Tony's house, Leicester.

Although I routinely turn down invitations to stag parties – I find the idea of male communal vomiting faintly depressing – I'd always assumed these last-ditch attempts at male bonding happened shortly before a man got hitched. Not so, according to Tony. His stag night parties have removed any pretence that you need to be getting married in order to gawp at naked ladies. Tony's clients include rugby clubs, cricket clubs and military bases, and it seems the latter is where he had his unfortunate run-in with the press.

'The RAF used to hold their annual knees-ups in the privacy of the barracks, away from prying lenses. But when they opened their gates to anyone with an invitation, members of the tabloid press were able to sneak in and make up all sorts of stories about naked debauchery and alcoholic intemperance amongst the armed forces.'

Tony still seems peeved by some of the negative publicity he's received.

'It's so ridiculous. These journalists, they just make up outrageous stories about my girls but the fact is, women have been stripping in front of men since the dawn of time. There's nothing closer to human nature right?'

Tony is keen to distance himself from the seamier side of the industry and assures me that his girls aren't as 'in your face' as some. He describes them as being much classier.

He starts flicking through *Reach for the Big Time* – and halfway through lets out a squeal of recognition.

Roy Baker

'Roy Baker has always caused a sensation, with people returning to see his fantastic hypnotic act again and again. Quick return bookings and standing ovations are the order of the day when Roy is around. He has made several TV appearances, has a superb cabaret act and with the flair of the complete showman does a fine one-man show. His excellent promotion material backed up by a first class performance makes him the ideal choice for Civic theatres and summer seasons. This year (1976) he has toured the Pontin Holiday Camps for the full summer season filling the Startime Cabaret Spot and has been asked to return to do the Christmas season for them.

Only first class offers considered

According to Tony, not only was Roy a talented hypnotist, he also revolutionised the world of stripping. Up until the late '60s it had been illegal for strippers to actually move on stage. But Roy found a way round this crazy law by placing his girls on a revolving podium. For the first time ever, tits and arse were given equal billing and everyone went home satisfied. Roy Baker and the Moving Nudes became a massive hit all across Britain.

Tony's stag shows have gone through several transformations over the past twenty years. 'Tony Tadman's Sexique Glamour Girl Show' is the latest reincarnation and, according to Tony, is the classiest show yet.

'I prefer to keep my ladies on stage away from prying hands, however if a girl chooses to pour hot oil over her body and have a man rub it in, then that is of course up to her. . . '

The latest Sexique promotional poster features a more corpulent, ruddy-cheeked Tony surrounded by a bevy of PVC-clad lovelies in knee-high plastic boots. Despite the naughty schoolboy grin, Tony seems to have lost the glint of earlier publicity shots. I guess the sight of a naked bosom loses its thrill after a while.

'To be honest it's a bit like those people who work in Mars Bar factories – the last thing they feel like at the end of the day is a bloody Mars Bar.'

He hands me the signed release and a rolled-up Sexique poster and wishes me well with the rest of my trip. . .

'By the way', he whispers 'all the contact details are on the poster if ever you want to – well – you know. . . '

21. Poggy Porkson and the Princess Pig's Party

Reach for the Deadline: three days to go. . .

Question time: Emu's partner – Roy Hudd or Roy Hull? Give up? Okay, the answer is. . . neither – it was Rod Hull. Always a tough one that.

For much of the 1970s and '80s, UK TV was overrun with puppet shows. We're talking Basil Brush, Lamb Chop, Emu, Orville, The Muppets, Bagpuss, The Woodentops, Bill and Ben, Spitting Image, Finger Bobs, Dusty Bin, Pipkin (what the hell was that all about?), Button Moon, Hector's House, The Clangers. . . I could go on, but you get the idea. BBC TV Centre must have been a nightmare of tangled string and fur. Hard to believe now but many of these shows became peak time family viewing. The Saturday night Basil Brush show for instance featured the biggest stars of the day, such as John Inman and Lauren Bacall, and would regularly attract audiences of twelve million. So what led to this obsession with all things foamy? Could it have had something to do with the awfulness of the non-puppets appearing on TV back then – remember Frank Bough anyone?

After several days of non-stop calling I've at last managed to get through to my two Mark Raffles leads – puppeteer Chris Smith and magical ventriloquist Roy Van Dyke. Both are still working and both have agreed to see me at short notice.

I'm on the M40 heading for Weston-Super-Mare, home of *Big*

Timer Roy Van Dyke. Cabaret has just broken the speed limit for the first time.

Roy Van Dyke
The Magical Comedian
Unusual Magic – Funny Gags – but above all it's entertainment all the way
Also Roy Van Dyke and the Merry Midgets puppets:
A unique presentation of unusual laugh-packed entertainment
Theatres, clubs, TV, Cruising, Advertising, OTMH, Dinners

My contact number for Roy turned out to be a magic shop in the West Country run by an American lady called Patti Clair, a good friend of Roy's. She kindly agreed to pass on my details to Roy. When he eventually called me back, he couldn't understand why I would want to travel all the way to Weston to talk to him about a book he knew nothing about. He had a point I suppose, but after some gentle persuasion I managed to get him to agree to meet me at the Royal Hotel next to the Winter Gardens where he'll be attending a magic seminar.

My concern is how I'm ever going to recognise him. In his photo he's wearing one of his 'Merry Midget' outfits consisting of a rag doll style puppet hanging around his neck to give the impression of being six inches tall with a huge head – you know the sort of thing.

'You'll have no problem spotting me' he says. 'Just look for a wheelchair – I'm the one without legs, you can't miss me. I'm afraid I won't be able to see you for very long as I have a strict routine I like to stick to. I'm nearly ninety you know.'

Routine seems to become ever more important with the onset of old age. My parents, for instance, have built a rigorous structure based around mealtimes and simple chores. A typical day begins with dad flopping out of bed at 9am to take the incontinent dog for a pee in the garden (this part of the routine needs a serious rethink if the yellow stink-stains in the kitchen are anything to go by). Breakfast consists of two bowls of Alpen, tea and toast. Dad eats his muesli downstairs, then takes a tray up to mum, along with Radio Four and the *Daily Telegraph*. After a brief potter in the garden, lunch will be served at 12.30 on the dot – Knorr Chicken Cuppa Soup for mum, toast and pate with sliced cucumber for dad. Pudding involves the ritual snapping of Ski yoghurt pots.

After a day of light errands – a visit to the post office, hair appointment for mum, another walk for the incontinent dog – it's time for a well-deserved sit-down with a mug of tea, a hot buttered bun and half an hour of wordplay. After *Countdown* the day's errands will be discussed and pondered over. Supper consists of oven-cooked chicken thighs with peas and boiled potatoes in front of *Coronation Street*. Dad then takes the dog out for yet another pointless pee and 'turns in' half an hour later – by which time mum is snoring gently to 'Sailing By' (on long-wave of course).

My other puppet-meister, Chris Smith lives just outside Reading so I've arranged to visit him on the way back from Weston-Super-Mare. According to 'Mapquest', The Winter Garden on Marine Parade is exactly 137.32 miles from my front door in Paddington. In a normal car this would only take a couple of hours but in Cabaret I need to leave at least three. So in theory I could have Roy and Chris signed up by mid afternoon leaving me time to. . . to what? Seems I'm all out of leads again. . .

All I know about Weston-Super-Mare is that it's the birthplace of John Cleese, although he apparently loathed the place. For Cleese this provincial little seaside town summed up all that was stifling about respectable middle-class Britain after the war – buttoned up men and tight-lipped women scurrying through closed and chilly lives. Talking of closed and chilly, I wonder what the seafront will be like at this time of year? Unfortunately I'm not about to find out.

During a Welcome Break stop just outside Swindon, I ring Roy, as promised, to let him know what time I'll be arriving, but something is wrong – he sounds flustered.

'Oh dear I'm so sorry', he says nervously. 'I thought there'd be time for us to meet but I'm afraid the magicians' convention is going on all day and I won't have a spare moment – we'll have to make it some other time.'

Please don't do this to me Roy – not now. . . .

'How about later in the day, after the convention?' I suggest.

'Not possible, I'm going into hospital for an operation tomorrow and need an early night. I'll call you once I'm up and about. Actually, why don't you just send me the release, I'm sure it's fine.'

I obviously don't want to take my frustration out on a ninety-year old man I've never met before and I'm grateful that he's agreed to sign the release, but couldn't he have told me this earlier?

I take the next exit off the M40, drive to the nearest post office and send Roy the release via the guaranteed next-day delivery service. I then call Chris Smith's landline to try and rearrange our meeting, but am put straight through to his incredibly polite voice mail:

'Hello there. I'm on answer-phone message at the moment but I'd like to help you with all your entertainment needs, so please leave your message, time of call and contact details after you hear the tone. Thanks so much for calling and toodle-pip.'

There's something of the Ealing comedy about Chris' voice – a sing-song, hey-ho-mustn't-grumble-worse-things-happen-at-sea kind of soft London accent straight out of the 1950s.

Chris Smith

The Vibrant Ventriloquial Virtuoso. A sophisticated combination of Comedy Ventriloquism, Novel Puppets plus audience participation, for television, cabaret, functions etc...

Like most elderly folk in possession of a mobile phone, Chris doesn't believe in actually turning the thing on (I reckon oldies must think it costs money to leave them switched on). Today however he must be feeling extravagant because he answers straight away.

'Hi Chris, I'm just outside Reading – there's been a change of plan. Roy Van Dyke is unable to see me today so I was wondering whether I could pop over to yours a bit earlier?'

'Actually James, I was about to call you. There's been a change of plan my end too. No need for you to come all the way out to Reading to see me because I'm on my way to London as we speak – I had a last-minute job offer to perform at a kiddies' fun day in Holborn. I could try and smuggle you in if you like?'

'Sounds good.'

'Great – I'll call you back with the details. . . By the way I'm also performing my *Punch and Judy* show next week at a shopping centre outside Reading – you could come along to that too if you'd like – should be a lot of fun.'

And with that I turn the car round and head straight back to London, almost managing to break the speed limit again.

I'm a bit nervous about meeting Chris – he looks quite dotty in his 1977 publicity photo – a bit like Rod Hull but with even madder hair and a dramatic pointy beard. His right arm is inside a large foam duck with long eyelashes and a feathery fringe.

He's just rung back to tell me he's going to be late for our appointment at the 'Sure Start Family Services Funday' in Holborn.

I'm already outside the gates but the grumpy lady in charge is refusing to let me in unless accompanied by a child. But Chris has come up with a plan – if I pretend to be his assistant, old grumpy-chops will have to let me in to help him set up.

Some of the mums queuing up outside the gates to the park have noticed me loitering and are becoming suspicious. Single man in a duffel coat lurking outside a kiddies' fun day? I must have 'paedophile' written all over me.

Suddenly a beige Dormobile comes screeching round the corner. Out jumps one of the smiliest, gnomiest men I've ever seen. Chris hasn't aged a bit – the long pointy beard is still long and pointy, as are the collars on his bright purple shirt and the tall wizardy hat perched on top of his head. There follows a brief but awkward show of fake bonhomie as I pretend to be his spotty assistant. He hands me a suitcase full of puppets and we march purposefully through the gates.

'I've put you both in the Band Room,' the organiser tells us 'you'll see I've painted a poster for you and stuck it on the door outside.'

The so-called 'poster' is actually just a scrap of orange paper with 'Puppet Show at 12.00 and 1.30' scribbled across it in felt-tip pen.

As we remove the last of the suitcases from the back of Chris' Dormobile, I notice a crumpled sleeping bag on the floor and a box of cakes on top of the fridge.

'I call it my home from home,' he tells me, 'this is where I stay when I have an out-of-town gig.'

Seeing Chris' old Dormobile reminds me of some of the chilly holidays we used to spend in the back of Dad's rented 'mobile home' – or 'Mr Whippy van' as he liked to call it. Sadly we rarely had anything as exotic as cake onboard. Edibles usually consisted of a few desultory scotch eggs, a couple of tins of Tyne Brand meat ('no lumps of fat or gristle guaranteed') and a bottle of Cresta lemonade ('It's frothy man!'). And that would have to see us through a week of sub zero temperatures, driving rain and endless arguments about who should sleep in the bunk bed.

Chris' Mr Whippy van isn't quite as basic as dad's but still, you wouldn't want to spend your holidays in it.

Chris (still dressed in his wizard outfit) and I head over to the bandstand, carefully avoiding the hordes of yelling toddlers. In a small wig-wam, a group of youngsters is sitting cross-legged singing 'See-Saw Marjorie Daw' at the top of their voices. Nearby are several thrift stalls selling cheap baby-clothes and newsagent-quality toys.

The 'Sure Start' scheme is a 'public services awareness initiative', set up by the local council to inform parents about the various child-care facilities available in the area – but for the parents it's just a good excuse to get the kids out of the house. And according to Chris there's nothing toddlers love more than a good old-fashioned puppet show. Chris should know, he's been working with puppets for over fifty years although if it had been up to his Dad – who loathed 'showbiz types' – Chris would still be working as a wigmaker in Reading.

'My job was to measure ladies' heads and fill in the bald spots. I also did a bit of hair-dying too.'

'But I thought only men went bald' I reply, unpacking yet another suitcase of puppets.

'Oh good heavens no, lots of ladies lose their hair due to illness or old age. I remember this one old dear of eighty had convinced herself that if I dyed her thinning grey hair jet black it would make her look thirty-five again. I tried to warn her against going through with it but she was terribly insistent. Well, as you can imagine, she ended up looking like a horrible corpse with this pale, wrinkly face and unnaturally black hair. I used to tell people you can never fool the ageing process.'

I can't resist asking whether his luxuriant thatch of ginger curls is all his own.

'Of course, every single hair.' He replies confidently. Well I had to ask. . .

Chris makes most of his puppets by hand out of old Fairy Liquid bottles, socks, bits of string and anything else that comes to hand. His 'number one puppet', Mrs Duck, features on nearly all his promotional material.

Each puppet is greeted like an old friend as he carefully unpacks them from the suitcase. I ask whether he ever thinks of them as more than just string and sock but he scoffs at the suggestion.

'When Harry Corbett was asked that very same question he replied: 'I stick my hand up Sooty's backside and wiggle my fingers about – I'd hardly do that if I thought he was human.'

But Chris does seem to hold a special place in his heart for Mrs Duck. He's even written a poem about how his feathery friend came to be:

I was looking in my loft one day
I wondered what I'd find
I came across a cushion there
Something came to mind. . .

Chris and his vast array of puppets were lucky enough to appear on

New Faces back in the late '70s.

'One of the most hair-raising moments of my life' he tells me with a shudder. 'But the panel particularly loved my Mr Dog puppet.' And with that he reaches into a large Sainsbury's bag and pulls out an enormous brown, slightly moth-eaten dog with long droopy ears and a felt tongue. He gazes lovingly into the dog's beady eyes, gives it a little stroke and smiles as if to say 'Ahh yes, those were the days. . . '

Then, back in the real world, he continues, 'After *New Faces* my phone didn't stop ringing for a week.'

The large echoey band-room is beginning to fill up with excitable toddlers and stressed-out mums but we haven't even finished putting up the small *Punch and Judy* style stage yet. Chris remains calm and genial as he attaches a collection of bizarre creatures to the inside of the tent. This afternoon's show will feature a moth-eaten monkey, a plasticine worm on a stick, two foam pigs (one with a crown), a tatty sock-dog, a bright green crocodile and a scary looking clown with demonic teeth.

As the last of the kids take their seats, Chris puts on a cassette of 'There's No Business Like Show Business' to get everyone in the mood. What follows is half an hour in the company of a puppet-man possessed.

Various glove puppets are wobbled, bounced and shaken across the tiny stage to the bewilderment of the audience. There's a story of sorts – something about a snail trying to return to its shell only to find a naughty worm has taken up residency. This sequence, worthy of a Terry Gilliam cartoon, lasts for about ten minutes and is accompanied by a tape of jolly Wurlitzer organ music. By the end, the worm is no closer to being evicted from the snail's shell and the story is abandoned in favour of a talking cigarette packet and a singing ukulele called Uke. After a brief song and dance routine, Uke and the fag packet are put to one side and replaced by the demonic clown and a small teddy. Now you'll have to bear with me as I try and explain what happens next, because it all gets a bit weird. The demonic clown tells Teddy to clean the stage of snail trails because a pig named Princess Pig will shortly be holding a grand party for all her piggy friends. Teddy, whose voice sounds like a cross between Fagin and Arthur Daly, dutifully clears up the snail slime and is rewarded with a deflated red balloon. But because Teddy doesn't have any lips, lungs or breath he's unable to blow into said balloon. So the scary clown offers to blow it up for him (clever use of a foot pump here). But naughty old Ted is acting up and keeps trying to grab the balloon back which really hacks off the clown who starts bellowing 'Stop it Teddy, I can't blow if you hold it like that. . . ', at which point I seem to be the only person in the audience sniggering. Teddy is suddenly out of the picture and replaced by another pig named Poggy Porkson (keep up at the back). Poggy is trying to find his way to Princess Pig's party but a wicked crocodile called Snappy keeps sending him in the wrong direction. Just as I'm wondering whether Poggy will ever make it to the party, there's another unexpected change of direction as Mrs Duck suddenly pops her head up and asks the confused audience if they'd like to hear her sing. Some of the kids nod, others it seems would rather be at home playing Death-Blade-Zombie-Killer on Playstation 2.

Chris suddenly emerges from behind the stage with sock-dog attached to his hand and his arm inside an empty Cornflakes packet... Sock-dog appears to be suffering from acute dyslexia. Chris tries to persuade the dog to say hello to the nice boys and girls but the mutt has a problem with the word 'girls' and keeps saying 'giggles' instead. I'm not sure if I should read anything into this, so I don't.

The audience, mostly made up of veiled Somalians with English as a second language, is becoming restless – the kids have started throwing sweet wrappers and some of the mothers are talking into mobile phones. Chris bravely struggles on but his quirky old-fashioned, end-of-pier style of kiddie's show seems woefully out of place in tough inner-city London. It's one of the strangest clashes of cultures I've ever seen. Multicultural Britain meets unreconstructed puppeteer from the '70s.

As the last of the prams trundle back out into the grey afternoon, I ask Chris how he thinks the show went.

'Could have been better' he replies, gently brushing Mrs Duck's fringe 'but you know I shouldn't grumble – I need the work. . . ' An hour later he'll be doing the show all over again in front of a different set of Somalians.

22. 'Ten More Minutes and the Money's Mine'

Reach for the Deadline: two days to go...
'Hi James – great news – I've found you a couple of leads for Dick Pleasant...'

In all the excitement I manage to spill a large glass of whisky over the *Big Time* family tree – but I don't care because this excellent news from Tony Tadman means I'm edging ever closer to my cover-star. Never mind that there are still eleven entertainers unaccounted for and no word yet from John Adrian.

The first of Tony's Dick Pleasant contacts, Strip King Entertainments, apparently used to book Dick for stag parties back in the early '70s. Unfortunately they aren't listed anywhere on the web and there's no joy from Directory Enquiries, which I guess means they must have gone out of business. Tony's other contact, Dukeries Entertainments, are still going strong. According to their website they were established in Nottingham back in 1973 as a 'consultancy and booking service for all types of entertainment. Our aim is to keep our reputation, not make it!'. I skim down their list of comics to find 'star comedy illusionist Brett Kite', 'top comedy impressionist Terry Joyce' and 'zany funny-men Tramp and Swank' but no Dick Pleasant. I know that Dick also sang and played Hawaiian guitar, so I click on 'male vocal groups' to find a list that sounds more like the inhabitants of an average high street: *Designer*, *Next*, *Intense Addiction*, *Spiral Scratch* and *Generation*

Gap are all available for weddings and corporate functions. Finally I check the list of male vocalists – there's a Kev 'Butch' Fletcher and a Gary 'C' but still no sign of Dick. My immediate thought is that he must have retired but then I remember – light entertainers never retire, they just stop working.

I call the Dukeries offices in Nottingham and am put straight through to the main man John Hudson.

'Yes, I remember Dickie. Wonderful comic. Gentle and kind and very, very funny. A good all rounder was Dick. He and I were born on the same day you know, 5th July. I even worked with him a couple of times when I was still performing.'

I take a deep breath before asking the vital question.

'Do you know where I can find him?'

He lets out a deafening laugh.

'Good God no – last time I saw Dickie we were on stage together up north, Scotland I think it was. Dickie was playing his beloved Hawaiian guitar of course. I remember he used to wear wreaths of fake flowers round his neck to give the act that extra bit of authenticity. He'd gig every single night of the year, sometimes twice in one night. His ability to adapt – stag show one night, kiddies' entertainer the next – was what kept him going for so long.'

'So what became of him?' I ask.

'Last thing I heard he was living in Staveley, a little town just outside Chesterfield. Try Directory Enquiries.'

'I already have but the operator just giggled when I mentioned Dick's name.' At this point John reveals something I have suspected all along – Dick Pleasant isn't his real name. His real name is in fact Richard Pheasant; he apparently changed it to Dick Pleasant because he thought it sounded catchier. So now at last I have something tangible to work with.

I thank John for his help, mop up the spilt whisky, pour myself another one and start calling my friends at Directory Enquiries.

'What name please?'

'Pheasant.'

'Pheasant? As in the bird?'

'Yep. . .'

'How are you spelling that?'

'Erm – as in the bird. . .'

'Right. . . Initial?'

'"D" – I mean "R" – as in Richard.'

'Town?'

'Staveley, near Chesterfield.'

After what seems like an eternity, the operator tells me there are no 'R Pheasants' living in Staveley. Damn it, I knew this was too good to be true. After another long pause he continues '. . . but I do have a T Pheasant living in Burton Joyce, which is in the same county – would you like that number?'

'Oh yes please.'

Could this be a relation possibly? I start dialling frantically. A man picks up; good start.

'Hello, Burton Joyce 5634.'

And he sounds old – even better.

'Could I speak to Mr Pheasant please?'

'This is he. How may I help you?'

. . . And so polite!

'I'm trying to track down a comedian by the name of Dick Pleasant, real name Richard Pheasant. '

'Oh dear, you must have the wrong number – I'm Timothy Pheasant.'

'Are you by any chance related to Richard or do you know of any other Pheasants living in the area?'

He pauses for a moment – 'I've only ever come across one. This fella' rang me up by mistake once – said his name was Pheasant – turned out he'd rung the wrong number – he was calling from Ilkeston. Extraordinary really. I mean what are the chances of a man named Pheasant ringing another man named Pheasant by accident?

I like Timothy Pheasant – he sounds like a game old bird. Okay, so that means there's another Pheasant possibly still living in the Ilkeston area. Come on Directory Enquiries – help me out here.

'Name please.'

'Pheasant. As in the bird.'

'Town?'

'Ilkeston.'

'Initial?'

'Ah, don't know.'

'Sorry we need an initial.'

'Couldn't you just give me the numbers for all the Pheasants living in the Ilkeston area?'

'Sorry, we're not supposed to do that. . . '

'But this is an emergency. Look, I doubt there's even a single one, right?'

'You're wrong. . . '

'Yes I know it's wrong in theory but can't you make an exception just this once?'

'No I mean you're wrong. . . there are two Pheasants living in the Ilkeston area. . . which one would you like? I have a C Pheasant living in Green Lane, Ilkeston. . . and a D Pheasant living in Little Hallam.'

'Sorry, did you say D or P Pheasant?'

'D – as in Dick.'

'You have a Dick?' I squeal. Long embarrassed pause followed by a polite cough. . .

'I don't know if he's actually called Dick. . . '

'But you just said. . . '

'I meant, as in D for Dick. . . I could have said D for David or Darren or Danielle.'

'So you're telling me you don't have a Dick? I mean, that he isn't called Dick?'

'I don't know. I don't even know if he's a he. He may be a she. All I can tell you is that he or she is definitely a D.'

At this point I say something I never thought I'd say to a Directory Enquiries employee. . .

'I love you.'

And I must really mean it because I say it again.

'I love you. . . whoever you are. And thank you.'

In my head, Dick's old hallmark catchphrase, 'Ten more minutes and the money's mine', keeps popping up again and again – I can't help but smirk at its poignancy.

I can't bring myself to ring D Pheasant right away so I try C Pheasant first. This has to be a relation of some sort. . .

'Is that Mr C Pheasant?'

'No – this is his son.'

'Oh, I wonder if you can help me – I'm trying to track down a Richard Pheasant, also know as Dick Pleasant – he's a comedian.'

'Hold on, I'll ask my dad. Hey dad, have you heard of a comedian called Richard Pheasant also known as Dick Peasant. . . ?'

'Pleasant. . . .' I correct him.

'Pardon?'

'His name is Pleasant not Peasant. . . '

'Sorry dad – he's Pleasant not Peasant.'

Long pause from dad. . .

'Never heard of either of them. . .'

Shit – okay, time for the big one – although I shouldn't get too excited, after all I'm looking for a Richard Pheasant or a Dick Pleasant, not necessarily a D Pheasant. As Mr Directory Enquiries himself put it, D could stand for anything – Donald, Debbie. . . even Doris. I pour myself another slug of whisky and wait as six long rings pass. . . Come on Dick, Debbie, Dottie or Daz – pick up. Damn it, another answer phone. I leave a message and spend the next hour pacing round my flat like a restless lion.

4.11pm – the phone rings – this has to be him.

'Hello?' I splutter. . . 'Hello??'

'Hello! Congratulations! You have been selected as a guaranteed winner of one of the following fantastic prizes: £25,000 in cash, a holiday to Disney World Florida, a DVD player or a genuine 9ct emerald. To claim your prize simply ring this number now. . . '

£25,000 in cash, eh? Could come in useful. I make a note of the premium rate number. . . just in case.

4.23pm – another call – this time I'm on the loo. 'Don't hang up!' I yell in the vain hope that whoever is on the other end of the line is wearing their bionic ears. I make a slow, undignified shuffle across the sitting room.

'Hello! Hello?' I yell, trousers trailing.

'Yes hello. You left a message on my answer phone earlier. . . I understand you're looking for Richard Pheasant. . . '

'Yes, yes, yes. . . are you him?' I ask a little too enthusiastically.

'Well no – he's my father. . . '

'You mean Mr D Pheasant – also known as Richard – is your father?'

'Yes, but he prefers the name Dick. . . '

Shitting hell, this has to be him. But hang on, this young man sounds incredibly posh to be the son of a northern comic – more Brideshead than Birkenhead.

'Is your dad there? I'd love a word.'

'He's with his cows at the moment over in the top field.'

Cows? Top field? I guess that means Dick must have retired. . . I mean 'moved' to the country.

'How long has he been out of 'the business?' I ask.

'What business?'

'*The* business – show business.'

'He was never in show business. Dad's a dairy farmer.'

'But, hang on, his name's Richard Pheasant right?'

'Right.'

'So how can that be?'

'I dunno, that's just his name and he's always been fond of cows. Am I right in thinking dad's not the man you're looking for?'

'Correct, but thanks anyway.'

This is absurd, how can there possibly be two unrelated Richard Pheasants living within twenty miles of each other? All this bloody phone bashing is getting me nowhere. I need to hit the road again.

Let's pray the good people of Staveley can help.

I'm seriously worried about Cabaret's health – I think she's had enough of all these long journeys. The exhaust is making a horrible clattering noise and the engine sounds like one of Richard Pheasant's cows being run over by a tractor. Half way up the M1 she decides enough is enough and conks out completely. The charming AA man who comes to my rescue is a big Capri fan but his diagnosis isn't good. He does manage to temporarily fix the dodgy fan belt but that's the least of my problems – the exhaust is exhausted, the carburettor isn't carburetting and the engine needs to take a trip to the breaker's yard. The question is, can I make it to Staveley and back to London in what is now essentially a broken kettle? The AA man is doubtful. But seeing as I'm so near the end of my journey I decide to chance it, which means driving at a steady twenty-seven miles an hour up the motorway. There is something deeply emasculating about snailing up the slow lane of the M1 in a car old enough to be most other cars' grandmother. Hulking great SUVs and low slung sports cars whoosh past in a gale of testosterone – even boring little Noddy cars leave me stranded.

Three hours forty minutes later I wheeze and splutter my way up the off ramp and onto the small 'B' road that will take me to Staveley. Clouds of black smoke belch from the exhaust whenever I put my foot down more than half an inch.

The long humiliating haul to this bleak corner of north Derbyshire has given me plenty of time to start panicking again about all the entertainers still unaccounted for. I've been leaving messages with John Adrian all day – tomorrow is crunch-time, my final day – and I really need to know whether he's managed to contact anyone.

I'm wandering round a small '60s shopping precinct looking for Staveley post office where I hope someone will be able to help me with my search. I nip into 'Wisebuys' next door for a pork pie and a bag of Revels. On the way out I show the shop assistant Dick's photo to see if it rings any bells. But she just shakes her head and starts giggling.

Staveley, once the heart of a proud mining community, has been in steady decline ever since the pits closed several years ago. The town's only other industry – a chemical works – has also recently gone under, leaving the large Somerfields supermarket as the main focal point of the town. Wooden benches have even been erected around the edge of the car park so that ex-miners and old ladies in headscarves can gather to watch endless shopping-trolleys sail by.

A long queue of chilly OAPs is waiting outside the small sub post office, pension-books at the ready. Seems I've come at a bad time. I squeeze to the front of the queue and ask the cashier if she's heard of Dick. She shakes her head and tells me to get to the back of the queue. Everyone in line looks at least seventy – surely someone here must have heard of local man Dick or at least recognise his distinctive features. I clear my throat and hold *Reach for the Big Time* aloft like some mad preacher. . .

'Excuse me everyone, sorry to bother you all but I need your help – I'm trying to find this man. He's a comic, goes by the name of Dick Pleasant – I understand he's from around these parts. Does anyone recognise him?'

Everyone reaches for their reading specs as I work my way up the line, stopping intermittently to allow everyone a closer look. An old man with two sticks makes a grunting sound that could be recognition but is in fact just a nasty cough. Suddenly a lady in a tea-cosy hat and plastic pinny grabs my arm.

'I'm sure I recognise the name but, hmmm. . . '; she gazes intently at the photo, but I think she's just trying to be helpful.

Halfway down the line, an elderly couple stop me in my tracks.

'We remember Dickie, don't we dear?' The woman turns to her husband and smiles. 'We had our first dance at one of Dick's shows right here in Staveley – you remember love?'

'Oh aye. He were great, were Dickie. Marvellous Hawaiian guitar player and very funny too. I believe we had our very first kiss that night an' all' – he turns to his wife and winks.

'Any idea where I might find him?'

Hubbie – tall, whiskery, three teeth the colour of Bisto – calls out to a weather-beaten man at the back of the queue.

'Oi, Tony – whatever 'appened to that comic Dicky Pleasant? Does he still live round here?'

'Haven't seen him in years,' replies Tony 'wasn't he over Hartington way?'

Another man in a cap and muddy donkey jacket interrupts.

'Last thing I heard he were living on the Gratton estate. . . '

The man scribbles down some directions for me on the back of an envelope and ten minutes later I'm outside Gratton Court – a bleak, nondescript set of rundown council blocks. I don't have an apartment number for Dicky so I head into the nearest block and ring on a random doorbell. A youngish woman with a bawling baby attached to her hip answers the door and suggests I try asking one of the older residents of the estate. She points me in the direction of Mr Birch, a lifelong resident of Gratton Court who doesn't get out much these days.

Mr Birch is nervous about opening his front door to strangers and so our entire conversation is held at ground level, through his tiny letterbox.

'I remember Dick. . . ' he tells me, lips pressed against the narrow metal slit.

'. . . Lived at number forty-seven. Only knew him to say hello to, mind. He moved, ohhh – eight or nine year ago I believe.'

'Any idea where he moved to?'

'Beg your pardon?'

I press my mouth against the letterbox until our lips are virtually kissing.

'Where's he moved to?' I yell.

'You'll need to ask his neighbour Mrs Bacon – she'll know.'

Mrs Bacon is equally reluctant about opening doors to strangers but, joy of joys, she does remember Dick and even has an address for him. Seems he moved to the nearby village of Woodthorpe, although Mrs Bacon is having difficulty reading her own handwriting. . .

'Northbriggs Road I think it says here – looks like number twenty-eight, or could be forty-eight or forty-nine. . . or is it sixteen?'

Woodthorpe is a short drive from Staveley through a rough and rugged North Derbyshire landscape. Northbriggs Road, a steep, winding lane with large detached houses on either side, is situated on the outskirts of the village. I park up outside number twenty-eight where a bearded man in cords is doing a spot of weeding. Last thing he'd heard, Richard was living at number fourteen but he hadn't seen him around for a while. I jog down the street to a large 1930s house with a wooded back garden. Before ringing the doorbell I take several deep breaths – please God let this be him. No answer. I tiptoe round the side and peer in through the kitchen window. The place looks deserted. In the drive of the house opposite a young woman is unloading her car.

'Excuse me!' I shout, 'Do you know if Richard Pheasant still lives here by any chance?'

'No mi duck, he moved to a big place over Froggart way – couldn't tell you where exactly. Modern house with gates – oh and lots of land.'

Either Dick has hit the big time late in life or else he's been involved in a major lottery rollover.

My mind is racing as I tear along the narrow lanes that lead to Froggart. Could I really be about to meet the star of my book? In my rush to get there I end up in the path of an oncoming tractor and have to swerve into the kerb to avoid a major farming accident.

Distressingly the village of Froggart seems to consist of nothing but large modern houses with impressive gates and extensive gardens – any one of which could belong to Dick. The girl in the local newsagent isn't much help – 'You'll have come back next week – I'm only part-time.'

I start hammering on various doors but there's no one around. I'm beginning to wonder about village life in Britain – or rather, the lack of it. Where is everyone? It seems villages have become little more than healthy graves.

I decide to head for the biggest house with the most impressive garden and hope for the best. It's a vast pile, built from local stone with a set of wide gates and a huge garden. If this does happen to be the place, old Dicky has done even better for himself than I thought.

A face at the window sees me fiddling with the gate.

'Can I help you at all?'

I give a little smile and a wave, trying my best not to look too much like a demented burglar with my five-day growth of stubble and scruffy leather jacket.

'Sorry to bother you, but does Richard Pheasant live here by any chance?'

'Yes, he's my husband – I'll fetch him. Wait there.'

She seems remarkably young to be Dick's wife. Mind you, pools winners and all that. . .

Suddenly from behind a high hedge, a man carrying a muddy spade appears.

'Hello, I'm Richard, what can I do you for?'

Well, he certainly looks like the man on the cover of my book – dark hair, round jolly features, kind eyes – all that's missing is the pencil moustache. . . but hang on, this Richard Pheasant only looks about fifty. My Dick would have to be at least eighty by now. Either I've entered some weird light-entertainment wormhole or this is yet another rogue Pheasant.

'Are you alright? Can I help you?' he asks. Confused, I blurt out the first thing that comes into my head.

'You've shaved your moustache off. . . ' Hardly the best way of introducing myself to a complete stranger. 'What I mean is – you look so well. . . and young and, and. . . everything. Are you still performing?'

He looks at his wife and shrugs. Then it clicks. . .

'You must be looking for Dick Pleasant the comedian?'

'Yes – and you're him, right?'

'Not exactly. . . I'm his son. . . '

Well I guess that would explain the youthfulness of his cheeks.

'Is your dad in?' I ask jauntily 'I'd love to meet him.'

He lowers his eyes. . .

'I'm afraid dad died seven years ago. . . '

'Died? But. . . '

'You'd better come in.'

I may never have actually met Dick but because he's been such a big part of my life for the past year, I really feel as though I know him. I even know what he sounds like in my head.

Dick Junior and I sit solemnly at the kitchen table looking through a box of Dick Senior memorabilia – flyers, publicity shots, local newspaper cuttings. Richard hands me an old, yellowing copy of the *Chesterfield Times*, which features an article all about Dick's sudden and unexpected break into TV. Dick is quoted as saying 'I just happened to be around at the right time and suddenly everyone in TV wanted me.' That same year Dick would appear alongside Derek Nimmo in *Life Begins at Forty*; as a bookmaker in *All Creatures Great and Small*; as a barman in *The D H Lawrence Affair*, and as an MP in *Lloyd George*. The article goes on to say that '. . . despite the fame and fortune Dick intends to stay with his comedy act and has just been booked for a six week summer season at Skegness.' Richard Junior is especially proud of his dad's late arrival into the world of TV walk-on work, as am I.

In a corner of the sitting room stands his father's pride and joy – a gleaming Hawaiian guitar. Funny to think of Dick twanging away, not on some balmy tropical beach, but in a smoky miner's club in drizzly old Derbyshire.

When he sees the cover of my book, Richard's face breaks into a broad, affectionate grin – much like the one his father is pulling back at him from the cover. I apologise for using the image without his permission but he just waves his hand as if to say 'That's fine. . . '

After a long, emotional pause Richard looks up and smiles.

'Funny, dad never intended becoming an entertainer – like most Staveley men, mining was his first love.'

But Dick's unusual love affair with Hawaiian music meant he was able to bring a ray of South Sea Island sunshine to the drab environs of the northern club circuit. It was only after he began dropping in the odd joke here and there in between songs that Dick realised there was more mileage to be had in comedy.

'He'd go wherever the work took him – cabarets, concert halls, theatres, holiday camps – his best season ever was at the Miners' Holiday Camp in Skegness.'

Over the years Dick took to the road with some of TV's best known stars including Bernard Manning, Lulu and Tony Christie. His deadpan, Les Dawson-style delivery and occasional 'blue' material went down well with the northern crowds. But when the industry began to change, Dick found himself out of favour with the 'alternative' set. He battled on for a few more years before his eventual move to walk-on TV heaven. But after suffering a serious stroke, Dick was forced to retire from showbiz all together

– although he never told anyone he'd retired of course.

Richard Junior never felt tempted to follow in his father's footsteps and decided instead to settle for the less risky world of financial advising. I guess people will always need advice on how best to invest their cash, whereas old comics like Dick are a much more expendable commodity. And the comparative rewards are here for all to see – the house, the land and those impressive gates are all a long way from Dick's poky council flat just outside Staveley.

Richard takes me out into the great swathe of garden that extends all the way down to a wide stretch of river. 'I've my dad to thank for all of this,' he tells me 'he was such a hard worker – an inspiration.'

And so with my cover-star on board, admittedly by proxy, all I need now is for John Adrian and *Loot* to come up trumps.

Before leaving Froggart, I give John a call. The news isn't good – although he's managed to pass on messages to six of the eleven outstanding acts, he still hasn't been able to trace '*Kat Mandu*', '*The Merry Monk of Magic*', 'John Marshall the Man with the X-ray Eyes', '*Gay Duo*' and '*Lips*'.

So that's it – after three weeks and six days I have singularly failed in my quest. That night I lie awake torturing myself about how I might have done things differently – a cacophony of 'should-haves' 'could-haves' and 'if-onlys' swirl round my head. I try to take comfort in the fact that I gave it my best shot. I may have failed to save the book but I did at least get to meet some of its characters and have an adventure along the way. But my brief moment of optimism is short-lived and soon the spectre of bankruptcy is hanging over me. I start picking over my life – as I so often do at this cruel hour of the night. Why had I never hit the big time? Maybe if I'd been a little spunkier, thrown caution to the wind more often. . .

In a moment of early morning, self-pitying panic, I'm reminded of what Johnny Clamp had said as we sat on his scruffy old sofa:

'When I go, the world won't miss a beat. . . '

23. Ambition is a Ravenous Beast

'It is a mistake to suppose that men succeed through success; they much oftener succeed through failures'
– Samuel Smiles

'Success consists of going from failure to failure without loss of enthusiasm' – Winston Churchill

The phone eventually rings at midday – by which time I'm so nervous I can hardly lift the receiver. But this isn't the dreaded call from my publisher that I'd been expecting – in fact it's an old friend ringing to ask if I'd like to accompany her to an awards ceremony that evening. Liz has been nominated for a Channel Four News report she directed about the Iraq war. I know it sounds heartless and probably selfish too, but quite frankly I'm in no mood to celebrate anyone else's success right now. But Liz reckons it will do me good to get out of the house and so after much huffing and puffing I agree to meet her at the National Film Theatre where the ceremony will be taking place.

Liz is pacing nervously outside the concrete edifice when I arrive. Over the course of the next hour she manages to smoke her way through two packets of full strength Camel. The poor girl is beside herself with nerves and doesn't seem particularly thrilled about her nomination. The world of TV news is highly competitive and awards like this are taken very seriously, so you'd think she'd be a bit excited at least. We stand around sipping cheap wine from plastic cups as beaming work colleagues rush over with fingers crossed. I do my best to match their enthusiasm but all I can feel is a compounded sense of my own failure.

I'm on my third glass of red wine when the phone rings – the caller display tells me the number has been withheld. If this is the publisher they've left it very late in the day to ring. Liz is beckoning me to follow her into the theatre so I ignore the call and attempt to remain upbeat for my friend. There's a real buzz of anticipation as we take out seats at the front of the auditorium.

The nominees for best foreign report are about to be announced. Liz is gripping the arm of her chair so hard that her knuckles have turned white. There are three nominees in all but she is the clear favourite. A short clip from each film is played before ITV newsreader and MC for the evening, Mark Austin, takes to the podium. . .

'And the winner for best foreign news report is...'

Back in the lobby Liz's colleagues are clambering to congratulate her on her success. . . This prize is going to stand her in good stead for future work – so why doesn't she look happier? As an ambitious young journalist I guess she must be thinking about the next job and whether she can top this award. . . ambition it seems is a ravenous beast. I think back to my old friend Keith Manifold and his thoughts about the futility of aiming too high....

As the crowd makes for the bar I leave Liz basking in her glory and take a wander over to the Millennium Wheel, which is still turning imperceptibly, despite the late hour. My phone begins to vibrate – a message is waiting. . . It's my editor and she's finding it hard to relay the bad news.

'We're so sorry it's come to this James, we really are. . .' She sounds genuinely upset. After all, she's the one who originally commissioned the book all those months ago. . . in a way this is her baby too.

'Isn't there anything we can do?' I ask forlornly. 'Couldn't you give me just one more month...?'

'Oh James, I wish there was a way but I'm afraid it's not up to me.'

'Or a few days at least? I've come this far. . .'

24. Pulp Friction

A bitterly cold Wednesday, winter 2004: half-past-four and a heavy gloom is descending.

Security won't let me in to watch the pulping, so I'm outside the gates, freezing my face off. I jump up and down, flapping to keep warm. There's nothing to be seen out here. The occasional ominous-looking truck is waved through heavy prison-like security gates – no doubt filled with remaindered copies of yet another celebrity autobiography; print run: 100 000, sales: thirty-nine, career: in tatters.

It's probably best that I don't witness the actual pulping. Nick thinks I'm mad to have come.

'You just want to wallow in self-pity', he'd said, as I wittered on about closure. But it was never going to be that easy. The fact is I am now liable for the £25,000 printing and pulping costs and have no idea how I'm ever going to raise the money. The pulping costs alone are exorbitant. I try to imagine what's going on behind the forbidding concrete walls. Some demonic thug in a sweaty vest, poking my books into the hungry jaws of the pulping machine with his pitchfork? What *can* they be doing in there? I came here to try and draw a line, but now I'm actually really curious to know what could possibly be costing me all that money. Idiotically I attempt to work it out in my head. How much could it be to hire a couple of printing press operators in a Taiwanese sweatshop? And as for the pulping itself – one heavily perspiring demon chucking 35 000 copies of my book into a big chomping machine? Minimum wage, surely. After all, I could have set fire to them in my own garden for nothing if they'd only asked.

And that's that, supposedly, and yet I still have a niggling feeling of unease. How do I know that the actual cost of the pulping isn't, say twenty-five quid, and the rest of the money is being spent on some fabulous pulping party? It's probably going on right now – behind those horrible grey walls, at my expense. And I haven't even been invited.

But it doesn't end with the pulping – apparently once the books have been mulched, they will then be recycled. . . but into what, exactly? Who knows. . . ? Next week's *Sunday Telegraph*, perhaps? So much lavatory roll? Could it be that Dick Pleasant, Keith Manifold et al. are about to end up as pages in the next *Harry Potter* book?

Icy rain begins to fall as I wander slowly back to my ever-faithful Capri. There on the passenger seat is my single copy of *Reach for the Big Time*. I pick it up and start flicking through the dog-eared pages. These are no longer just old photographs but real, three dimensional people, many of whom I'd now be honoured to call friends.

Then suddenly it hits me – an idea that could turn this whole sorry saga around. After so many weeks on the road, I now have all the material I need to bring these fading images back to life. Early on, I made a promise to Keith Manifold that I would save *Reach for the Big Time*, not just for him, but for everyone involved. Well, I may have failed to salvage this particular book, but what if I was to write another book – a book *about* the book?

Surely that would be a story worth telling. . .

Postscript

- Although Capri Cabaret's problems have worsened steadily, she isn't finished yet and is hoping for a kind restorer to rescue her from the small ads pages of *Practical Classics*.
- Ford are planning to launch an updated version of the Capri in late 2007.
- Having lost the Bunny-Lewis-gender-bet, James spent a week prancing around Paddington in a sequinned frock. He is now an expert stiletto-walker and occasionally wears a touch of rouge on his cheeks.
- Nick-the-Cynic sold his R2-D2 autograph for £37 on eBay.
- Sadly James failed to win the £25,000 telephone lottery. Instead he received a small misshapen emerald worth about 50p. He's still hoping to win the big prize. . .
- His quest to track down the remaining stars of *Reach for the Big Time* continues. Any information on the whereabouts of the following would be gratefully received:

Gay Duo
Merry Monk of Magic
Kat Mandu
Lips
Disco Kid
John Marshall *The Man with the X ray Eyes*
Candy Rock
Tony *Shades* Valence

David Noble – who *'The ladies love to love and the men can't help but admire'*
Laughing Larry Larkin
Homer Noodleman
Roy Baker
Tony Durant – the best bird impressionist in the business

James Innes Smith 2007